You Are What You Love

This book Is Dedicated to . . .
Elliot Malach and Paul Hoffman.
You have taught me the True meaning
of Generosity and Success!
Without you . . . my life as well as this book
would not be possible.

May we always Live as One!

He Told Me A Joke.
My Lord told me a joke
and seeing Him laugh has done more for me
than any scripture I will ever read.
– Meister Eckhart

Publisher: Vaishali and Elliot Malach, Purple Haze Press™

Project Director/Editor: Bethany Argisle, Argisle Enterprises Inc.

Book Design, Layout and Cover Design: Albert Howell, Meta4 Productions

Wave Illustration: Brian Narelle, Narelle Creative

Editorial Staff: Orion Torney, Jessica Brunner

Special Thanks to: Tina Davis, Abacus Imprints, and Robert Bergman, Spirit Boxer

First Printing, April 2006.

Library of Congress Cataloging in Public Data

Vaishali, 1959 -

You Are What You Love

ISBN 0-9773200-0-6

1. Love 2. Self-Help 3. Spirituality 4. Consciousness Education

Quote Releases and Permissions

References

The works of Emanuel Swedenborg, supported by the Swedenborg Foundation, West Chester, PA.

Argisleizms used with permission by Bethany Argisle, Argisle Enterprises Inc., San Rafael, CA.

Dr. Michael Coleman, Huntington, CA.

The Dr. Phil Show, supported by Dr. Phil McGraw, Los Angeles CA.

The Lucidity Institute, supported by Dr. Stephen La Berge, Palto Alto, CA.

The works of Elson Haas M.D., supported by Celestial Arts Publishing, Berkeley, CA.

Acknowledgments

This book has taught me that truly, no one individual can produce any book by themselves except, of course, Swedenborg... (Keep reading you'll get it, and on the re-read you'll find it very funny!). This book is the fruit of the labor of many people to whom my heart goes out with many "Thanks." Without these key people, this sharing, this book, this creative expression would not have been possible! Thank you Angels! Thank you Heaven! Thank you Life! So it is and so it goes.

Elliot Malach, Pela Tomasello, Sarah Bartholomew and Marie Loverich put in countless hours, tirelessly and selflessly. With Bethany and Jet Argisle at the helm of the Beam Team, Jessica Brunner and Albert Howell/Meta4 Productions, the bookcooks extraordinaire in the book brick factory. Stephanie Buenger, Kathryn and Dannion Brinkley, Digi Rob, Brian Narelle, Orion Freedomsong, and Spirit Boxer, you have been the guardian Angels of this book! For your support. Thank You! Thank You! Thank You!

To all my friends and family, you know who you are! To all the health care providers who have worked tirelessly and often times for no money to keep me alive and functioning since that devastating 1998 car-accident, Thank You!

Without the love, generosity and basic human kindness you have all freely given, I would have zero quality of life, not to mention my physical body would be dead. When this book helps or improves the quality of even one being's

life, then we all share in that success!
Thank you! Thank you! Eternally . . . Thank You!

You can contact me at the following addresses:

www.purplehazepress.com

www.youarewhatyoulove.com

If the only prayer you say in your whole life is 'Thank You' it would suffice.
–Master Eckhart

Table of Contents

Foreword ix

Authors Notes xi

Introduction xiv

Two Bodies, Two Minds 1

Ultimate Truth & Ultimate Lies 33

Everything Is Mind 73

Mastery of the Human Experience 115

Forgiveness & Equability 163

Surrender & Neutrality 193

Dreaming 227

Inner Space: The Real Final Frontier 259

Perception Is A Choice 297

Agreements 335

Moving Forward 357

Suggested Readings 381

Glossary 382

Foreword: Very Vaishali

Vaishali is a presence, an awareness of love living, viable, tangible, applicable, now is love is Vaishali.

I began work on Vaishali's first book when she showed me what was on her heart's mind – we shared and traded her amazing skills as a healer of Chi Nei Tsang and my publishing abilities. We kept one another (and still do) going through many a life challenge, called love in one form or another we gave our mutual attention to arriving now.

I was named after a place on Earth by my Mother, who said later she thought she saw the name on a milk truck on the way to the hospital. I found out that Bethany means House of God or Home of the Poor or Bringer of Wealth. The town is where Jesus raised Lazarus from the Dead and where Mary and Martha lived and danced and dreamed and shared. The town of Bethany is said to be a favorite of Jesus'.

Vaishali's namesake is that of the town named after King Vashal, whose heroic deeds are in the Ramayana. Vaishali is credited with being the World's first Republic to have a duly elected assembly of representatives and efficient administration. The Lord Buddha set foot on the soil of Vashali, lightning and thunder followed by heavy downpour and purged the plagued city. Vaishali is where Buddha preached his last sermon. According to history, Vaishali is twice blessed as Jainism too, has its origins at Vaishali.

So, two women with place in their hearts are the lions at the gate where rangels have danced and have all contributed to this wondrous work, of Vaishali turning herself inside out on these pages for the blest best offering YOU ARE WHAT YOU LOVE . . . .

Join us in this adventure as LOVE unfolds, embraces, upholds those who know that LOVE IS THE GOLD AT THE END OF THE RAINBOW.

Bethany Argisle
Project Director

Feel your soul rise
no longer fear's demise
Welcome to the LOVE Department store
ONE LOVE: ONE SIZE FITS 4EVER'S More
—Argisle

Author's Notes – Vaishali's Victory

Greetings, beloved reader, welcome to a labor of great love. I have spent my adult life seeking esoteric wisdom and studying as many different spiritual and religious expressions of God consciousness as I could find. Heaven has been most generous over the years in providing a virtual unending parade of gifted and enlightened teachers that I have learned from. For most people this type of focus finds no place in their everyday lives. Between children, business meetings, soccer games and laundry, the average person has a hard time finding time to contemplate what a philosophy that is thousands of years old has to say about the relevance of God in our everyday life.

However, if we live without having any real understanding of *what* we are, and *why* we are here, we will never have a life worth living. Some of us live and learn while others merely exist, repeating the same old tired lessons over and over again. No matter what is ultimately given you: children, no children, huge bank account, no bank account, large breasts or small breasts, all of us, without exception, have to discover for ourselves a way through the labyrinth of life. All of us are responsible for finding our own way home. The information contained within this book is designed to that end.

There is nothing in this book that has not already been stated by many other voices since before the beginning of recorded humankind. What this book does advertise is that you will *experience* wisdom in a style and manner that is clearly "something new under the sun." Anyone who says they have not heard any good stories lately, simply hasn't heard a good storyteller. This book is designed to solve that temporal problem.

This book is intended for those who would like the benefit of having explored the spiritual realm all their life, but were too busy doing other things. Imagine how nice it would be to receive the benefit of someone else going into surgery or the gym for you. Well, that is not going to happen here. However, if you would like the benefits of having universal wisdom on how to create a life worth living reviewed, then brilliantly summed up and handed over on a silver platter, this book *is* for you.

The construction of this book brought with it some inherent problems not normally found in books: trying to describe the difference between temporal and eternal or illusion versus reality. For example, there is a use of capitalization within the book we should discuss. Chinese medicine has adopted a commonly accepted style of capitalization I am borrowing. Any time you see the word Heart, I am not talking about the organ beating in your chest. I am talking on an energy level only. I am referring to the *feeling/knowing place within.* The place where the human and divine meet and are seated within the human experience. Any time you see the word heart, I am referring to the organ, the physical pump in your chest.

Also, in order to enhance eternal, God-like qualities, I have created a non-traditional use of capitalization. Every time you read the word Heaven, you will always find it capitalized. Every time you read the word hell it will not be capitalized. The intention is to visually underscore the unlimited and infinite nature of Heaven while contrasting it to the tiny nature of hell. I'm sure many of you reading this have your own definition of Heaven and hell, however, for the purpose of this book, we are defining Heaven as a place or state of being beyond limitation. And we are defining hell as the opposite, a place or state of being that is limited.

That is the end of this book's definition of Heaven and hell, so reader beware, any other interpretation, slant or charge on these words is your own contribution, and not those of the author.

Another inherent problem in sharing information of this type is that it requires a great deal of repetition in order for the wisdom to become familiar, coherent and clear. So please bear with me if it seems we are covering territory we have already viewed earlier. It will all come together at some point to create an extended vista that can only occur when the information has a chance to build upon itself. There is also a glossary in the back. Should you discover in reading that a reference has been made to something or someone that you are not familiar with go ahead and look it up in the back. Usually these references are made in relation to something humorous, and I wouldn't want for you to miss the joke.

Read the book slowly; take your time. Although the ideas are not new, the perspective is and therefore requires time to become familiar. Also please feel free to pick up the book and use it like the I-Ching, opening it up randomly and seeing where your eye falls. My prayer is that you enjoy this book, share the stories with your friends, and have fun with it for the inner adventure it was meant to be. Blessings to you all! And so it is and so it goes.

Vaishali – January 2006

Introduction

There once lived a very wise, compassionate and patient person. The gift of understanding the secrets and mysteries of both the physical world and the spiritual realm had been given to this man. This person had permission from the highest level of Heaven to travel freely into all of the spiritual dimensions, and to discourse at length with the beings that make up all levels of spiritual existence. The purpose of this person's life was to act as a human bridge for knowledge and wisdom from the spiritual realm to our physical world. He recorded all that had been revealed to him about spiritual operation, organization and the relationship with human existence. This wisdom would enable humankind to gain insight into the nature of Ultimate Truth, into the nature of mind.

We would finally be able to answer the big questions:

❋ What is the purpose of all created life?
❋ Who are we?
❋ Why are we here?
❋ Why do we need to find our consciousness residing in a physical body, while hanging out on a rock that is simultaneously spinning and hurtling itself at insane speeds through space?

Why do we need this? Why?

This living bridge of transformational wisdom is available in the prolific writings left behind by this spiritualist. We can actually read his mind-transforming accounts of how the spiritual realm works, and start practicing mastery of the physical and spiritual worlds now in this very moment. Over two hundred years after this person's death, we now stand in the light of this timeless wisdom aligning ourselves with the illumination and confidence of knowing who we are and why we are here.

This person is the great Swedish mystic Emanuel Swedenborg. When D. T. Suzuki, a Master of Zen Buddhist teaching, first read Swedenborg's spiritually sophisticated writings, he proclaimed Swedenborg to be the most enlightened Westerner he had ever read. D.T. Suzuki even wrote a book honoring Swedenborg and the truth he came to share. He titled the book: *Swedenborg, Buddha of the North*. Guess that says it all. No room for misinterpretation there.

Swedenborg actually started out his professional career as a scientist. He began mastering every known science of his era. (Swedenborg died in 1772.) He was the first to determine the purpose of the cerebellum in the human brain. He wrote three volumes on the human brain that included the most accurate drawings of his time. He perfected the lunar method of latitude and longitude we use today[1]. He foretold of Einstein's theory of relativity, more than one hundred years before the birth of Einstein himself[2]. He learned lens building and constructed a microscope and a telescope, both incredibly advanced for that era. He wrote over 150 scientific works on various topics including: color, fire, units of measure, soil erosion, and

1. *Secrets of the Masters*, by Michael Coleman, PhD. circa 1980.

2. *The Ghost of Flight 401*, by John G. Fuller, Berkeley Publishing Corp.1976.

money. He was also a metallurgist, and invented many of the mining safety improvements used in the 1700s and later. In addition to all that, he was a member of Sweden's Parliament, and even though he traveled frequently, he never missed a meeting.

According to Swedenborg, what launched him on his mission to master every known science in his lifetime was he *needed* to know where the soul resided in the human experience. After years of approaching this question from the scientific point of view, he realized that all of his scientific background was actually not useful in resolving this dilemma. Swedenborg described his realization of the scientific mental process as a huge burden. He compared its oppression to having to pull a large wagon full of heavy stones around with him everywhere he went. So, at the age of fifty-six, Swedenborg abandoned his scientific career to focus all his attention exclusively on his spiritual travels using inwardly controlled breathing. Since he was a small child, Swedenborg had been able to slow down his breathing until he would enter into a trance-like state.

What inspired this life altering epiphany? Swedenborg says that Heaven gave him permission to break through to the purely spiritual dimension: where there is nothing physical or mortal, only spiritual beings that make up the various levels of Heaven and hell. His encounters and experiences are described in detail in his many writings. It was D.T. Suzuki who figured out that if you gathered together all of Swedenborg's spiritual writings, put them together in a row, and after every five hundred pages you said, "Stop here, that's volume one," then counted off another five hundred pages and made that volume two, etc., you would have over sixty volumes of work. Of course, we are only talking about his spiritual, not scientific writings. That is impressive with or without a computer, and Swedenborg's contribution was clearly before the age of computers.

Swedenborg, however, never made a big deal about his prolific offerings. He said it was easy and simple. He said he did not originally put his name on his writings, as he felt the information was not his per se, but rather the angels had dictated it to him. All that was required of him was to put pen to paper. Don't we all wish our experiences of writing timeless wisdom were that painless and entertaining! Swedenborg did resolve the mystery of where the soul resides in the human experience, but that answer is for another time and another book . . . only kidding, only kidding. Swedenborg's brilliant forensic examination of spirit and the soul goes like this: you do not *have* a soul. I do not *have* a soul. Even the politicians in Washington do not *have* souls. (I know, I know . . . tell you something you didn't already know.) Rather, Swedenborg would assert, we *are* a soul, and the soul is the sum total of one's will, love, service and life purpose. We do not *have* a soul, because the soul is not a possession or an object. The soul cannot be lost somewhere, like a cheap pair of sunglasses left in a gas station restroom. Thank God for that, or we'd all be in trouble. No, the truth is we *are* a soul. We bring our soul with us when we come to planet Earth, and we take it with us when we leave; the soul is the very fabric and nature of our being.

The primary quality of any soul is what Swedenborg calls one's *Ruling Love*. To see this, let's take Jesus or Buddha. We see a spiritual being that is governed by a *Ruling Love* of equability, honesty, sharing, openness, carefree, unconditionally loving and of great joy. Now let's examine the

Ruling Love of a Hitler. What we would see is a spiritual being who is possessed by a *Ruling Love* of hatred, lies, deception, raging insecurity, mistrust, and, of course, the ever popular unconditional infliction of judgment and suffering upon others. So exactly what is it that makes or determines one's Ruling Love? Swedenborg simply stated says, "You are what you love. You do not exist or live separately from what you love. You are what you love and you love whatever you are giving your attention to."

If you are going through your everyday life, giving your attention to worrying about bills, health, the kids, the car, etc., then you love worrying. If you give your attention to not telling others the truth about anything, then you love lying. If you give your attention to stories about how you cannot do things right, or how you are inferior, then you love being *less than.* Shocking, isn't it!?! You can clearly see that if what Swedenborg says is true, that *you are what you love,* then if you love the same things that hell loves, such as worry, *less than,* lying and deception, you will surely find yourself living in hell. If we are all honest, it is not hard to see then why worry, lying and feeling *less than* are all such hellish qualities of existence.

The saving grace is that the converse also holds true. If you love what Heaven loves, such as honesty, open sharing, equability, good and healthy trust in life and love, then you will surely abide in Heaven, deeply and completely. So how do we do this? How do we go from living in hell, or at the very least from frequenting hell on a daily basis, to living in a place beyond suffering and limitation? First, we learn to observe and understand the nature of mind itself. We realize what it means to be a spiritual being experiencing itself in a physical reality.

In this psychodrama called the movement of life, it is essential we learn what we, as spirit, really are, without confusing *what we are* with *what we have come here to let go of and leave behind.*

It Is A Lie

It is a lie – any talk of God

that does not comfort you.

– By Meister Eckhart

Chapter One

Two Bodies,

Two Minds

There is only One; There is always infinite abundance

When we experience life here on the Earth, we find ourselves involved with two of the most exciting fashion accessories available in the universe: two bodies and two forms of consciousness. The first body is the spiritual body. This is our essence before we arrived on the planet, and it will be us when we leave. When we come into the physical world we inherit the second body, the physical body, from our physical parents. This is where most people, as Jimi Hendrix accurately predicted, get caught in cross-town traffic on the way to enlightenment. They do not realize that they have two bodies and two forms of consciousness. Most people have realized only the one body and the one form of consciousness; the most limited and the most temporal of each.

All unrealized spiritual beings get distracted with the temporal, the physical level of awareness. It is the physical body that gets most people's attention: washing, clothing, haircuts, doctor exams, sleeping, eating, etc. Most of us take better care of our cars than we do our spiritual bodies! It seems that the longer something lasts, the more we take it for granted. As Mickey Mantle put it, "If I knew I was going to live this long, I'd have taken better care of my body." Since our spiritual body will be with us through eternity, we need to take the "Mickey Mentality" to the next level.

How many of us spend any time nurturing our spiritual bodies? Does anyone even know how? First we must realize that we do not have a spiritual body, we are a spiritual body. Second we need to consciously nurture it by giving our attention to the truth, independent of the gyrations in the physical world.

Just as we are experiencing two bodies, we are also experiencing two forms of consciousness. The highest form of consciousness is eternal - unlimited, and spiritual in nature. The other form of consciousness, the lower form, is temporal - limited and physically based.

The eternal form of consciousness is our spiritual body. We bring it with us when we come here. We actually do not have eternal consciousness; we are eternal consciousness. What eternal consciousness is, what we really are, is love, acceptance, forgiveness, flexibility, creativity, compassion, tolerance, the present moment, patience, and understanding.

The temporal form of consciousness we all experience is what we call the ego: any form of information or communication that is subject to change, the inner critic, the voice of limitation.

The reason we experience two forms of consciousness, and the reason we experience two forms of bodies is the same. Each one is designed to solve a different kind of problem. We use our eternal consciousness for solving our eternal problems: "Why am I here? What is the meaning and purpose of my life and relationships? What

ETERNAL	TEMPORAL
Love	ego
Forgiveness	thoughts
Acceptance	words
Tolerance	beliefs
Present Moment	accumulated information
Flexibility	info. learned in schools
Patience	media exposed
Responsive	reactionary

is my value? What is my power? What is my worth?" These are our eternal problems, and these problems require the use of eternal consciousness exclusively in order to finally resolve them. Although we really are an eternal form of consciousness, here to solve eternal problems, we find ourselves in a limited, ever-changing physical world requiring a limited form of intelligence in order to solve our temporal everyday problems. The ego's realm is solving these temporal problems: "What's for dinner? What shall I wear? Does this dress make me look fat? What do I do with a 1040 form? Do I buy this stock, or do I just throw my money out the window? Do I choose less filling or great taste?" This is temporal intelligence.

No one will ever solve any eternal problem by giving their attention to a temporal and limited form consciousness-to the thoughts and beliefs of the ego. When you try using temporal consciousness to solve eternal problems . . . well, we call that suffering. Specifically, we have the root cause of all suffering - the ultimate in trying to shove a square peg into a round hole.

But how do we tell the difference between the two voices, or two forms of consciousness? If you hear words in your mind, that is the ego talking to you. The ego is what you learned about yourself, life and relationships from school, home, peers, and the media at large. All ego information is limited. There is no complete encyclopedia or dictionary anywhere; additions and modifications are always being made; new things are always being discovered. There is no complete form of limited information anywhere. The ego is in the head, completely dis-embodied from the wisdom of the Heart. Conversely, eternal consciousness is the intelligence of the Heart. Love is a feeling/knowing.

Don't just make up your mind, make up your Heart
– Argisle

As Sogyal Rinpoche, the Tibetan Buddhist teacher and author of *The Tibetan Book of Living and Dying* describes it:

Two people have been living in you all your life. One is the ego, garrulous, demanding, hysterical, calculating; the other is the hidden spiritual being, whose still voice of wisdom you have only rarely heard or attended to.

When the truth is realized, it can be seen everywhere. Every sacred symbol reflects it.

The yin/yang, symbol of Taoism: All of life appears to be made up of opposing energies: up, down, day, night, hot, cold, male, female, temporal, eternal. The truth is . . . it is all One. There is not a day planet, and a night planet . . . it is all One. The two meet and become One in the present moment.

 The Star of David, symbol of the Jewish faith: There appears to be two opposing energies making up all of life. Mastery of life is to reconcile the two into the One. The meeting point of two into the One occurs in the present moment.

The Cross, symbol of Christianity: There appears to be two movements making up life: up, down, left, right, in, out. The horizontal line represents the movement of the temporal. The vertical line represents the eternal, and the two meet and become One in the present moment. The four lines, also represent the four directions which converge in the present moment.

There is a relationship with the present moment that fuses both forms of consciousness into Oneness. That critical relationship with the present moment can best be understood as the contents of an angel's mind. Swedenborg says all angels were human at one time. Just like us they had to tough it out here on Earth. They had the same stresses, desires, pressures, urges, needs, fears and experiences. In fact, all angels had to go through what we are presently mastering: temporal vs. eternal.

So what exactly creates angels out of mortals? The same relationship with the present moment that fuses the mind into Oneness: loyalty and devotion to using eternal consciousness for solving only eternal problems, and temporal consciousness for solving only temporal problems. Another way to say this is that mind is focused on loving, accepting, and trusting the reality that Heaven determines everything. We are designed to forgive our way through life from the Heart, instead of thinking, be-

7

lieving, and strategically controlling our way through life from the head.

> **This means going through life without giving your attention to thoughts or beliefs about what it all means:**
>
> ❀ What is your power?
> ❀ What is your worth?
> ❀ What is your value?
> ❀ What is the meaning of this moment?
> ❀ What is the value, power and worth of others?

You live your life like it was one big free fall through the cosmos, with loving and trusting as your sole parachute, guiding your information and natural response to all of life. Pretty tricky, huh?!

It is absolutely imperative that we realize that we have two forms of consciousness. Our attention needs to be committed to the eternal portion of the program. The purpose of arriving here is to begin to deprogram our deep and abiding habituation to limitation: to thinking and believing our way through life. Instead, we must accustom our minds to loving, accepting, relaxing, and trusting our way through life. We do this by focusing our attention on the truth that our value, power and worth is that we are a force of love, right here, right now, independent of the ego's opinion.

A mind that is focusing exclusively on the truth, is a mind that uses eternal consciousness for solving eternal problems and temporal consciousness for solving temporal problems. A mind focused on the truth knows at any given moment whether it is solving a temporal or eternal problem; it knows which form of consciousness it is giving its attention to in order to resolve and overcome each challenge. Sacred traditions say that we are actually solving temporal problems only 5% of our day. We are solving eternal problems approximately 95% of the time. This should come as no surprise because we did not come here to solve limited problems in a temporal world. We came here to realize we are love and nothing else.

The great love teacher Jesus reminds us to not have a thought or belief about how we are going to live, or where we will get our clothes. He asks us to consider the birds. They do not have a thought or belief about anything in the temporal world, yet they are fed. Consider the lilies of the field. They do not toil or spin. They do not have a work ethic. They never punch a time clock. They produce nothing. Yet even King Solomon did not have clothes finer than what God gave the flowers. The birds and the flowers are all temporal. They have no egos. They are here today and gone tomorrow. The point is that all they do is show up, without a thought or belief, and they are taken care of. You are eternal. How could you not know that you are taken care of?

If you are coming from thoughts and beliefs, then that limited form of consciousness will rob you of your higher knowing, because true knowing is an unlimited form of consciousness. Everyone has had the experience of a feeling/knowing you could not put into words. You could not explain it in any temporal terms. You just knew something; it was a gut feeling/knowing. You could not logically or rationally show where or how the details came together.

Yet, you just knew. We all know what it feels like to honor that feeling/knowing, and to witness it come to pass. We also know what it feels like to dishonor that feeling/knowing and witness that reality. The former feels more expansive and empowering than the latter; this feeling/knowing is a vastly higher intelligence than any thought or any belief.

No one ever said it better than Antoine De Saint-Exupery in his brilliant book, *The Little Prince*, "It is only with the heart that one can see rightly. What is essential is invisible to the eye." This is the knowing, the universal feeling/knowing that Jesus is referring to when he asks, "How could you not know you are taken care of?" He is saying if you are coming from a thought and belief, that limited form of consciousness will sabotage you from giving your attention to the truth, to unlimited eternal consciousness.

You cannot be giving your attention to limited consciousness and unlimited at the same time. You cannot simultaneously be worrying about life, and still feel you are fully supported and completely taken care of because you are eternal love. One of these movements of mind will become senior over the other depending on what you are giving your attention to.

All of our relationship challenges are eternal, and therefore will require love, tolerance, patience and understanding intelligence in order to solve them. This means all relationships: the relationships with family, friends, co-workers, neighbors, fellow citizens of the same planet, the relationship with abundance, happiness, and the present moment. All relationships are eternal.

Sacred traditions say that you can prove this to yourself. Just ask yourself if you will always be in relationship with yourself. Will that ever change? When you hear yourself answering, "No, that will never change, I will always be in relationship with myself." You have just heard yourself give the correct answer. You have just proven to yourself that relationship is an eternal problem requiring eternal consciousness to reconcile. This means you will never solve a single relationship challenge by having thoughts and beliefs about the relationship. All you need to know is that you show up from your Heart. For therein lies the exact wisdom you are looking for.

When we look around the Earth, we do not see a lot of problems being instigated by people who are coming from their Hearts, speaking truth openly and honestly. The people coming from their heads, however, can lie, cheat, steal, attack, and re-create all manner of difficulty and suffering for everyone. Ask yourself when is it that you become confused, uncertain and insecure? Is it when you are lost in your head, swimming in an agitated pool of thoughts and beliefs? Or are you more likely to be confused about how to respond to life when you are centered in the Heart, feeling one with love, and connected to life itself?

Suppose we had a spiritual MRI machine that could examine the contents of a person's mind, similar to the X-ray machines at airports that examine the contents of a bag without opening it.

If we put an average unenlightened person through our machine, what we would see is a collection of thoughts and beliefs that would look something like this:

※ I am going to be left out and alone.

※ I am the person that my parents reject.

※ It is going to work out for everyone but me.

※ I'm the person that always gets dumped in relationships.

※ I am the person that always gets overlooked for promotion.

※ I always get in the slowest line at the supermarket checkout.

※ No matter how much money I make, I never seem to have enough.

※ I am not going to have enough time, money, love, or the opportunity to get through life.

※ No matter how many times I change lanes on the freeway, I always get stuck in the slowest moving lane."

Sound familiar?

Thoughts and beliefs – just exactly who is working for whom? As Jesus says, "You cannot serve two masters." You cannot give your attention to the limited consciousness of the ego (thoughts and beliefs) and give your attention to unlimited consciousness (love, abundance, and good faith) at the same time. Do you know whom you are serving?

Zen Buddhist Masters are aware that we have two forms of consciousness. They have developed a very useful technique to reveal this reality to the students. These Masters have the same response to any question a student might ask, and the response is, "Who is asking?" No matter what the student asks, over and over again the Master's response is, "Who is asking? Who is asking?" The Master is not asking for the student's temporal name, ID on their library card, or driver's license.

The Master is asking, "Do you know you have two forms of consciousness? Do you know who is talking to you at any given moment? Do you know who is asking this question, temporal or eternal consciousness? Who is asking? Who are you trained to give your attention to? Do you know? Do you know who you are serving?"

If someone tied a blindfold around your eyes, and then proceeded to inform you about how you were to navigate your way through life, how you were going to understand your power, your nature, your purpose, the very first thing you would do is ask, "Excuse me, but who are you? Whose information is this? Are you Homer of the Odyssey fame or Homer of the Simpson's fame? Are you Karl Marx, or Groucho Marx? Mark Twain or Shania Twain? Are you Moses who parted the Red Sea, or Grandma Moses who painted red flowers? Are you Buddha? Shiva? Jesus? Who?"

Zen Buddhism reminds us that we would not live five seconds of our exterior life this way - taking extremely important information from an unknown source. Yet we live all of our interior life not knowing who is communicating with us? Why is that?

The great spiritual teacher J. Krishnamurti once phrased it something like this

> *So, that instrument which is thought has produced this world. The chaos, the wars, which very few will accept. It's not valid (thought). Most of all now, it is producing problem after problem. The politicians try to solve one problem, in the very solution of that problem, they are increasing multiple problems. The scientist are doing the same . . . So understand that instrument which human beings have used for thousands of years is worn out, is no longer valid, is no longer worthwhile. Both outwardly and inwardly we are in tremendous crisis. And all this is brought about by thought . . . Then we must look for another instrument. Is there another instrument, or is man condemned forever to this way of life, which is brought about by thought . . . Thought has not solved a single human problem, psychological problem[3].*

One problem within human consciousness is that we are still killing each other, the planet and ourselves. After a million plus years, not only have we not solved a single problem, but we have made all these problems worse. Why? We are using the wrong form of consciousness. We are not awake enough to know we have two! We are not awake enough to use the most appropriate one at the most appropriate time.

When we hear the voice in our heads telling us about our power, our value, and our worth, we do not consider "who is asking?" We simply respond by giving it all of our attention. This is what we have practiced with our love. Since we are what we love and we love what we give our

3. This quote comes from the New Dimensions Radio program number 1782

14

attention to, we are living in our very own ego-recreated hell. We just don't know any better. As long as we give all of our attention to the temporal, to the voice in our heads, we'll be living in hell instead of Heaven. Remember we are spirit, pure awareness. Like the soul, we do not have awareness, we are awareness. We are not our hair, bank account, or clothing. We are not our experiences, thoughts, beliefs, or emotions. All these things come and go. We are eternal. We cannot be anything in the temporal world; we are really awareness experiencing itself. We are using the temporal world only as a mirror, or device for self-reflection.

Krishnamurti used to compare thoughts and beliefs to the illumination of a single candle. He would ask his audience, *"Why would you live your life by the illumination of a single candle, when you could have the sun?"* He also liked to ask:

> *Why should one have belief at all about anything? You don't believe the sun rises and the sun sets. You don't believe in the constallation of Orion. You don't believe London esists, it's THERE! Beliefs like ideology have divided man!*[4]

Krishnamurti is suggesting that life, truth, and self exist independent of our thoughts and beliefs about them. It is only in our letting go of our thoughts and beliefs about what is and ourselves that real authentic life, truth, and self can find us. When we let go of illusion we can find true reality, meet it, touch it, and become One with it. Krishnamurti used to say *"to learn language thought is necessary! To go from here to there, there thought is necessary. But psychologically and inwardly thought has no place."*[5]

4/5. These quotes comes from the New Dimensions Radio program number 1782

This is such a great question. Why do we have this neurotic need to manufacture beliefs? The answer is only because we are deeply habituated to do so; only because we are brainwashed to live in our heads and not in our Hearts. As a result, we become unconsciously programmed to the lower form of consciousness; to think and believe our way through life, instead of using the higher consciousness to feel, love and trust our way in life.

Why can't we just be in the present moment with an open Heart creating the space for reality to tell us something about its true self-evident nature? Why don't we shift our focus to eternal consciousness, to the ever increasing, ever expansive form of consciousness, instead of limiting ourselves to the ego-based information of thinking and believing? What if we shifted to knowing the truth by giving it our unconditional attention? Then we could become One with this higher form of consciousness, and thus end all of our problems.

Why is feeling the love and wisdom of Heaven a higher and greater form of intelligence than all the thoughts and beliefs ever had by everyone combined? Thoughts and beliefs are only useful for solving limited, temporal problems in the limited, physical world. If used to solve eternal problems, they will rob you of the very thing you seek to create. To illustrate this point, let's take two different scenarios. One involves right use of consciousness, and the other does not.

First imagine you are an eternal being here to master the journey out of the head, and into the Heart - mastering the use of only eternal consciousness to solve your eternal problems, and the use of only temporal consciousness to solve your temporal problems. You are a realized being knowing and experiencing two forms of consciousness. You know which form of consciousness is talking to you at any given moment, exactly how much attention to give each form of consciousness, and when to give it.

As a realized being in right relationship with your mind, you will also find you are in right relationship with the emotions of life. (Yes folks, there is a connection.) What you are doing with your attention is determining whether you live in Heaven or hell. And trust me on this one . . . you are going to feel a wide difference between living in Heaven and living in hell. When you are in right relationship with *what is* – you will be One with the feeling/knowing of love. You will be One with the present moment, confident, self-assured, nurtured, carefree, expansive, powerful, grounded, fully capable, and fully supported in all aspects of life. You will be aligned at all times with the truth that you are pure love. You will be experiencing the deep healing comfort that comes from knowing that Heaven is in command of all things and all people. You will have practiced trusting the movement of love's wisdom as it manifests itself on Earth, to the exclusion of all the ego's noise.

In our second scenario, you are a spiritual creature that does not realize you have two forms of consciousness, and you do not know what attention to give to each. You would be giving all your attention to what you think and believe you are. Usually this is simply the memory in mind deferring to some old out-dated experiences, stories and feelings that the ego then uses to inform you of what your capability and worth are. You would be thinking and believing your way through life:

I can't do this. I'm a failure. How come that jackass in

marketing got the promotion instead of me? Why is it that no matter what stock I buy it always goes down? I'm going bald and no one will go out with me. My butt is getting so big it is now dense enough to generate its own gravitational field. I'm always broke. I'm always on a diet, and I always buy the losing lottery ticket(s).

More importantly with the second scenario is that you would be feeling contracted, unsupported and worried. These are not the feelings manifested by giving attention to a higher consciousness. Your body would also be reflecting this attention to limitation in the form of contraction: your stomach knotting, your throat and jaw constricting, your muscles tightening, and your blood pressure rising. The nervous system, not to be left out, would be screaming, "Whew! Do I need a drink or a smoke!" What the body is really feeling is nature's form of biofeedback, mirroring back to us what we are doing with our attention. Here on the rock all life forms have signed up for the "sentient school" of learning. Here we all physically experience what we are doing with our mind and with our love in order to become fully awake. God, not to be out done, has always had very effective ways of inviting us to get real about what we are doing with our consciousness.

Swedenborg likes to visualize the mind in the image of a wave. Imagine a wave on the ocean. Only the very top 10% of the wave, the crest, is what we call "consciousness" or "awakened consciousness." Everything under that top 10% of the crest of the wave down to the trough, is the 90% of mind that represents the unconscious or subconscious. We are here because having a sentient body is the best way to become conscious of the remaining 90% of our wave that is hidden. How do we do this? How do we become conscious of something that is invisible and we are unaware of?

This is how – by paying attention to how you feel. Whatever the 90% of the invisible unconscious mind is doing, it is going to have to be felt by you. That is how you can tell from the 10% that is conscious, what you are unconsciously focusing on with the other 90%. According to Swedenborg, our feelings are our higher consciousness. That makes what you feel your highest truth barometer, your greatest truth divining rod. What you are feeling, here on the Earth, is the contents of your mind. What you're feeling is the ultimate form of biofeedback available anywhere. What you are feeling is what you are giving your attention to.

Specifically what you are feeling is how your mind is organized. According to how you feel, your mind is either organized to match the same loves, affections and affinities as Heaven or as hell.

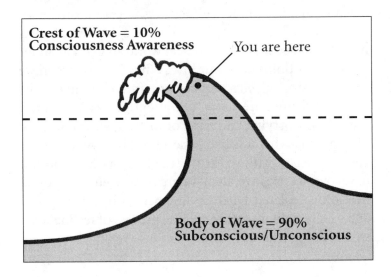

Crest of Wave = 10%
Consciousness Awareness

You are here

Body of Wave = 90%
Subconscious/Unconscious

"Feelings: What I used to think about, now I feel"
– Argisle

Ever wonder what that white, frothy, foam-like substance is that rides on the top of the ocean waves? Swedenborg says that in our image of mind as a wave on the ocean, the white frothy foam corresponds to thoughts and beliefs. They are nothing more than this superficial foam. This is a particularly fascinating comment from a man of science. Most of us have our awareness surfing almost exclusively at the crest, or top of the wave. Even more limiting than that, most of us spend all our time hanging ten on the froth, never even penetrating into the greater mysteries of the wave. Bobbing along on the froth instead of swimming through the wave brings a whole new definition of a shallow and meaningless existence brought to you by the limiting power of thoughts and beliefs.

We are here to fully realize our mind; here to discover the true contents of the entire wave. Without exception, the true meaning and purpose, the very nature of every person's life, is to practice focusing unconditionally on what Heaven loves instead of what the ego loves. There is no better place than the physical world to get real about what we are doing with our love. Why? Because when we get here, we are given a nervous system, so we can feel the truth of what we are giving our attention to. We can feel the hell of worrying and lying or instead, we can feel the difference in what it is like to be a force of love. When we align ourselves with the truth, the truth that we do not have love, we are love, then we are in Heaven. Everything here on the planet Earth is designed to help us get real and to remain honest through the process of feeling what we are doing with our love.

So what do we do with all the unresolved inner critic re-created stories, impressions, "truths" which we have told ourselves about life, and others? Why, we unconsciously stuff this litter into the subconscious 90% of the wave, of course!

After depositing the litter of what we think and believe into the bulk of the wave for lifetimes, how do we now begin to develop the needed process of inner-wave house cleaning? How do we get our conscious hands on our unconscious and invisible trash and recycle it? By feeling where the clutter and the garbage is.

We answer the question by turning our attention inward, to observing how the stimulation of life affects our feeling or emotional body. Swedenborg suggests we can become conscious of what we love, of what the unconscious is focusing on, by mindfully monitoring how we feel. Anytime we are aware of the emotional body feeling fearful, anxiety riddled, anxious, ungrounded, wound up too tight, or any other limiting sensations, we are really feeling the unrealized 90% of the wave, our subconscious, trying to use temporal consciousness to solve eternal problems. It is our feelings, not the ego, with the inner communication that does not lie. With our mind reflected back to us in a physically based reality, we can now use reality to feel as well as to see the invisible.

The Buddhists say the unrealized portion of mind is projecting its story out in a three-dimensional reality so that we may realize the relationship we have with mind; the relationship of loyalty and dependence we have trained ourselves to have with the ego and fear-based information. When we practice focusing on the truth to the exclusion of everything else, we are separating ourselves from the tyranny of the ego and its need to generate fear within our wave. This is when we become fully self-realizing.

The spiritual purpose of the Earth is to provide a physical feeling based reflective arena, in which our unresolved inner states of mind become manifested outwardly so that we may practice realizing our unconscious mind. Anytime we are looking at a situation going on in front of our eyeballs, the only way that this dynamic can be happening is if the same situation is occurring behind our eyeballs. Nothing can exist physically in an exterior reality unless we have that same relationship going on within ourselves.

In order for anything to exist outside of us, it must first exist within us as an interior reality. If we are feeling judged, criticized or unaccepted by others, what we are authentically experiencing is the relationship that we are having with our own mind. Our unrealized mind, or wave, is projecting this relationship, this dynamic of judging, criticizing and non-acceptance of ourselves out onto others. It now becomes the real life story of what others are doing to us. This is not bad. This is not good. This is simply how unrealized beings relate to each other. The mind has developed this response to judge, criticize, and to not accept life in its entirety as a side effect of its habitual use of temporal consciousness to solve eternal problems. We all do it until we realize ourselves. The nature of an unrealized wave is to project its unconscious contents out into the three-dimensional world so that it may become self-aware. It is through this self-awareness process that we discover that we are what we love, and we love whatever we are giving our attention to at this very moment. Remember we are here to realize that everything is mind being reflected back for self-realization. There is nothing else.

Jesus once said, "You know a tree by its fruits." The unrealized mind, or wave, has a relationship with the ego that bears this out. Cheech and Chong unknowingly interpreted Jesus' saying in one of their early comedy routines:

The two are walking down the street, and Cheech says to Chong, "*Hey man, is that shit there on the sidewalk?*" Chong replies, "*Yeah, I think it is.*" Cheech then suggests, "*Well, why don't you smell it?*" Chong protests, but he eventually leans over and deeply inhales. "*Yep,*" He informs his buddy, "*It smells like shit, all right!*" Cheech then suggests to Chong that he taste it to be sure. Again Chong protests, only more strongly this time, and again he finally concedes to tasting the evidence. "*Yep,*" he again informs his buddy, "*It tastes like shit all right!*" Cheech then, quite brilliantly, concludes, "*It looks like shit, it smells like shit, it tastes like shit. It must be shit! Good thing we didn't step in it!*" Chong immediately supports this conclusion, "*Yeah, good thing we didn't step in it!*"

If what you hear from the voice in your head feels limiting, smells limiting, looks limiting, and tastes limiting, you're listening to the ego's shit. There's not much fruit on that tree, and certainly no need to taste it, unless you've developed a fine taste for shit. If you are giving your attention to something that feels expansive, such as trusting in divine love, then your tree will bear unlimited fruit, such as patience and happiness. Jesus would love this Cheech and Chong routine. It flawlessly, albeit a little graphically, illustrates the truth: you do indeed know a tree by its fruits. Bon appetite!

Reflect back on when you were a kid. When you became confused and asked for guidance, how many teachers or parents told you, "You come complete. You have everything within you that you need to know. Just drop into your Heart and reveal it to yourself." This is rare. Instead how many teachers or parents smacked you on the back of the head and yelled, "You got a brain, use it!" All the emphasis and value is on the process of thinking and believing your way through life. There has not been much support or appreciation in the modern world for loving and trusting your way through life, huh!

We have all been deeply brainwashed from birth to become thought and belief dependent, to over-ride our feeling/knowing truths. Remember when you were in kindergarten? The first thing you learned was to put on your thinking cap. Well it is time we loosened the grip of that fashion accessory and let some real love flow through.

We are here in a body to practice de-programming the wave from the unconscious habit of thinking and believing our way through life. We are here to admit that we do not know what reality is. If you think we know what reality is, how come if there are five witnesses to a car accident, every witness gives a different version of "reality"? If we knew what reality was, we would have ended our suffering by now. In admitting that we do not know what reality is, we lay down all our thoughts and beliefs about it. Instead of formulating thoughts and beliefs about reality, we need to let reality show us what it is.

As Dr. Phil McGraw, a modern day relationship teacher, is so fond of saying, *"We have the relationship with others that we have trained them to have."* This statement is so true and accurate, it applies to every level of mind. We have the relationship with our ego that we have trained it to have with us. If we are racked with worry, anger, and fear, then we have trained the ego that it can come right in and take over. We have trained the ego to tyrannize spirit's relationship with happiness and the present moment. We have trained the ego to put a story, or memory of limitation, in front of our attention. We then respond by abandoning the truth and turning toward this ego-based illusion, a very familiar deeply trained response indeed.

Internationally renown Tibetan Buddhist teacher Sogyal Rinpoche in his New York Times best-selling book, *The Tibetan Book of Living and Dying* says it like this:

> *The Buddhist meditation masters know how flexible and workable the mind is. If we train it, anything is possible. In fact, we are already perfectly trained by and for samsara, (a state of suffering and limitation) trained to get jealous, trained to grasp, trained to be anxious and sad and desperate and greedy, trained to react angrily to whatever provokes us. We are trained, in fact, to such an extent that these negative emotions rise spontaneously, without our even trying to generate them. So everything is a question of training and the power of habit. Devote the mind to confusion and we know only too well, if we're honest, that it will become a dark master of confusion, adept in its addictions, subtle and perversely supple in its slaveries. Devote it in meditation to the task of freeing itself from illusion, and we will find that with time, patience, discipline, and the right training, our mind will begin to unknot itself and know its essential bliss and clarity.*

The purpose of everyone's life is to shatter this tyranny. Break the bond and transform that relationship into an unconditional Oneness with Heaven. We can do this by consciously choosing what we are giving our attention to at any given moment, by realizing whether we are solving a temporal problem or an eternal one.

Realize we have two forms of consciousness, and recognize when we are giving our attention to something other than the truth. Surrender our addiction to thinking and believing our way through life and relationships. Practice negotiating from our Hearts not our heads. Give up all of our memories and stories, especially those that do not support the truth - that we do not have love, we are love. Embody the truth that we are love until that is all we feel. Then Heaven becomes the exclusive contents of mind, the exclusive contents of the wave. Only then will we experience that the wave is truly One with the ocean, One with the same loving truth as the ocean. So make yourself comfortable, please, because the show is not over till the enlightenment lady sings, or until the fat lady becomes 'enlightened', whichever comes first.

The following story is originally taken from Leo Tolstoy. This story is a jewel that beautifully sets into right context the formation we have been sharing.

One day it occurred to a certain emperor that if he only knew the answers to three questions, he would never stray in any matter.

What is the best time to do each thing?

Who are the most important people to work with?

What is the most important thing to do at all times?

The emperor issued a decree throughout his kingdom announcing that whoever could answer the questions would receive a great reward. Many who read the decree made their way to the palace at once, each person with a different answer.

In reply to the first question, one person advised that the emperor make up a thorough time schedule. Consecrate every hour, day, month and year for certain tasks, then follow the schedule to the letter. Only then could he hope to do every task at the right time.

Another person replied that it was impossible to plan in advance. He suggested that the emperor should put all vain amusements aside, remaining attentive to everything, in order to know what to do, at what time.

Someone else insisted that, by himself, the emperor could never hope to have all the foresight and competence necessary to decide when to do each and every task. What he really needed was to set up a Council of the Wise and then act according to their advice.

Someone else said that certain matters required an immediate decision and could not wait for consultation. If he wanted to know in advance what was going to happen, he should consult magicians and soothsayers.

The responses to the second question also lacked accord.

One person said that the emperor needed to place all his trust in administrators. Another urged reliance in priests and monks, while others recommended physicians. Still others put their faith in warriors.

The third question drew a similar variety of answers.

Some said science was the most important pursuit. Others insisted on religion. Yet others claimed the most important thing was military skill. The emperor was not pleased with any of the answers, and no reward was given.

After several nights of reflection, the emperor resolved to visit a hermit who lived up on the mountain and was said to be an enlightened man. The emperor wished to find the hermit to ask him the three questions even though he knew the hermit never left the mountains. He was known to receive only the poor, refusing to have anything to do with persons of wealth or power. So the emperor disguised himself as a simple peasant, ordering his attendants to wait for him at the foot of the mountain. He then climbed the slope alone to seek the hermit.

Reaching the holy man's dwelling place, the emperor found the hermit digging a garden in front of his hut. When the hermit saw the stranger, he nodded his head in greeting and continued to dig. The labor was obviously hard on him. He was an old man, and each time he thrust his spade into the ground to turn the Earth, he heaved heavily. The emperor approached him and said, "I have come here to ask your help with three questions: What is the best time to do each thing? Who are the most important people to work with? What is the most important thing to do at all times?"

The hermit listened attentively but only patted the emperor on the shoulder and continued digging. The emperor said, "You must be tired. Here, let me give you a hand with that." The hermit thanked him, handed the emperor the spade, and then sat down on the ground to rest.

After he had dug two rows, the emperor stopped and turned to the hermit and repeated his three questions. The hermit still did not answer. Instead he stood up and pointed to the space and said, "Why don't you rest now? I can take over again." But the emperor continued to dig. One hour passed, then two. Finally the sun began to set behind the mountain. The emperor put down the spade and said to the hermit, "I came here to ask if you could answer my three questions. If you can't give me any answer, please let me know, so that I can get on my way home!"

The hermit lifted his head and asked the emperor, "Do you hear someone running over there?" The emperor turned his head. They both saw a man with a long white beard emerge from the woods. He ran wildly, pressing his hands against a bloody wound in his stomach. The man ran toward the emperor before falling unconscious to the ground, where he lay groaning. Opening the man's clothing, the emperor and hermit saw the man had received a deep gash. The emperor cleaned the wound thoroughly and then used his own shirt to bandage it. The blood completely soaked it within minutes. He rinsed the shirt out and bandaged the wound a second time and continued to do so until the flow of blood had stopped.

At last the wounded man regained consciousness and asked for a drink of water. The emperor ran down to the stream and brought back a jug of fresh water. Meanwhile, the sun had disappeared and the night air had begun to turn cold. The hermit gave the emperor a hand in carrying the man into the hut where they laid him down on the hermit's bed. The man closed his eyes and lay quietly. The emperor was worn out from a long day of climbing the mountain and digging the garden. Leaning against the doorway, he fell asleep. When he arose, the sun had already risen over the mountain. For a moment he forgot where he was and what he had come here for. He looked over to the bed and saw the wounded man also looking around him in confusion. When he saw the emperor, he stared at him intently and then said in a faint whisper, "Please forgive me." "But what have you done that I should forgive you?" asked the emperor. "You do not know me, your majesty, but I know you. I was your sworn enemy, and I had vowed to take vengeance on you. For during the last war you killed my brother and seized my property. When I learned that you were coming alone to the mountain to meet the hermit, I resolved to surprise you on your way back and kill you. But after waiting a long time there was still no sign of you, and so I left my ambush in order to seek you out. Instead of finding you, I came across your attendants, who recognized me, giving me this wound. Luckily, I escaped and ran here. If I hadn't met you, I would surely be dead by now. I had intended to kill you, and instead you saved my life! I am ashamed and grateful beyond words. If I live, I vow to be your servant for the rest of my life. I will bid my children and grandchildren to do the same. Please grant me your forgiveness."

The emperor was overjoyed to see that he was so easily reconciled with a former enemy. He not only forgave the man but promised to return all the man's property and send his own physician and servants to wait on the man until he was completely healed. After ordering his attendants to take the man home, the emperor returned to see the hermit. Before returning to the palace, the emperor wanted to repeat his three questions one last time. He found the hermit sowing seeds in the Earth they had dug the day before. The hermit stood up and looked at the emperor. "But your questions have already been answered." "How's that?" the emperor asked, puzzled.

"Yesterday, if you had not taken pity on my age and given me a hand with digging these beds, you would have been attacked by that man on your way home. Then you would have deeply regretted not staying with me. Therefore the most important time was the time you were digging in the beds. The most important person was myself. The most important pursuit was to help me. Later, when the wounded man ran up here, the most important time was the time you spent dressing his wound, for if you had not cared for him he would have died. You would have lost the chance to be reconciled with him. Likewise, he was the most important person, and the most important pursuit was taking care of his wound. Remember that there is only one important time and that is now. The present moment is the only time over which we have dominion. The most important person is always the person with whom you are, who is right before you, for who knows if you will have dealings with any other person in the future. The most important pursuit is making that person, the one standing at your side, happy. For that alone is the pursuit of life!"

An Image That Makes Them Sad

How long will grown men and

women in this world

keep drawing in their coloring books

an image of God that makes them sad?

—By Meister Eckhart

Chapter Two

Ultimate Truth &
Ultimate Lies

there is always infinite abundance

there is only the One,

Chinese Medicine and Ayurveda are two of the oldest known methods of self-healing on the planet. These structures of self-knowledge were in practice long before the spiritual was separated from the physical. Ayurveda, from Eastern India, is Sanskrit for "the science of daily life." The idea being that there is a science to the mastery of every-day life, and that this mastery is a required step in the eventual mastery of the wave, of mind as a whole. These ancient Eastern healing sciences, including Tibetan Medicine, all describe an original disease from which stem all other diseases. These healing practices say that once this original disease has been healed in a person's wave, that person will never be sick again. They will not only have perfect physical, mental, and emotional health, they will have completely fulfilled their life purpose: they will have reached enlightenment.

These ancient healing traditions say that every person on the planet is born with this disease, and if it is not resolved in their lifetime, they will die with this disease. If a person does not heal themselves of this disease, when the body dies, this unresolved disease will cause the spirit to reincarnate over and over again, until the disease *is* terminated within the wave. Every person who is not fully enlightened is suffering from this disease. Every wave that has ever been here on the rock has had this disease. Everyone you have ever known, or will ever know, has this disease. The sole purpose of the creation of the planet Earth is to offer spiritual beings a place to go with an opportunity to practice ending this disease. This disease is what keeps a wave from realizing it is not a wave at all; it is the ocean. When the disease is removed, there are no waves, only the ocean, only the One. This disease has nothing to do with germs or airborne viruses. This disease cannot be passed from one to another through touch, bodily fluids, or intimate contact. Neither the American Medical Association nor any Western allopathic doctor you have ever seen has acknowledged this disease. It cannot be treated with vaccines or modern pharmaceuticals. It cannot be seen with x-rays, ultrasound, or cat scans. It cannot be grown in a petri dish or placed in a particle accelerator. Yet this disease is the root cause of all the pain, all of the other diseases, all of the suffering, and all of the violence on the planet. This disease is a spiritual malady that enters into the wave through the doorway of perception. Remember that you are what you love, and you love whatever you are giving your attention to. When you love anything limited, anything that lives outside of Heaven, anything not in alignment with the truth that there is only the One, then you love this disease. Because you *live* according to your Ruling Love, if you love this disease, then you must also *live* with it. The ancient healing systems have a name for this disease. They call it the disease of duality.

Look out at the exterior world. If we think and believe it is real, that it has nothing to do with us personally and how we relate to mind, then we are asleep; we are caught in the disease of duality. We are giving our attention to the ego instead of to Ultimate Truth. Duality keeps us from realizing Ultimate Truth.

Without intending to, Albert Einstein left us a beautiful description of the effects of the disease of duality:

> *A human being is a part of the whole, called by us "Universe," a part limited in time and space. He experiences himself, his thoughts and feelings as something separated from the rest – a kind of optical delusion of his consciousness. The striving to free oneself from this delusion is the one issue of true religion. Not to nourish the delusion but to try to overcome it is the way to reach the attainable measure of peace of mind.*

If we were to be so rude and crude as to reduce Ultimate Truth to two sentences, then according to sacred traditions, it would look like this:

Ultimate Truth

　1. There is only the One.

　2. There is always infinite abundance.

This is the entire contents of an angel's or enlightened being's mind. Period. If we put an angel or enlightened being through the spiritual MRI machine that we talked about in *Chapter One,* what we would see on the screen is: There is only the One (self beyond duality); there is always infinite abundance. That is it. The mind has been completely emptied of everything temporal, illusory, and ego re-created. There is only truth. No fillers, no additives, no preservatives, or artificial colorings.

Ayurveda, Chinese, and Tibetan Medicine all define an enlightened being as one who has healed mind (the wave) of the disease of duality; an *unenlightened* being is one who has not healed mind of the disease of duality. From an Eastern perspective this is the most basic definition of enlightenment: a perception of self and life that exists separate from duality.

What is duality? It is the psychological ether you and everyone else are ignorantly swimming in. Duality is subject/object orientation. I am over here, and I am separate from everything else. I am the subject. Everything around me that I experience is the object – something other than me. We come into this world and relate to it right from the gate in subject/object. I am so and so, son or daughter of so and so. I am a mother/father. These are my children. Those are my neighbors, boss, co-workers, etc. I am here, and everybody else is out there. "I" being the subject in the relationship, and everything else being the "object."

This gives rise to the illusion that there is more than one of us here. The truth is, there is only the One: One life, One present moment, One God consciousness, and One source of real happiness and abundance that we are all *sharing*. The truth is that whatever you have done to another, you have done to yourself, because there is only One of us here.

Alan Watts, a humorous interpreter of Eastern philosophies, used to talk about what he called the "Let's all remember we're God game!" God was hanging out, being all knowing and all seeing. Things got a little dull, so God decided to break up Its own consciousness into little bits or sparks, and then to take away the memory from the bits or sparks. By doing this, He took away the memory that they are collectively God. What we have left over is the "Let's all remember we're God game." It is not like you are God, and I am God. It is more like we *all* are God, for there is only the One.

The "Let's all remember we're God game" is like the Beatles. John is a Beatle, as is George, Paul, and Ringo. Is John a Beatle by himself? Of course, but he is not "The Beatles" by himself. That requires the collective performing and living as One to be the Beatles. Yeah, yeah, yeaaaaahhhh!

The Tibetan Buddhist teacher Sogyal Rinpoche articulates beyond duality as follows:

> *Saints and mystics throughout history have adorned their realizations with different names and given them different faces and interpretations, but what they are all fundamentally experiencing is the essential nature of mind. Christians and Jews call it "God"; Hindus call it "the Self," "Shiva," "Brahman," and "Vishnu"; Sufi mystics name it "the Hidden Essence"; and Buddhists call it "Buddha nature." At the heart of all religions is the certainty that there is a fundamental truth that this life is a sacred opportunity to evolve and realize it.*

Spirit lives and grows strong in alignment with the One. The ego lives and grows larger and stronger in the petri dish of duality. The ego loves and needs duality in order to survive, in the same way the physical body needs oxygen to survive. The ego requires duality in order to maintain its tyranny against mind. Without the tyranny of duality, how could any wave experience *more than* or *less than?* Without duality, there would be no difference between *more powerful* or *less powerful.* All feelings, impressions, stories and memories of worthy, unworthy, lovable, unlovable, capable, not capable, abandoned, supported, good or bad are all held together in mind by the disease of duality. The disease is the illusion that there is a *you* separate from the One. If there was no you and no me, no subject, no object, then there would only be the One, and Ultimate Truth: there is only the One, there is always infinite abundance.

The discussion about duality, or of true self as *beyond* duality, is most predominately seen in the Eastern traditions such as Taoism (which is inseparable from Chinese Medicine), and Buddhism (which is inseparable from Tibetan Medicine). It is also seen in many other sacred traditions as well. In Christianity, we see it as Jesus' proclamation, "The Father and I are One!" and in the statement, "Whatever you have done to the lest of my brethren, you have done to me." In the Jewish/Arabic traditions we see it in the expression, "There is no God, but God." Thus a renunciation of the temporal, with full attention given to the eternal. There is only the One. There is only eternal God consciousness.

The Sufi tradition, a Middle Eastern mystical sect, is most poetic and magical in its depiction of self existing as Pure Awareness. What the Sufis, as well as others, speak of is a *Flame of Pure Awareness.* The Judeo/Christian tradition refers to the experience of *self as a Flame,* as in the appearance of the burning bush to Moses. The *Flame of Pure Awareness is the universal existence of self beyond duality.* The *Flame of Pure Awareness* is our spiritual body, the one we brought with us when we came to the physical world, and the one we take with us when we go. The *Flame of Pure Awareness* is what we really are when temporal thoughts and beliefs, experiences, emotions and memories are stripped away. The *Flame of Pure Awareness* is the universally well-known "white light" that we will all move into when our human experience is over. The *Flame of Pure Awareness* is what is passed on from reincarnation to reincarnation. It is the spirit that dwells within the temple of the body.

When awareness is trapped in duality, awareness experiences incomplete action, our thoughts and beliefs. This incomplete action then makes an impression or mark on the psyche. The great sacred traditions speak of an unenlightened mind as filled with *impressions* or *wounds*. The Sanskrit word is *samskaras*. The purpose of life is to realize and empty the mind of these impressions, stories, conclusions, thoughts and beliefs, or wounds. All of life on the Earth in a physical form is the creative practice of performing self-soul surgery: removing the stuff we are here to get over. This spiritual surgical technique is called *witnessing*.

All spiritual beings, while having a physical experience, acquire impressions in the wave from the disease of duality. This is all part of the karma of moving through life while asleep. The mind, the wave, is giving all of its attention to what the ego is telling us. As long as the mind listens, the ego will proceed to tell us what our power, value and worth is, and how much of it we have permission to embody at any given moment.

> **The ego, the voice of limitation, tells us that life basically boils down to an equation:**
>
> We = screwed + indebted + in trouble + out of control
>
> Others = powerful + more fortunate
> We < Others

Solving the equation is easy: we are screwed, in debt, in trouble, and out-of-control. Others are more powerful and fortunate than we are. Therefore we are less than others. (And you thought math was hard!)

The ego will always direct us towards the limited outcome just like we trained it to do. These ego-based stories, conclusions, thoughts and beliefs are now charged with the energy of our attention, which makes the wound in the wave. The use of awareness that makes this impression or mark on the psyche is an *incomplete action*. In Hinduism and Buddhism, incomplete action, or incomplete cause and effect, is called *karma*.

We can visualize these *impressions* as a kind of karmic map of mind. If we want to know what our biggest, nastiest karma is, just look at what our biggest, nastiest belief is about ourselves, about life, about relationship, about others, and we've hit pay dirt. The ego is a lot like CNN but without the commercials. If you watch your mind, your wave, it will parade in front of you all the news you have trained it to program and air over and over again, ad nausea.

There is a relationship between being unconscious and accumulating karma, and being conscious and burning off karma. It all depends upon what you are doing with your awareness. Let us approach understanding what happens when we are unconscious as the accumulation of *incomplete cause and effects*. When we are unconscious, we are not in the present moment, we are not accepting *what is* from an open Heart. When we are unconscious we are listening to the ego's limited, tiny version of reality from the head place. This is *not* what we came here to do with our will, love, service and life purpose. It is therefore an *incomplete action*.

When we are conscious we are in the present moment with *what is* from an open Heart. When we are conscious it is the *Flame of Pure Awareness,* the Heartfelt wisdom from the feeling place within, that observes with gratitude the perfection of every given moment. Since this level of conscious practice is the highest function behind the design and creation of the physical world, it is what we came here to do. It is therefore a *complete action.* Witnessing *what is* from the Heart is a conscious action that burns off negative and incomplete karma, which accumulates when we listen to the ego from the head.

Incomplete action or duality happening within the wave would look like this: I give my attention to thoughts and beliefs about who and what I am; I give my attention to thoughts and beliefs about who others are, what life and relationship(s) are; I understand myself, life, world and value system through the deeply trained habit of seeing everything from a subject/object perspective. This would appear internally as an inner dialog that sounds like, "I am a successful attorney, superior to the dregs I squash in court. My power is that I command respect and am a force to be reckoned with in the courtroom, even though I respect no one other than myself. I drive a sixty foot long Mercedes and I live in a multi-million dollar mansion, in case you were interested in seeing my value and worth measured against yours. This behavior and these possessions make the appropriate statements about my obvious superiority and importance." The dialog could run in the reverse direction, "I am a lowly piece of shit that no one could possibly love or respect."

With incomplete action, a person's awareness goes out into the exterior world and touches an object: another person, a house, a car, whatever. Incomplete action occurs when the awareness coming back to the person tells them that whatever they perceive is exactly what they think and believe it is. No one came here to listen to the ego's version of reality; that is an *incomplete action*. In doing so, we re-create a story of duality: another person with so much power and worth, who in turn affects my sense of power and worth. It is all cause and effect: thoughts and beliefs re-create limitation, which re-creates more thoughts and beliefs, which re-creates more limitations. It just keeps spiraling downwards until it is out-of-control.

The action is incomplete because it was not witnessed by the aspect of mind we recognize as the *Flame of Pure Awareness*. The action was witnessed instead by the ego, by the disease of duality. So when the action is witnessed by the disease we are all here to get over, it fragments the mind. It creates more duality, which in turn drives every known and unknown disease and limitation even deeper into the wave. We've created our own personal hell.

The action needs to be witnessed by the aspect of mind

that has the inherent power to return our mind to a state of wholeness, beyond the illusory grasp of duality, which fragments mind into many tiny pieces. This action can only occur when we give our awareness to eternal consciousness for solving our eternal problems, without a thought or belief, because that is the action we came to the rock to complete. That is the sole action that makes the *Flame of Pure Awareness* the senior witnessing force in our lives.

The action is made complete only when awareness going out into the exterior world touches something, and the awareness coming back to the person is then run through the *Flame of Pure Awareness* in the Heart, not through the ego-head filter. The *Flame of Pure Awareness* keeps the person in witnessing mode. Without it, we would fall immediately back into the limitation of what we think and believe life and self are. The *Flame of Pure Awareness* is beyond duality intelligence, beyond subject/object orientation. It is the unifying, indivisible quality of authentic intelligence, which reveals, recognizes, and realizes the interior through the process of witnessing it in the exterior.

The *Flame of Pure Awareness* is the intelligence that *sees* and *gets real* about how mind is organized by witnessing itself reflected back in the medium of the physical world. This is what Jesus means when he refers to "Those who have eyes to see;" those who *see* not illusion, but rather the movement of realized love, movement of the One everywhere.

When awareness realizes itself, it is purified, and that is the action we came here to complete. When mind becomes self-realizing the action is complete. The purpose of all created life, the purpose of a physical world, is for self-realization. It is to fully realize we are what we love, and we love whatever we are giving our attention to. Once we realize what we are doing with our love, manifesting either Heaven or hell on a moment to moment basis, then the action is complete. The purpose of being here has been realized.

When mind realizes it is looking at itself, the seeds of karma become purified, or roasted by the *Flame of Pure Awareness*. Then, no karma sprouts up and grows from this action. The action is complete because we got from it what we came here to realize. Karma is repeating whatever you need to, until you get it. In future chapters we will refer to the karma of an incomplete action as re-creation. Anything born from a limited intelligence, such as the ego, will only have the capacity to re-create what is already here, which is itself limiting. Only healthy God consciousness is unlimited and can therefore create something new, manifest something from nothing. We all came here to create a new response to ultimate lies, to end the limitations we are all here to get over. Eternal consciousness has the power to create a new response to any old or new problem. The ego, on the other hand, can only re-create over and over again. It cannot create something new. It is a limited form of consciousness. What do you want from it? If the ego is providing the answers to all of your eternal problems, there is only one possible outcome for you. Look up *futile* in the dictionary, if you have not already guessed what that outcome will be.

Understand that this whole shootin' match was created for the convenience of your enlightenment. As God consciousness, as eternal consciousness, if there were a better, faster, easier way to reach enlightenment, you'd be doing it. You'd already be there. If you do not understand that everything you are experiencing here is the exact, perfect reflection of the relationship you have with your own mind, then you will be destined to re-create what you think and believe it is. That would be re-creating the limitation you are here to get over. *This will continue until you realize that what you are looking at is your own mind, and then choose to move on from that place of truth.*

In the name of integrating this idea of self as the *Flame of Pure Awareness,* the Sufi's have a saying, "Remember you are the *fire* and not the wood." The meaning behind the saying is true self is what you really are, not what you think and believe you are. Authentic self exists independent of what you think and believe. This is the *Flame of Pure Awareness.* It burns away all illusion, all duality, all toxicity in mind re-created by giving our attention to temporal consciousness (the ego) to solve our eternal problems (who am I, why am I here?). You, your true self, are the fire. You are not the illusion, the wood, the projection of mind that is being destroyed, burned away and purified.

You are not the body, divorce, bankruptcy, the diagnoses of a disease, anger, worry, less than, powerless, memories, feelings, thoughts, beliefs, or the things you've learned. Everything that is temporal will change. That is its nature. You are not any of these things. You are eternal consciousness; you are the part of the program that does not change. You are the eternal awareness that is constantly flowing from you. You are the witnessor of everything that changes. Being eternal, you cannot be anything that changes. You have come to witness the end of self re-created illusion. You, as true self beyond duality, have come to destroy the karma that holds these self re-created illusions together by running it through the *Flame of Pure Awareness.*

Instead of identifying with the wood (the dream, duality, what we think and believe reality is, what we think and believe we are), we wake up to Oneness with the dream maker, with our higher self. We wake up to the consciousness that has been dreaming and projecting it all, instead of being stuck in the illusion that we are the dream, or stuck in the invisible trap of thinking and believing we are some character within the dream. We wake up to the aspect of mind that is creating the whole dream. We realize ourselves as the producer and manufacturer of the dream instead of thinking we are a tiny part within the dream.

Giving our attention to the *Flame of Pure Awareness* is called *self-witnessing*; it is the ending of karma, the annihilation of subject/object orientation, the completion of self-realization. Witnessing occurs in life when we look at the physical realm, the exterior, and see how it is a mirror of our interior. For as it is above, so it is below; as it is within, so it is without. Self-witnessing *sees* how our mind is organized: what form of consciousness we are giving our attention to and why. What problem are we solving? Is it a temporal or eternal problem? It is in this action of self-witnessing that we realize the relationship we have with mind. It is this fully realized or recognized state that ends karma. If we do not wake up from duality and recognize it, then we will repeat the karma, the incomplete action, the cycle, the story, the pattern, the limitation, the suffering. We will repeat it until we do get it.

There is absolutely no way around this repetitive process, as the planet Earth was created precisely for this opportunity to practice the mastery of complete action. This is the place, with all of its physical distractions, to practice the truth that we are pure love, and absolutely nothing else. The limited, unrealized relationship we have trained ourselves to have with the *Flame of Pure Awareness* is what we bring with us to the Earth plane to work on until it becomes fully realized. Like the song *New York*, "if you can make it here, you can make it anywhere."

The Eastern traditions speak of enlightenment as perfect nothingness. This means enlightenment is self-realization beyond duality. The word nothingness here in the West can best be understood as no - thing - ness: no subject/object perception that creates a thing. No subject, no object, no thing: just the One. Self-realization is beyond the mind's involvement with subject/object. The mind no longer perceives subject/object. There is no other thing; there is only self; there is only the One.

Everything we see, touch, taste, smell, experience, and feel is the movement of the One love. We are dreaming each other. In the same way, when we dream at night, we are everything in our dream. We are the sky, the roads, the other dream characters. We are projecting mind out in the form of a dream story. When we awaken from our nocturnal dream, Buddhism would argue that we are not really awake at all. We are still asleep within the dream. We have not yet *awakened* to the true nature of reality that we are all really pure love. We are still attached to knowing reality through the most limited form of consciousness. We are still attached to our stories and memories of what we think and believe life and self is.

In the story of the Buddha, he is asked if he is God. The Buddha responds, "No, not the way you think and believe." "Well are you a planet come in a human form?"

the people would ask. And the Buddha would reply, "No, not the way you think and believe." The people would then ask, "Well, what are you?" And the Buddha would answer, "I am awake. The only difference between you and I is that I'm fully awake"(no longer caught asleep in the disease of duality).

The state of a fully awakened mind the Buddha is referring to, is not what you and I would call awake. The reality we call "awake" is defined as getting up out of bed and going through our every day life. Buddhism would understand this state as still *asleep* or *un-awakened* to the true nature of self and reality, because you are literally asleep at the wheel; you are *sleepwalking* when you are still thinking and believing your way through life. You are not *awake* to the reality that you have two forms of consciousness. Are you not *awake* to which form of consciousness solves which problem; not *awake* to which forms of consciousness you willingly choose to serve; not *awake* to the universal law that you are what you love, and you love whatever you are giving your attention to.

The Buddha's fully awakened state is also the Chinese Medicine and Ayurvedic definition of enlightenment: a mind that has healed itself of the disease of duality. Awakened and beyond duality are One, just as duality and asleep are one.

Taoism says "Our true nature and the eternal Tao are One." The temporal Tao can be named, because temporal consciousness, duality, and words are all a limited form of intelligence. The eternal Tao cannot be named, because words exist only in duality. The eternal Tao is beyond duality. True self is beyond duality, beyond words, thoughts, or labels.

In the 1980's a few years before he died, J. Krishnamurti was on the *New Dimensions* (radio program number 1782), Meditation Mastery: A dialogue with Krishnamurti. He talked about what the world would be like if everyone on the planet knew the true nature of our inter-connectedness; if everyone lived and related to each other from the Heartfelt place of Oneness!

> *If we could go into the question of what is thinking? Why thought has made life so utterly wearisome, cruel, beastly for what it is not. If you once admit, not only logically, but actually, that human consciousness is not individual consciousness, it is the consciousness of all humanity. That is very difficult to not only intellectually accept it, but to feel it. Then you become tremendously responsible for what you are doing . . . To have peace on Earth, one has to live peacefully, and that peace can not be brought about by legislation . . . Intelligence can not exist without love . . . through thought you can not achieve the immensity of life.*

All wars are created by conflict in thoughts and beliefs. *My* God, *My* Country! We must realize that we are neither defending God nor country. We are defending merely what we think and believe God is or is not, what we think and believe our country is or is not. We are engaging in a most violent and unhealthy relationship with mind in order to protect and defend our illusions, our projections of mind, and our stories of duality. We give our attention and love to investing in lies in order to protect the very stuff we came here to get over. Shocking isn't?

Krishnamurti went on to detail how we have the capability with today's technology, wealth, and means to distribute food, clothing, shelter and generally to provide everyone on the planet with an equitable standard of living. Because we are all One, as long as there are others on the planet who are in life and death situations, mind is still trapped in the pain and tyranny of limitation and survival. We are sabotaging mind by living the ugly lie that our lives, health, and happiness are somehow separate from the universal life force of others residing on the planet. The true nature of all suffering is a mind trapped in the tyranny of duality, re-created by giving attention to thinking and believing our way through life, instead of loving, accepting, and trusting.

Krishnamurti described a world where all beings *know* the One; living the truth that your happiness depends on supporting the happiness of the One. Your living completely requires loving the life of the One in its infinite expressions. The One is everything. The One is everyone here now. The One is everything and everyone that has gone before, and everything and everyone that will follow. How wonderful to lucidly live a life of such clarity. Truly the only way spirit lives and actively embodies such truth is when spirit gives all attention to the truth, and nothing else. As Swedenborg reminds us, we are what we love. We do not live or exist separate from what we love. And we love whatever we are giving our attention to.

Putting duality, itself, under the microscope of awareness can be tricky. As the saying goes, "Fish are the last ones to know they live in water." When mind is caught in duality, the Catch 22 is to realize the subject/object perception (the water) in which you live. When you live in the water of duality, you do not see the duality. What you see is subject/object orientation that is familiar. Relating to *what is* through the filter of subject/object is how you know who you are from the rest of the world.

Subject/object perception is how the wave has been brainwashed or rather wave washed to see *normally.* You do not *see* that the disease *is* subject/object perspective itself. Subject/object as the disease itself separates your attention from the direct experience of the One, which is beyond the subject/object mirage.

The disease of duality has an extremely insidious, invisible grip on the unconscious portion of every wave. This is why it is essential for everyone to practice ending it now. Respond by practicing coming from the Heart and not the head: by practicing loving and trusting that Heaven is running everything, by practicing remembering that reality is not what we neurotically think and believe it to be. For without practicing *seeing* life through the *Flame of Pure Awareness,* how will we ever gain right perspective and thereby end our suffering, enabling us to move on from the rock? This is the key to successful living. This is the real secret of a life worth living. This is the definition of a fearless life.

Infinite Abundance

All unrealized, unenlightened beings are filled with memories, stories, thoughts and beliefs about how self, life, and relationships are riddled with scarcity: not enough love, not enough time, not enough money, not enough opportunity, etc. Heard this before?

The truth is that we are One with love, and as love, we therefore must be One with infinite abundance. How could we be love, and not be infinitely abundant at the same time? If we are love, how could we be lacking in anything? The only way we could be experiencing the illusion of not having enough of anything is if the limited thinking that we are here to get over dilutes our focus. This is the place where the suffering is drastically reduced when you practice knowing the difference between what you really are, and what is the crap that you are here to get over. By confusing what we really are, with the shit we are to leave behind, we re-create endless misery and unhappiness, not to mention what confusing the two does to our experience of value, power, and worth.

Our job is to become self-realizing about what we love; what we are giving our attention to. From the awareness that we have two forms of consciousness, we train the wave to give its attention exclusively to Ultimate Truth. Our job is to do a *core dump* of any and all information that does not match and support Ultimate Truth. Everything else is illusion, the stuff we are here to get over. It is our conscious relationship with the truth that allows us to have a life worth living.

Here is a wonderful story from Swedenborg's life about letting go of self re-created limitations:

A man, who was a big Swedenborg fan, was being sent on a business trip to Stockholm where Swedenborg lived. The man wrote to Swedenborg to inquire if it would be possible for the two of them to meet while he was in town. Swedenborg, being the embodiment of Heaven's love, invited the man to visit. When the man arrived, he explained to Swedenborg that he had read all of Swedenborg's writings about the spiritual realm. The man went on to explain that he had heard all the amazing things Swedenborg had to share about spirit and the nature of the soul. He just needed it proven to him personally.

The man told Swedenborg about a friend of his who had

died. He explained to Swedenborg that he was the only one in the room when his friend died, so he is the only living person who knew what they were talking about at the time of his friend's death. The man wanted Swedenborg to journey into the spiritual realm, find his friend, and ask him what they were talking about at the time of his death. Then Swedenborg would confirm the dialog with him, the only living witness.

Swedenborg, in addition to his vastly numerous writings, also experienced what he called "minor miracles." Swedenborg did not write about these "minor miracles" himself. We know about them because of other people who were astonished by them, and wrote about them. One such person was the German philosopher Immanuel Kant, who was one of the first to observe and research the otherworldly abilities of the then elderly scientist and statesman.

Swedenborg asked the man if he had heard of his journeying into the realm of spirit for important information for such notables as the Queen of Sweden, as well as others. The man informed Swedenborg he had indeed heard these stories, but implored Swedenborg that he needed the situation made *up-close and personal.* Swedenborg told the man to return in a few days so that he could look into his request.

When asked a question, Swedenborg would always go into a trance-like state to consult with the higher order angels of the spiritual realm. If he was informed that the question had benefit for all sentient beings, then he would be given the answer. However, if the angels Swedenborg consulted informed him the question put forth was simply a game of mental masturbation (I'm paraphrasing, of course), then Swedenborg would tell those inquiring that the information was not given. They would then simply go away empty handed.

The man returned a few days later. Swedenborg shared that he had been given permission to find the man's friend in the spiritual world of Heaven and hell, and he was able to ask what the two were discussing at his time of death. The man became every excited. When Swedenborg revealed what the two men had been talking about, all of the truth of Swedenborg's writings came to bear on the man's mind.

The man said, "Then it is all true. Everything you've said about Heaven and hell, you are what you love, and you love whatever you give your attention to; this is all true! So, please, tell me," the man said, "that my friend you found is in a level of Heaven?" "I'm sorry," Swedenborg replied, "but your friend is in a level of hell." "But why?" the man asked, "It is not like he was a bad person that went around deliberately hurting others." "Your friend is in a level of hell," Swedenborg lovingly explained, "because of the very things the two of you were talking about at the time of his death. Because of the things you think and believe about yourself and others." The man was totally shocked. He asked Swedenborg, "You mean we take those things with us into the afterworld?" "Oh yes," Swedenborg replied, "and in the spiritual realm it is extremely difficult to make separation from our stories. *So, why don't we agree in this moment to put down our limitations. Here. Now. While we can*[6]."

6. The Presence of Other Worlds, by Wilson Van Dussen

Look at all the time and energy we individually and collectively give to the story that we do not have enough. We, as a people, are consistently worshipping the self re-created story that we do not have enough time. We tell everyone we meet, "I don't have enough time. There are not enough hours in the day." We defer life, under the guise that we don't have enough time to really live, because we have all this stuff to do. We organize our day, week, year, and finally our lifetime around the lie - we don't have enough. Not enough time, money, love, and opportunity; these are the four big relationships we keep insisting will never be there for us. After empowering this lie for years, for lifetimes, with all of our awareness, is it really that surprising that this is the self re-created hell we live in?

The truth there is always infinite abundance, means each person, each spirit, has the free will needed to recognize and remove the obstacles that keep mind from being infinitely abundant right now, in this and every present moment. We are not restricting infinitely abundant to a mere superficial definition that stops at the monetary level. Oh, no. We are expanding infinitely abundant to a qualitative, as well as a quantitative, dimension of experience. We are talking about infinite abundance in every aspect of life: abundant health, abundant good faith in the movement of love in all things, abundant creativity, and abundant time. Most importantly we are talking about abundant caring, nurturing, honest, happy relationships everywhere in our lives.

What would it look like if a spiritual being, having a human experience, were to *know* there is only the One, there is always infinite abundance? Just exactly how would that look? It would appear as a Jesus turning water into wine, raising Lazarus, dividing a few fish and loafs of bread to feed thousands of people. It would appear as a Jesus shattering the greatest limiting illusion of all - the illusion of a personal death. It would appear as a Buddha also shattering the illusion of death, by coming back into the poisoned physical body on his deathbed to answer questions before finally discarding the physical shell. It would appear as a Milarepa, the great Buddhist saint, who lived for years off of nettles and the song of the Heart. After being heavily poisoned, he did not leave the body until he lovingly transformed and liberated the mind of the man who poisoned him. It would look like a Joan of Arc, whose heart would not burn with the rest of her physical body. It would look like all the saints who gave unconditionally, and yet were never touched or diminished by the suffering and horror raging on around them. There is always enough God (eternal) consciousness in every moment. When you give that truth your attention, you are One with that truth, because you are what you love, and you love whatever you are giving your attention to.

To intimately *know* Ultimate Truth with our awareness, that there is only the One, there is always infinite abundance, is to connect our wave with the ocean. It is to unconditionally unify spirit with source, with true power and strength, and with the unlimited mind. It is from this place of Oneness, of unification, that real tolerance, compassion, patience, and trust can blossom. It can flow freely from Heart to Heart, soul to soul and life to life. Why? Because we are ultimately One.

With the advent of modern diagnostic equipment, scientists have been able to verifiably measure that the average person uses only 5% - 10% of their brain. Modern science knows this, but they do not know why. Chinese and

Ayurvedic medicine, thousands of years ago, without all the fancy equipment, also realized that people used only a very small portion of their entire brain. The primary difference is that these ancient healing sciences know why we access such a limited portion of our potential. Our relationship with the right use of temporal and eternal consciousness is so poor! We lose so much of our energy thinking and believing our way through life, that we literally do not have the energy to access the rest of our mind. We have poured all of our water into the sand. The way we live our lives is so unconscious, that we are ignorantly flushing all our life force down the drain. We are doing this all in the name of solving our problems and being more efficient. Ironic as hell, isn't it?

As *The Beatles* point out, we need to *"fix the hole(s) where the rain gets in, and stop our mind from wandering where it will go."* We must first live the only appropriate relationship with eternal consciousness by giving our attention to love. The only way we can possible have access to the energy we need to live an unconditional life is to be One with the energy of infinite abundance; to be One with Ultimate Truth. To be One with Ultimate Truth is to give it our exclusive attention because we are what we love, and we love whatever we are giving our attention to.

Ultimate Lies

The ego, otherwise known as limited consciousness, has its own version of Ultimate Truth – Ultimate Lies. The karmic effect of spirit giving attention to Ultimate Truth is liberation, freedom, and unconditional happiness. The karmic effect of spirit giving attention to ultimate lies is the exact opposite: duality, limitation, suffering, and unconditional unhappiness.

Because the ego is a limited form of consciousness, its version of the truth, what we recognize as ultimate lies, is extremely limited in imagination. The ego's ultimate lies can be summed up in two sentences as well:

Ultimate Lies

1. You are separate from love because you didn't do it right, and you're not good enough.
2. There is not enough love, time, money, opportunity . . .

It is not brain surgery to see that these lies are the exact opposite of Ultimate Truth, and that these lies are extremely familiar, because they are systemic in our world. Spirit cannot be giving attention to both the truth and the lies at the same time.

When examining the ultimate lies of the ego, we can clearly see the source of all our suffering, insecurity, worry, struggle, stories of abandonment and less than, and victim-hood. If we examine everything in our lives that makes us unhappy, we will find the story, the lies, that we are not love, and that there will not be enough of

_____.

(*Fill in the blank*)

Why have we trained the ego to give our attention to these lies? Because we have trained the ego that we will understand ourselves, others, and all of collective life through the insidiously diseased filter of *didn't do it right, not good enough, not enough.* We construct an infrastructure of suffering and limitation in our lives when we give attention to the ego's lies as a benchmark for understanding and determining the reality of our value, power, and worth.

In witnessing the movement of the wave, you will find every thought and belief based bit of information is steeped in duality. It is aligned with the agenda that, "I'm over here, and love is over there, and there is a mountain of not deserving and unworthiness between the two of us." The ego will point out that it can *prove* to us that we do not deserve love.

The ego will prove its point by giving us a blow-by-blow description of where it believes we did not do it right:

1. You could have done better.
2. Compared to others, you just do not measure up.
3. A five-year-old in a coma could have done better.
4. Why can't you do anything right?

That voice doesn't *feel* good, does it? It feels more like the shit on the bottom of your shoe and smells like it too.

Now the real truth is that we do not have love, we are love. We do not have power, we are power. We do not have value and worth, we are value and worth. We do not have divine consciousness, we are divine consciousness! How can God consciousness possibly create a learning experience of itself it did not need? As God consciousness, we cannot create a learning experience that we do not need, and we cannot create these learning experiences before or after we need them. So where did we *not do it right?* How could we possibly be *not good enough?* This information, *didn't do it right* or *not good enough,* is so horribly limited that it could only have come from one place, one very limited place: hell; the home of all that is limited; the home of the ego's excrement. And we know this, because we know a tree by its fruits.

In his writings, Swedenborg talks about why we can only practice unconditional love on the physical plane until we fully realize it, and why we cannot practice this evolutionary necessity in the spiritual realm. According to him, it is only on the planet Earth that a spiritual creature can hide or cover up their Ruling Love (this is what Swedenborg calls the main or primary aspect of a person's soul). Because of this physical aspect a person can deceive you; they can put on a con artist face. The bottom line is *you can be lied to here.* In the spiritual realm, it is a completely different story.

In the spiritual realm, everyone can see clearly up front everyone else's Ruling Love. No one can lie to another there, because lying only happens if someone involved does not realize the truth. When everyone can see the truth, you can't lie, or at least you can't get away with it like you can here. Swedenborg indicates that whenever there is a dispute, or conflict about the truth being spoken in the spiritual world, a higher order angel appears and speaks the truth so that it will be known by all. That would come in real handy here when buying a car, swimsuit, or dating.

There is a purpose for living in a place where you could be fooled, and you *know* you can be fooled. Here on the Earth, because you can be deceived and betrayed, each spirit has the opportunity to practice honestly showing up from the Heart, trusting that Heaven determines everything. It is here on the rock that we practice showing up from the Heart because we want to, even knowing we can be hurt. No one and nothing else has any power over us in our lives except Heaven. Being that Heaven is the most powerful force around, it wins!

The rock is the only place where we can practice showing up, no matter what others do, no matter what events occur, and still continue to give our attention to honesty, good faith in life and love, tolerance, and compassion. Why? Because in this arena we cannot fake it. This is the only place where we can practice living in Heaven, because we love living in Heaven, and for no other reason. When living in Heaven is its own reward, you cannot be sabotaged into giving something else your attention. When you love giving your attention to what Heaven loves, for no other reason, for no other pay off, than this is what you love, then and only then can you no longer be corrupted, or distracted from living unconditionally in Heaven.

We practice loving unconditionally here because we must. This is the only place where you can find yourself caught in the crosshairs, so this is the only place you can practice being immune to victim-hood, less than and unhappiness. Earth is where we come to practice choosing love, and to practice aligning the wave with generosity, regardless of what temporal threats arise. We require an arena we cannot fake it in, in order to practice being One with love and generosity for no other reason than this is what we love. For as we have no doubt already experienced, in the physical world of illusions, the person or persons you are loving and being generous with may turn around at any moment and betray you right to your face!

You can be lied to and betrayed by your husband, wife, children, teacher, boss, elected official, dogcatcher, whatever. On the rock, we learn to love in a way we cannot in the spiritual realm. In the spiritual realm we can see the deception coming. Here we learn to love and give because that is what we feel right about, and for no other reason. We are all familiar with situations on Earth that could come back and bite us on the ass later. We are here because this is the only place where we can practice being fearless. We came here to practice showing up from the Heart, because it feels right. No matter how others treat us. No matter what they say. No matter what they do.

This world was constructed for the purpose of practicing the fine art of being the best possible person that we can be. When asked for help, we respond, even if it turns out that it was a lie, and we got burned. We would help and give fearlessly to each other, because we want to live in a world where the inhabitants show up to help and support each other. We worship Ultimate Truth. We choose to respond to mind unconditionally, because there is only the One, and there is always infinite abundance. It is only by giving our attention to Ultimate Truth that we can have the energy and support we need to unconditionally master a loving mind.

Not Enough

The second part of ultimate lies is that there is *not enough*. It permeates our suffering as well as the lyrics to our *didn't do it right, not good enough* song. The *not enough* singers harmonize with the *separate from love* melody until we have a very ugly noise: "I have all these bills and all these responsibilities; I have all this work, and never enough time and money to do the things that I want; I'm single, and I want to meet someone, but all the *good ones* are taken; I can't change this; I'm not strong, smart, or privileged enough; oh, this situation will never change; this relationship will never change; my unhappiness will never change." Sound familiar? All of this rhythmic music is brought to you courtesy of the ultimate lies concert series.

Our job is to realize where we have given our attention to the ego's lies. We need to dismantle the toxic relationship we have with our attention by realizing *what* we are loving, and then shifting our attention to Ultimate Truth, because the truth heals every lie the ego has ever told us.

The ego's job, in effect, is to rob us of truth, happiness, real power, and the present moment. The ego is looking for the same job security that everyone else in the temporal world wants. If the voice of limitation sabotages our relationship with truth and gets our attention with its lies, then it remains the senior influence of mind. The ego is, in fact, so limited that without our attention it fails to exist. However, when we give it our attention instead of starving and reducing it, the ego becomes the ruling master. We serve it and feed it more and more by thinking and believing our way through life. We set our attention on autopilot to the ego's lies, and all we accomplish is to further set-up the ego. Now it lives in its own gated community with a swimming pool, a hot tub and plenty of attitude. Never to leave, never to be evicted without a lot of drama, kicking and screaming.

Ayurveda has some fascinating observations about the ego's relationship with happiness. According to Ayurvedic psychology, the best inroad to destroying our present dysfunctional relationship with the inner critic is to be happy. The ego, being a limited form of consciousness, thrives off of limited thoughts and emotions. The most limited of all states of being is unhappiness. That is the ego's favorite food. It loves to manufacture stories and beliefs that will eventually take us to a very unhappy place. The really insulting thing about all this is that the ego will use the very power of our attention to strand us on the unhappy fantasy island. And yes, this one comes without the tall friendly looking guy in the white suit and the little guy screaming, "da plane, boss!"

Ayurveda describes the process of giving our attention to Ultimate Truth, as a process that will take us to a very happy and unlimited place. Giving our attention to the truth is like throwing water on the Wicked Witch of the West from the Wizard of Oz. The truth will melt the ego's ugliness and set free our innocence to return home. Ayurveda says that when you are happy, you are in the present moment, and you do not have a problem with it. Ayurveda also says that enlightened beings are in the present moment without a problem. So when we are happy we are practicing an enlightened state of mind. We are practicing liberating the wave, hanging ten in the curl. Cowabunga, Dude!

Ayurveda describes the ego as hating two things. The first is the present moment. Ayurveda suggests that we see this for ourselves in our everyday relationship with the present moment. Just try taking one day out of your life to examine your awareness. We need to stop ourselves at different points in the day to sample where our consciousness is on the time continuum. How much of the time are we here now? How much of the time are we projecting off into the future, or back into the past? If we are being really honest, we will see that very little of the time are we here now.

What we are experiencing with this time projecting phenomena is the ego's subtle, covert hatred for the present moment. If we will reflect back on the temporal and eternal list, *(Chapter One)* the interesting detail we will find is that we really are the present moment. Please, do not take the ego's hatred of you personally. There is nothing personal in it. The ego just happens to hate anything that is unlimited, infinite and eternal. Why? Because limited never did learn to play nicely with unlimited, that's why it's limited!

The second thing the ego hates is the imperfection, or flaws it perceives life to be riddled with. It relentlessly blames the present moment for all of these. The ignorance of the ego dictates that the present moment is deeply and inherently problematic, screwed-up, wrong, flawed. It is too fat, too thin, too little, too big, too ugly, too beautiful, not big enough, not small enough, etc. The ego has a judgment about how and why this present moment is not acceptable, not good enough, not the perfect divine food it actually is. According to the inner critic the present moment is not delivering the *right* outcome that it has an attachment to controlling. The ego cannot be with *what is* in the present moment with an open Heart.

Ayurvedic psychology describes the ego as an *empty shell,* similar to the empty shell of a circus tent. For enlightened beings, the circus tent looks like the tent has been collapsed, and the contents have all been removed. All unenlightened beings, by virtue of the attention they are giving the ego, have succeeded in keeping the drama on-going. The circus tent is completely puffed up, the smell of animal waste is in the air, and the three-rings are full, complete with clowns and jugglers. Unenlightened beings do not *see* the circus tent for the empty shell that it truly is. Duality, subject/object identification keeps the unenlightened wave asleep, playing out whatever role the disease would dictate within the tent. That is how we find ourselves stepping in the ego's shit, over and over again. We are like the man who sweeps up behind the elephants at the circus. When his friends ask him why he does not quit his crappy job, he is shocked. In horror he replies, "What! And give up show business?"

We need to ask ourselves how we will ever create an end to worry or any other limitation in our lives if we keep giving the ego our love and attention? If you went to a five-star resort and were offered the finest food and lodging, would you leave? When we give our attention to the ego we are freely offering it the most incredible succulent sustenance and the most luxurious living conditions. Why would it leave?

We need be awake in our everyday life to know who is talking to us, and how much attention to give to which form of consciousness. Each deserves its right and appropriate due. If we are not balancing our checkbook, or solving some other temporal problem in the temporal world, then we do not need to be giving the voice of limitation our attention. We need to learn to live in a manner in which we know what intelligence is needed to solve what problem, and what intelligence we are giving our attention to at any given moment.

A realized person would not step in the trap of ultimate lies, and therefore would not get caught in the tyranny of the ego and duality. Why? Because when the *separate from love* voice started to speak, a realized person would then tell the ego, "Excuse me, ego, but I do not have love. *I am love.* I do not have power. *I am power.* Love is the very fabric and nature of my being-ness. Love is nothing that could be lost or taken away. Only the voice of limitation could tell me that. So ego, you have a choice: you can either become love and Ultimate Truth because that is where I put my attention, or leave this nervous system . . . Don't let the door hit you on the way out."

A realized mind would transform the ego's story by recognizing the lies and then shifting attention immediately to Ultimate Truth. How do we get to this place of real self-witnessing, to this inner place of dismantling the relationship with suffering we have trained the ego to re-create? The same way we get to Carnegie Hall. Practice! Practice!

Begin by practicing making mind your friend (what a concept!). When we unconsciously give our attention to the ego, the wave is no longer a friendly or comfortable place to live. When we make the ego our greatest love, by giving it the greatest portion of our attention, then we live in the hell of limitation, scarcity, and duality. We need to develop a relationship with awareness itself that serves us.

We can retrain our relationship with the ego so that it works for us. We want the voice of the ego to remind us of where our focus has unconsciously wandered off to, so that we may consciously return it to Ultimate Truth to self beyond duality. That is how we create an ending to limitation and suffering, how we master the practice of remembering to love what Heaven loves, until the only place we live and visit is Heaven.

When the inner limitation alarm system goes off, when limiting, fear-based information hits the nervous system, its presence there is actually designed to awaken us. It is to remind us to be aware of what we are doing with our attention. This is the truth behind the existence of all suffering. It is nature's way of saying, "There is inappropriate form of consciousness being used here. Examine your life. Examine mind. Examine where you are placing your attention." Suffering is nature's way of saying, "Put the weapon of thoughts and beliefs down. Step away from that inappropriate form of consciousness, and no one will get hurt."

The self-witnessing process is, in fact, the Heart and soul of most sitting meditation practices. When a person is practicing most sitting styles of meditation, the person is sitting upright, eyes usually closed, attention turned inward, and all awareness is watching the breath: the inhale, the exhale. Watching the breath brings the person into the present moment. Why? Because breathing does not happen in the past or in the future. Breathing is happening now. Breathing only exists in the present moment.

We practice watching the breath, watching the movement of the wave. When a thought or belief goes off (which it will), mind then witnesses this action. Mind recognizes it as a thought or belief, *then lets it go.* The attention is then brought back to the breath, back to the present moment. Thus we practice being in relationship to self without a thought or belief. We practice recognizing which form of consciousness we are giving our attention to. Most importantly, we practice making continuous separation from the tyranny of what we think and believe as real. We practice coming back innocently into the Heart, to be with *what is* in the present moment with an open Heart.

Beyond the formal meditation practice is the big living meditation of life. As our awareness moves through life, we become aware of our own inner dialog as well as communication from the outer world around us. Our job and joy is to remember there is only the One. What we are becoming aware of is *mind*. What we are looking at is the *relationship we have with our own mind*. What we are listening to is the charge we have re-created about ourselves, so that by becoming self-realizing, we may create an ending to the stuff we came here to transcend.

The meditation of life requires we remain awake to self-witnessing, and not get caught asleep in the dream of duality when the ego starts telling us what reality is while we are working, driving, shopping, cooking, cleaning, or talking on the phone. In the flow of our everyday life is when we must remember Ultimate Truth. We must remember that we are what we love, and that we love whatever we are giving our attention to. We must also remember that we live according to what we love. In the midst of our daily life, if we suddenly also find ourselves in the midst of hell, we must ask, "What are we doing with our love? What have we done with our awareness that has put us in the express elevator straight to hell?"

When Swedenborg was asked, " What can a person do to have a life worth living?" His reply was that it had nothing to do with *doing*. It is not a doing thing. It is an awareness thing. It is a remembering and a forgetting thing. Remembering to give awareness to the truth, to love, to freely and willingly bring our awareness into the present moment. Remembering to share the love and aware-ness of Heaven, thereby joining forever the wave and the ocean, and to simply forget everything else.

Surfers call <u>it</u> "Getting Tubed (Entubarse)" (inside the Wave.) – Argisle

Chapter Three

Everything Is Mind

There is always infinite abundance

There is only the One

Divine love and wisdom are the most powerful forces in the universe. They created *what is*, – everything that is or ever has been. The everything that is or ever has been is mind being reflected back to itself for the purpose of self-realization. There is nothing other than mind, and the movement of mind. You see these forces mirrored back to us universally as well. The physical manifestation of a physical world with physical bodies, and physically based experiences is simply to support the embodiment of this process of self-realization. This is the sole purpose of all created life.

All of life is a mirror, reflecting back our relationship with the temporal and the eternal, so that we can *see* it and *feel* it honestly in an arena that we cannot fake. Earlier we examined how we could see mind, and the movement of the temporal and eternal. Where these forces meet and become One, in the present moment, is when we are with *what is* with an open Heart. This movement is also mirrored back in the symbols from Taoism, and Judaism, as well as the Christian traditions.

The Real Food of Life

All these traditions speak of life, everything that touches us here on the rock, as a form of food. Chinese medicine and Ayurveda also refer to the contents of life as a form of food as well. These great healing traditions say that our bodies are really an incredible digestive phenomena and intelligence. The body is actually a physically amassed collection of different kinds of digestive intelligences working together as one. Everything that touches us is a form of food. Everything we touch, taste, feel, experience and think is a form of food. We, as spirit having a physically-based experience, come fully equipped with a stylish assortment of digestive features and accessories for every occasion and for every form of food that will ever be served to us.

Buddhism and Tibetan medicine refer to a human as an "aggregate" of digestive intelligences. Our eyes digest light waves and particles in order to make perceptual sense of our world. Our ears digest sound waves so that we may hear our loved one's call, answer the phone, or enjoy the Beatles and Jimi Hendrix. We have all experienced our skin as digestive in the following way: anyone who has ever been in love knows when they run their hands and fingers through their lover's hair or across their skin, something big is going on there. Our hands are digesting the intimacy, the closeness through the digestive vehicle of the nervous system and the phenomena of touch.

We come from the manufacturer this way, because everything we experience here *is* the evolutionary divine food from Heaven, designed to feed our soul. The first thing we must be able to do with this food (our emotions, thoughts, experiences, perceptions, everything that happens to us here) is to swallow it; then we need to be able to stomach it; finally we must pull from it what we need and release the rest as waste.

Unrealized beings do not understand that what they think and believe about themselves and others *is* the waste portion of the program. They hold on to the waste. That is the way their mind is organized. They think and believe they need it. They do not know they have two forms of consciousness. They do not know they are using the most inherently limited form to solve the most inherently unlimited problems.

The amount of physical toxins found in the average person's physical body corresponds to the spiritual toxicity that has accumulated in the wave over time. This happens when we give our attention to the ego to tell us who we are, what our power and worth is, why we are here. The ego is a limited form of consciousness. The answer it provides us will always be limited, and that will always affect us in a limiting way. In other words, the emotional net result of the karmic incomplete action of listening to the ego is always going to be addiction to suffering and toxicity.

We see this reality reflected back to us with so many people suffering from colon cancer, irritable bowel syndrome, constipation, and other colon related diseases due to the unreleased waste. Why does the physical waste get backed up, trapped, dried on, attached, and built up in unreleased pockets? Why does the body recognize some toxins and dump them, but does not recognize all the toxins.

The body, like everything else here on the rock, is mirroring back to us what we are doing spiritually with our love. The first truth being reflected back to us is that we cannot tell the divine food from the unresolved waste! (We *really* don't know shit from shinola!). As a result we are deeply committed to unconsciously thinking and believing our way through life. We have become addicted, over time, to the toxicity. The bottom line is we are spiritually constipated.

We are asleep because we are unaware of the higher reality, that there are two forms of consciousness at play here for solving two very different forms of problems. All of our experiences and interactions is mind being reflected back for self-realization. There is nothing else. If you are under the impression that you are presently experiencing something else, then what you are really experiencing is the myopic responses re-created by your thought and belief system. You are experiencing the stuff you are here to get over, instead of experiencing the truth that everything is mind reflected back for your dining and dancing pleasure.

We think and believe we need the "crap" of criticism. We think and believe we need the contaminating influence of *didn't do it right,* and *not good enough* in order to end our relationship problems. Without critical judgment of ourselves and others how will we be able to distinguish the dregs and losers from the good, right and responsible people? How will we know who to like and dislike? How will we know who to blame? How will we know who to put down and who to make superior to the rest? We have made thinking and criticism the familiar foundation of our everyday lives. That is not the healthiest spiritual choice we could be making with our attention. We have not awakened to the reality that when we try to solve our relationship problems by making another inferior, all we seem to accomplish is a very successful shit slinging contest just like the monkeys do at the zoo, but without as much fun.

We approach life with a strategy that if we could only get more into our heads, we would finally be happy; if we could manipulate and control *what is* from this place of mistrust, in our heads, everything would turn out okay. *Wrong!* The way we have our love organized, we cannot tell the temporal from the eternal. We need to realize this approach is the waste portion of the program, and somehow separate ourselves from it. Hello, front desk of life? We need a *wake-up call!*

> *No matter what we think we know . . . We grow*
> *—Argisle*

Everything in the temporal world *is* a form of food that we need in order to reach enlightenment. We are *only* sent the food we *need to grow,* and only *when we need it.* Do we really want to live a life where the ego rules and responds to eternal consciousness with, "I do not like your food, it is all wrong. I positively will not accept it. And I most certainly will not be grateful for it." The ego will never stop judging Heaven's food as inferior. The ego's agenda is to make all of life look and feel as limiting and unhappy as it can possibly make it. Is that really the relationship we consciously wish to create with this perfect food that is the evolution of our soul?

Let us begin to recognize and trust our divinely sent food. We know that if we needed to be doing or living something else in order to reach enlightenment, we would be. As God consciousness we cannot create an experience, or food for our souls, that we do not need. We can trust our lives. We can trust, embrace, and be grateful for all of the divine food sent to us to end our suffering, no matter how it looks or feels, no matter how it is interpreted by the ego/the inner critic.

We have a tendency to think and believe that the things in the illusory or temporal world are more powerful than we are. We think the stuff that we are here to get over, like emotions, bills, experiences, etc. are really endowed with some special juice. Relating to these temporal things as more powerful than we are, is like sitting down to our lunch, and thinking and believing that the tuna fish sandwich has more authority and relevance than we do. This is not a useful or serving relationship to be having with our food. Relax! We can be the senior movement with an open and loving Heart to any temporal food we are served. Whatever it is, it came from Heaven's kitchen, so you know it has to be perfect.

Let's look at this from the perspective of Chinese Medicine. Chinese Medicine works with the idea of the Five Elements. Briefly, the Five Elements theory is this: everything that is living, be it the planet, you, me, or Homer Simpson from Springfield, has the Five Elements in common. With the Five Elements, there is life. Without the Five Elements, there is no life. Life is the Five Elements coming together in the temporal world. Death is the Five Elements leaving the body, or falling apart. That is what life and death in the temporal world are, according to Chinese Medicine. The Five Elements are: Fire, Earth, Metal, Water and Wood.

Wood Element

 Basically the Wood Element governs the liver and gall bladder, as well as the nervous system and certain mental functions. The main quality of the Wood Element is regeneration. If you cut it off, it will grow back . . . just like wood in nature.

The liver in Chinese Medicine is called "The General;" it is the energetic coordinator and equalizer of the body. Modern medicine knows of over five hundred functions that the liver controls. Modern medicine also admits there is still a great deal that is not known about the liver. A body can have a portion of the physical liver removed, and it will grow back. The liver is the only organ that can be as much as 80% surgically removed, and it will still grow back!

The Wood Element also governs our nails; if they get cut off, they grow back. A woman can get pregnant, miscarry and then get pregnant again. She can grow another life back. A person can even be sharing a thought or an idea, get interrupted, have that thought cut off, then grow the thought right back again, continuing on.

The universal quality the Wood Element is reflecting back to us is resilience. Our true nature is One with growing beyond what has hurt us. Our true response to the whole of life must be to move forward unconditionally.

Seen through the filter of the Wood Element there is a strong relationship between the physical liver and certain mental activities. If you do not realize that you have two forms of consciousness, and if you are trying to solve your eternal problems with the guidance of the ego, your liver is going to get stressed. The liver cannot digest our eternal problems using temporal tools like thoughts and beliefs. These problems require love; energy from the Heart not the head. When the liver cannot resolve eternal problems using temporal tools, it becomes dis-at-ease; it becomes stressed or unhealthy. Only in recognizing who is talking to us at any given moment, only in remembering to use eternal consciousness for solving eternal problems, and temporal consciousness for solving temporal problems, is the Wood Element liberated and mastered. There is an obscure idea in Chinese Medicine that when the Wood Element is mastered, enlightenment is instantly reached.

Have you ever wondered why we know that Jesus was a carpenter? We don't walk into a furniture store and say, "Wow, what a great piece of furniture. Looks like something a Jesus would have made." So why do we know that Jesus was a carpenter? We know this because a carpenter is one who has mastered the Wood Element.

What most advanced beings did for a living is not relevant. Do you know what Socrates did for a living? He was a stonemason. He laid stones, tile and grout. Yet we don't get into a nice shower and say, "Wow, nice job. Socrates could have done this." Like Jesus, what Socrates did for a living has nothing to do with the Heart and soul of the gift that he left us: the Socratic cry that, *"an unexamined life is not worth living."*

Jesus

Let's examine the end of Jesus' life, starting with the last supper Jesus shared with the disciples. Jesus knows that his physical body will be dead soon. Before the crucifixion, however, there will be torture, rejection and finally abandonment from those who profess to love him the most. Jesus also knows that before the meal is over, Judas, one of his disciples, will sneak out and betray him to the Jewish religious authorities, for thirty pieces of silver. The Jewish priests plan in turn to hand Jesus over to the local Roman military machine.

The Jewish religious authorities have feared Jesus for some time. These same authority figures very badly mishandled a man who came just before Jesus, and they were afraid of another "John the Baptist" incident. They did not want another situation that could blow up in their faces, like John the Baptist, who had the favor of the people, but not the favor of the religious authorities. These religious authority figures wanted Jesus dead as soon as possible. Their problem was that Jewish law has no provisions for killing men . . . only women. A woman caught committing adultery would be stoned to death, but not the man. So, to let the Romans do their dirty work for them, the religious powers-that-be, had to make up a false charge against Jesus and then conveniently hand him over to the Romans, who had a zillion laws and provisions for killing people.

Jesus knows all this is about to come to pass. He waits for what is about to come, with the sleeping disciples in the garden of Gethsemane. Judas arrives bringing the temple guards with him. Judas informs the guards that he will walk up to Jesus and give him a kiss on the cheek so that they will know who out of the group of men is the one they have come for.

The disciples are shocked and angered by Judas' blatant betrayal. One of the disciples grabs a sword and cuts off an arresting guard's ear. Jesus advocates neutrality, surrender and acceptance. Jesus heals the injured man's ear and offers no resistance. Jesus is shuttled back and forth between the local Roman military man, Pilate, and the regional Jewish leader King Herod. Every time he is moved, he is spit on, kicked, beaten and generally humiliated by anyone who has the opportunity to do so.

We will come back and examine the details of Gethsemane and Jesus and Judas' relationship in a moment. However in our story of Jesus' last day alive, after he has been handed over to the Roman procurator Pilate for the last time, he is then set up before the Jewish community for a vote. Jesus, a man of peace and non-violence, is set before the community with a man named Barabbas, who is a terrorist, a man of great violence. Pilate orders the community to decide who shall be crucified, Jesus or Barabbas. The religious authorities have stacked the deck against Jesus from the start, so it is no big surprise when their voice choosing Barabbas as the person who must be set free, is the primary voice heard.

Jesus is tied and nailed to the Roman version of a cross, which really looks more like scaffolding. While in unimaginable pain and dying slowly, Jesus looks up from the cross to see his mother crying. Jesus asks his brother and disciples to comfort her. Even in his last moments alive he treats others as he would want to be treated. There are not many souls on the rock who would have the spiritual maturity to consider the feelings of others at such a point in time. Jesus models forgiveness and unconditionality for us before he gives up the ghost under the most horrific of temporal circumstances. He models giving attention to what Heaven loves right until the absolute end. Jesus surrenders his soul without a thought or belief. Jesus victoriously embodies love consciousness that cannot die, be killed or extinguished.

Looking at the life of Jesus of Nazareth, we can see what using eternal consciousness to solve eternal problems might look like. Imagine that Jesus represents eternal consciousness. (I know it is type casting, but bear with me.) What we will see in the closer examination that follows is Jesus modeling for us where we get trapped in the tyranny of the ego, in the limitation of thoughts and beliefs. We will also see Jesus model for us the answer to ending this vicious cycle, which is to bring our awareness back from the temporal, and return it to the eternal. What else would you expect from a being who has mastered the Wood Element?

What we see in examining Gethsemane, is Jesus showing us where we get stuck in resisting Heaven's perfect food, where we pass up drinking from the evolutionary *cup* of enlightenment. We will also see where Jesus corrects this incomplete action and models for us right relationship with mind.

No matter how intense and life threatening things get, Jesus is never caught in the dream of duality: of subject/object identification. Jesus does not get trapped in fear, re-created by thinking and believing one's way through life. Jesus knows not to identify with anything in the temporal realm. He allows the temporal to come and go and change without becoming disturbed either inwardly or outwardly. Jesus' awareness is inseparable from the truth: the reality that there is only the One; there is always infinite abundance. Jesus does not fear the process of recognizing mind. He models for us being with *what is* in the present moment with an open Heart without a thought or belief. Jesus models for us how mind shatters the ultimate illusion of limitation for us; what we in the West understand as a personal death.

Judas represents temporal consciousness. Do you know what Judas did for a living? He was a scribe, the keeper and dispenser of temporal consciousness. Talk about worshipping thoughts and beliefs. And what better way to describe the relationship with misguided temporal-based consciousness then as the quintessential betrayer, complete with thirty pieces of silver and a kiss.

What we see when we look at the relationship between the two men is what the relationship between temporal and eternal consciousness looks like in mind, in the wave. Judas does not realize Jesus' true nature. When Jesus informs Judas that the priests and elders of the temple mean to kill him, Judas cannot see it. Judas cannot hear the truth of it. He argues with Jesus, "I will go to the temple and set everything right. I will fix it and manipulate it, and it will all turn out the way I think and believe it should." What Judas (representing temporal consciousness) does is say to eternal consciousness (Jesus), "You do not know *what is,* I alone know *what is.* I alone will fix everything according to my thoughts and beliefs, and make it right. Why? Because controlling and manipulating others is always how problems are solved."

Judas informs Jesus that he knows the priests and elders merely wish to engage Jesus in fair and open dialog, which, of course, is not how it all plays out. It plays out just as Jesus said it would. Judas does not *know.* Judas does not *see,* because he is representing the ego, and limited consciousness cannot *see* or recognize the truth or the reality of unlimited consciousness. If thoughts and beliefs were going to solve all our problems, like Judas,' it would have by now. Instead the problems, like Judas,' keep getting more intense and life diminishing.

In our story of Jesus and Judas, there is no other possible outcome for Judas than self-extinction. When we give our attention to thinking and believing our way through life, we might as well put a noose around our neck and swing from the highest tree. When we live like Judas, thinking and manipulating our way through life instead of loving and trusting, we are committing an extremely painful form of spiritual suicide. Giving our attention to temporal consciousness to solve our eternal problems, like Judas in this story, is not in any way, shape, or form a life-sustaining relationship with our own mind.

Living like Judas is to remain painfully, unconsciously, asleep in the disease of duality; thinking and believing one's way through life. Judas made the same mistake with his awareness, that all unenlightened beings are making with their awareness: they focus on the limited form of consciousness to such an extent that the real uncondi-tional love that lives directly within all of us is never felt, never seen, never heard, never surrendered to. Why? No one can give attention to eternal and temporal conscious-ness at the same time. No one can serve the limited ego, and give their attention to serving unlimited love at the same time. Judas did not know which master he served.

Now let us examine what happened at the garden of Gethsemane. Contained herein is one of the most com-pelling aspects of the story of mind being reflected back. Jesus and the twelve disciples have just finished their last meal together. During the meal, Jesus foretold that one of the twelve disciples will betray him, and that Peter will deny even knowing him before the cock can crow three times at dawn.

We pick up the story, Jesus is in the garden, it is late and the others have all fallen asleep. Jesus is aware that soon the temple guards led by Judas will come and arrest him. Jesus is also aware that his body will soon be dead, but not until the body has been beaten, whipped with a cat of nine tails, spit on, jeered at, rejected, and betrayed by not only his people, but also by his most intimate relationships. Jesus knows he is presently about to experience the most challenging portion of the program.

Here, in this moment, is when Jesus asks eternal consciousness, "If I may fulfill my life's purpose without drinking from this cup, let it pass from me." When Jesus says, "Let this cup pass from me," he is using "this cup" as a metaphor for the food about to be passed to him, to partake of. The food "this cup" contains is the temporal portion of the program: our thoughts, beliefs, feelings, memories, emotions, experiences and perceptions.

The entire purpose of Jesus asking if "this cup may pass" from him is so that he may show us what we are all doing with our food. We are all saying to eternal consciousness, "I'm scared of my food. Take it away! The tuna fish sandwich is too scary! I want to end all the suffering and create a life worth living, but I am not willing to do it with the perfect food divine love and wisdom has sent me." This is a not a useful dialog for us to get stuck in, especially if we are not even consciously aware that we are stuck in a fear-based dialog at all.

The entire purpose of Gethsemane is for Jesus to model for us *where* and *how* we miss the mark with our awareness. Jesus is walking us through where we forget to give our attention to the eternal and get caught up in the pain of duality. He then demonstrates the most important part. Jesus shatters that cycle of forgetfulness, ends the tyranny of limitation and establishes right relationship with mind. Jesus is modeling for us Swedenborg's concept of enlightenment: that it is a remembering and a forgetting thing. Jesus is teaching us alignment with higher wisdom, so that we may witness a living mastery over both the physical and spiritual realms. Yahoo!

Again, the whole purpose of a physically created world is so the ethereal, the hidden, the invisible, the unconscious interior can be made tangibly exteriorized, revealed, visible, and conscious. Everything in the physical world is a mirror. Everything is mind being reflected back to us, so that we may see it. Jesus, as eternal consciousness made human, modeled this for us in an absolutely clear conscious manner. He shows us how we can recognize and transform the misunderstanding we have all developed with our divinely perfect food.

We identify with our food. We think we are our hair, our bank account, our social status. However, we say that we do not identify with our food. We say that we know we are not these temporal things. But if we lost all of our money, we lost our job, and could not find employment, then as a final straw, all of our hair fell out, we would probably encounter a great deal of suffering. Our suffering is re-created to the degree that we unconsciously identify with these temporal things. Suffering is nature's way of asking us to get real, to become aware of what we are identifying with, what we are giving our attention to, what we love. Hell feels hellish. Heaven feels expansive. Heaven feels at peace.

Unrealized beings are not in right relationship with the divine food of life. Unrealized beings practice packaging Heaven's divine food as lacking in any authentic liberating or nurturing value, as a cruel personal affront made upon them by life itself. The divine food of life is much easier to enjoy and swallow, as well as provides us with the nurturing energy we need when we are in right relationship with it. We are here to recognize the divine food sent to us as not only non-threatening, but as actually liberating and as a source of great gratitude.

Jesus does not identify with his food. He does not judge or criticize his food. He willing, gratefully and openly takes it in, pulls what he needs from it, and lets the rest go. Jesus gives his attention to Ultimate Truth and says, (paraphrasing, again) "Wait a minute. I am the senior movement here, because I do not have love, I am love. Everything that I am experiencing is bringing enlightenment to mind, or Heaven would not have given it permission to happen. I can be with this food! I can trust that this is just the food I most need right now to grow. It is the food of liberation! *I can drink from this cup*, as I do not identify with anything temporal, only the eternal. I am beyond this!"

During Jesus' trial, he is asked if he is the King of the Jews. He is asked to show his power. Jesus remains silent, undisturbed and beyond agitation. Jesus models for us the kingdom and power that is beyond duality based consciousness. Jesus remains in the present moment, without thoughts and beliefs about his physical body's mortality, or what all this temporal stuff means regarding his value, power and worth. Jesus trusts that everything unfolding in every present moment is perfect. Jesus embodies for us right relationship with the divine food of life, even when it comes packaged in its most challenging form and context.

The people at Jesus' trial did not see the true nature of an enlightened mind that Jesus modeled for them. Why? Because they were coming from thoughts and beliefs. They were not giving their attention to loving, forgiving, tolerance, compassion, or mercy. They were not giving their attention to eternal consciousness for solving the eternal relationship problem they were experiencing with Jesus. They were not giving each form of consciousness its appropriate due. They had made temporal consciousness their exclusive filter for all understanding. As we have established, we cannot serve two masters. If temporal consciousness is what is getting our attention, then we cannot see, hear, recognize or understand the eternal. Limited is never going to *get* or *appreciate* unlimited.

Acceptance Intelligence

Jesus models another quality of beingness for us - what we have been describing as being with *what is* in the present moment with an open Heart. It is acceptance! The power of acceptance is the Heart and soul of Christ consciousness. Acceptance is deeply supported by the movement of beyond duality intelligence in mind. Jesus so beautifully shows us how to accept our mind. Acceptance of *what is* as perfect given by Heaven, is easier to swallow then the suffering of duality that we experience as: bankruptcy, divorce, physical pain or illness, surgery, the trauma of lies and betrayal.

Acceptance gets an incredibly bad rap in today's world. Most people in the West interpret acceptance intelligence as settling for, compromising, or grudgingly taking something you really do not want. Nothing could be further from the truth. We in the West also use the word acceptance when we want to manipulate an outcome. How many times were you told to accept something graciously? Which at the time translated to your feelings being completely ignored, so you could cater to someone else's agenda. "My feelings do not matter; I am disposable; it's not fair."

This is not at all what acceptance means. Acceptance means, "I accept that the present moment looks this way and feels this way." That is it! You are not to take anything personal, you are not judging it; you are not giving all of your attention to a temporal interpretation of *what is.* You are simply accepting the divine food as it is being given. If you will not accept the divine food of life, how will the wave ever realize it is really the ocean? How will you complete your life purpose mission if all you love is resisting the means of liberation that Heaven is providing you?

This paradox is like the joke about the man who was caught in his house during a flood. First, his neighbors drive by in a very large bus and offer to rescue the man. The man, however, politely refuses informing the busload of people that, "God will provide. God will provide." About thirty minutes later, as the water line is swiftly rising, a boat comes by. Again the people in the boat offer the man trapped in his house a safe exit. Once again the man refuses help, justifying the action with, "God will provide. God will provide." After another hour the man is forced on to the rooftop of his quickly submerging house. As he is perched on the last available shingle, a helicopter comes by to offer assistance. Again the man refuses, mouthing the words, "God will provide," as he slips under the flood waters and disappears. The man dies and goes to Heaven. There he confronts God with the question, "How could you just let me die like that?" God answers, "What do you mean 'just let you die'? I sent you three rescue parties: first a bus, then a boat and finally a helicopter!" This joke perfectly illustrates the wisdom of divinely accepting *what is* given; resistance is futile. Lack of gratitude is ignorant.

Acceptance means honestly accepting that the present moment looks this way and feels this way! Period! End of sentence! Acceptance does not mean that we should no longer advocate for right relationship, or speak our truth. We can accept that a painful situation is occurring and still speak and negotiate honestly with others and ourselves. "I cannot agree to inequality. I accept that this is happening, and I accept that I feel this way about it. However, I do not condone destructive and harmful behavior. I do not support any lying or stealing, etc." In this way we acknowledge and share our truth, while accepting the cup as it is being passed to us from Heaven. Acceptance does not mean you play victim or agree to anything *less than* or non-life sustaining. Acceptance lives in Heaven; when aligned with the acceptance of *what is,* then and only then do you live in Heaven as well.

Acceptance intelligence is the wisdom that allows us to be self-witnessing, thereby ending all self re-created suffering. When you are accepting mind as it unfolds in every eternal present moment, without getting distracted by a thought or a belief, without getting lost in duality, without a judgment or criticism, then you are *remembering* to witness the contents of your own wave. You are *remembering,* to observe, while witnessing the movement of mind. You are *remembering* to release the habit of interpreting reality through the process of buying into the ego's line of BS. As you witness and realize the investment in the lies, you are simultaneously roasting the seeds of karma, and creating right relationship with the divine food of life.

When you are in right relationship with the power of acceptance, you are finally getting down to the business of what we all came here to master. Every spiritual being, without exception, is here to accept mind. To accept the contents of the wave, you must first be aligned with acceptance intelligence. When we accept *what is* in the present moment with an open Heart, we realize that the stories and judgments that we have been projecting out onto others, are really a reflection of the relationship we have with our own wave. It is the unresolved relationships we have with our own mind that is being reflected back to us, as reality everywhere.

At the risk of being redundant, understand that in order to end suffering, we must first practice *seeing* and *recognizing* what is holding the suffering together. We must learn to align our attention with acceptance intelligence. If we are going to master the practice of self-witnessing, we must first be honest about what we are witnessing. Before we can remove an obstacle, we must first accept that the obstacle or limitation exists. Then we must accept that the stuff we are here to get over looks and feels exactly like what is being reflected back. How else can we know what we are resolving, and making peace with? How can the wave release and heal anything it has not become conscious of?

Remember, the truth is: we do not have consciousness we are consciousness. Reality, here on the rock, is consciously evolving to become fully conscious, that is the name of the game.

The bigger question is how do we know what we are here to accept? The answer is simple. We are here to accept anything and everything that is happening around and within the wave. Why do we have to practice accepting *exactly* what is being reflected back? Because the pattern we're here to accept looks and feels *exactly* like what is being reflected back. By bringing acceptance to the fact that the human experience looks this way and feels this way, we are making a complete action. We are healing and transforming the inner issue we came here to get over.

The complete action of healing and realization occurs by accepting exactly the lesson Heaven would give, when Heaven would give it. That is why practicing acceptance of everything *exactly* as it is happening is essential. What is happening in the exterior is the perfect reflection of what is happening in the interior. If I will not accept *what is,* I cannot heal and transform the very issues I am here to make whole through the power of self-realization. Without acceptance intelligence, I will not be accepting any of life's lessons or the evolutionary divine food of my soul. This level of non-acceptance is *exactly* what Socrates meant by a life not worth living.

When we are not accepting *what is* we are flailing about in the dream of duality. We are unconsciously looking in the mirror, and we see the reflection. But we do not realize this higher truth, because our awareness is thinking and believing the reflection is real. Acceptance breaks this illusion; acceptance intelligence breaks the grasp the disease of duality has over mind. Acceptance is to stop this flailing around in illusion. With acceptance, we can now *see* the Oneness of all life, of all mind.

Acceptance is the calm wind that tames the raging waves. Acceptance finally puts your hands on the limiting thing itself, and moves it out of mind. Spirit cannot do any real meaningful interior house cleaning without it. Without acceptance intelligence, the clutter of thoughts and beliefs will quickly fill the spaciousness of mind making it rigid, inflexible, heavy, depressed, and extremely unhappy.

You cannot create a learning experience that you do not need, and every learning experience is bringing us all enlightenment. So what is there not to accept? Again, *acceptance does not mean you have to like what is happening, or that you have to continue doing something.*

Acceptance is simply accepting that this moment comes complete with this look and this feel. Acceptance is the wave accepting Heaven's gifts as they are sent. There is absolutely no downside to this action.

As a general rule, all of life on the planet Earth works this way: whatever aspect of the wave, whatever aspect of mind, that has not been witnessed and accepted (and thus integrated into the whole of mind) will be re-created over and over again, ceaselessly, until spirit gets it, sees it and accepts it. Only this action of self-witnessing will end the cycle of unrealized self re-created suffering. What is holding all the world's suffering together is a conscious lack of acceptance for the perfection of what is given. It is that simple. Not what you were expecting?

Acceptance intelligence does not resist *what is,* as this intelligence only recognizes *what is* as the perfect divine food of Heaven. Acceptance is a Heart-felt intelligence, not a gray matter processed conclusion. Our ego does not need to complete its wish list before we can accept this moment as perfect. Acceptance does not respond to life with intentions of controlling an outcome. Acceptance intelligence does not love to control or manipulate anything for that matter. In fact, acceptance intelligence has no attachments, zero, zilch, nil, nada, nothing. No attachments to any outcome anywhere, at anytime, for any reason. For acceptance intelligence, this point is non-negotiable.

Acceptance intelligence never gives attention to the ego's stories that *what is* needs *fixing* or is *wrong*. Acceptance intelligence will never poison us with the lie that most of life contains experiences that we would have all been better off never having. That is a job for the voice of limitation; that is the ego's job. That is why the ego's misused contribution smells, looks, and tastes so bad.

Not accepting the process, and the means by which we are all invited to end our suffering, is the ultimate in limitation. Let's see . . . resisting and judging acceptance intelligence . . . hmmmmmm, it sounds limiting, feels limiting, tastes limiting, forces us to live in a hellishly limited place . . . where could this information have come from? Clearly, it is the ego's shit! Don't step in it!.

A wave cannot serve two masters. You cannot be giving attention to *didn't do it right, not good enough, not enough time, love, money, and opportunity,* and at the same time be accepting *what is* in the present moment with an open Heart. Acceptance means not having a thought or belief about yourself, others, or life. Acceptance is love, tolerance and patience felt internally. Acceptance is eternal consciousness shared freely and lovingly in the moment. Acceptance intelligence transforms the wave into a spiritual living embodiment of trust; trusting that Heaven runs everything; trusting that everything is perfect. What is really required of spirit is that we freely align our Ruling Love with showing up and caring for all of life here, as if we were all One. Why? Because the truth is we are One.

Shiva and Jesus as One

In the Hindu tradition, there is a story about why Shiva is considered to be the most powerful aspect of God consciousness. The larger idea is that due to the infinite nature of God, the best way to understand divine consciousness is to divide it up into pieces and then define each aspect as a separate personality. By understanding each personality, and the quality of the different personalities and their interactions and relationships as God consciousness in motion, we may begin to form and realize an ultimate gestalt. There are many personalities in the Hindu religion and each divine personality represents an aspect of God consciousness, just as Zeus and Hera and the other personalities that reside on Mount Olympus represent the same spiritual gestalt in action only from the Hellenistic religion of ancient Greece.

According to Hinduism, Shiva is the one out of all the aspects of God consciousness in the infinite space of Heaven, who offered to resolve all suffering by freely stepping forward, taking a cup filled with the world's poison, and drinking from it. Shiva, by being with *what is* in the present moment with an open Heart, transforms the world's poison into unconditional love, because that is what Shiva loves, and for no other reason. It is that quality of unconditional love that makes Shiva the most powerful aspect of God consciousness in the universe, and that is nice work when you can find it.

Say, got deja'vu? Where have we seen this before? Looks and feels exactly like what Christ consciousness just performed for us in the garden of Gethsemane. It looks and feels like One, because we are looking at the movement of the One, dreaming itself endlessly over and over again for the purpose of self-realization. Shiva represents unconditional acceptance of *what is* in the present moment with an open Heart. Shiva represents this because that is how the wave learns to transform the compost into the ever-blooming flower of enlightenment.

Since the higher reality is that everything is mind being reflected back for the ultimate in gestalts, everything we encounter here is spiritually relevant. Shiva's favorite color is purple. Purple is the color of the transformational action made complete by the power of unconditionally accepting *what is* in the present moment with an open Heart.

Red is the color associated with Christ consciousness. Red is the color that represents a quality of consciousness that removes all obstacles. The quality of consciousness that removes all obstacles is unconditional acceptance of *what is* in the present moment with an open Heart. If it looks like the One, acts like the One, walks like the One, talks like the One, it must be the One!

Acceptance and Christ/Shiva consciousness are inseparable. It is One intelligence. When we are going through our everyday life not in right relationship with accepting the divine food sent us; when we are judging, criticizing and contracting around *what is,* then we are saying to Christ/Shiva consciousness, "Get out of here! You do not understand the problem. You do not understand the solution. I know what is going on here. You do not. I am not going to live my life listening to you. I have no respect for your wisdom!" This is not a useful or serving relationship to have with eternal consciousness. However, it is one that will keep the ego fat, happy, and in the senior position, driving your life deeper into the land of unhappiness.

When we are accepting our lives, we are making Christ/Shiva consciousness the senior navigating and guiding intelligence. We are making eternal consciousness the focus of our attention for solving our eternal problems.

The Eastern word for illusion is *Maya.* In the West we think of illusion as meaning a trick, or slight of hand, smoke and mirrors. Maya as illusion means simply that reality is not what you think and believe it is. When you are accepting *what is* in the present moment with an open Heart, you are shattering illusion by witnessing mind. You now finally have the "hands on" power you have been searching for to shift any issue or limitation, and move it out of your life. When you witness the source of self re-created suffering, you are simultaneously creating an end to it. **Ending this cycle of suffering is the purpose of all human creation and existence.** The illusion, the limitations, the lies only stay in mind and re-create suffering for us if we do not destroy them through the process of self-witnessing.

Divine Correspondence

Swedenborg describes the reality of everything as mind being reflected back in the idea he calls *Divine Correspondence*. The idea is this: the physical world does not really exist in the way that we typically think and believe it does. (No big surprise there!) The only reason the physical world does exist at all is because it is Corresponding to or mirroring a spiritual reality.

When we can experience the exterior world, while simultaneously realizing what the experience is Corresponding to in the spiritual world (or interior realm), then the mastery of both worlds comes into place. The only way we can master Divine Correspondence is to forget everything we have already learned about life, self, and others. To master Divine Correspondence is to remember to give our attention to truth, to self beyond duality.

An established relationship with self, beyond duality, is absolutely critical. Without *seeing* that everything is mind and the movement of mind; without *seeing* the Oneness of all life, Divine Correspondence will never make any sense. Divine Correspondence requires beyond-duality consciousness in order to make the greatest gestalt, that what we are looking at *is* mind. Without imagining, knowing, or understanding that real self is beyond duality, Divine Correspondence will never be the self-reflective vehicle it was meant to be.

What is the value behind understanding Divine Correspondence? Understanding Divine Correspondence is essential for us to know what we are witnessing on the inside. If we have no idea what the exterior world is Corresponding to, how will we ever be able to relate to the physical world as the map of the interior it really is?

Most everyone has already heard an expression indig-enous to all of the sacred traditions, that everything that happens here on the rock is *perfect*. Without understand-ing Divine Correspondence, no one could ever under-stand the wisdom and truth of what is meant by *perfect*. Everything that happens here on the rock is *perfect,* but not in the way you think and believe (who didn't see that one coming?). Everything that happens here is exactly the *perfect* lesson that we need in order to wake up and realize mind. Everything that happens here occurs in the exact or *perfect time* it needs to occur for our liberation. This is one way we can understand that everything truly is *perfect*. However, Divine Correspondence can take us even deeper into this truth.

How could Hitler, the Nazis, and the concentration camps, how could any of that possibly, even remotely be considered *perfect?* Everything is mind. Everything that happens is a running commentary on our relationship between the temporal and eternal. Hitler represents the movement of the ego. Hitler is the *perfect* mirror of ha-tred for acceptance, and love for judgment and criticism made physical in the exterior world, so that we can see it. Everytime you tell yourself or another, *you did not do it right, you are not good enough,* you are putting a bullet in the chamber and shooting a part of your mind. Every time you see yourself or others as inferior, disposable, worthless, you are putting a part of your mind in the showers and turning on the gas. Every time you feel jus-tified in labeling yourself or others as not measuring up, or as *less than,* you are placing a part of your mind in the oven and mercilessly incinerating it. Is any of this looking even vaguely familiar?

How can the concentration camps be *perfect?* The people in the concentration camps were all innocent people. They were all rounded up without due process, without being able to confront their accusers or understand what crime they had committed. They were all imprisoned because they were guilty of being alive. They were tortured because they dared to take up space on the planet as a living, breathing entity. When we have thoughts and beliefs about ourselves, we are killing off these innocent people in the concentration camp of our minds, just like the Nazis did in the physical world. When we think and believe, control and manipulate our way through life, we become our own inner Hitler, committing horrendous acts of self-violence against our mind. When thoughts and beliefs are used for solving eternal problems it becomes the present moment nazi.

Hitler, the Nazis regimen, the camps it is all *perfect* in this way. If we are ever going to *stop* the tyranny of the ego, we must first see it for what it is. It is Hitler. It is the concentration camps. It is the mindless, senseless love of destruction and suffering. Every time you think and believe you need the ego to solve your eternal problems, just look at Hitler and make the Divine Correspondence to where you engage in a manner that does not accept and treat all of life equally.

Hitler and the Nazis are all working *perfectly* for us. They are here to liberate us. They are here to show us what we are doing with our love. When you realize that mistrust comes from listening to the poisonous lies of the ego, when you understand that *all* violence comes from aligning the wave with the ego instead of aligning the wave with love, when you see ultimate lies and the damage it causes in your life as all being *perfectly* reflected back in the form of Hitler and his minions, then you have made a complete action.

Without Hitler, without the Nazis, without the camps how could we *see* it for what it really is? How could we know, without experiencing it directly for ourselves, how truly hideously ugly and evil living in our heads actually is? Now, hopefully, we will be grateful for what we have learned, and honor the price that mind has paid to learn it. Maybe now we will make the commitment to ourselves that is needed to end the tyranny of the head. Maybe now we will freely put our shoulder to the karmic wheel by showing up in the present moment from an open Heart, without a thought or belief.

Anytime you want to reach for judgment, criticism, impatience, *didn't do it right, not good enough* to solve any relationship problem, stop! Look at Hitler. Ask yourself if this is really what you want to be doing with your will, love, service and life purpose? Ask yourself if you have already learned everything you need to know from hell or do you still require more from that learning experience? If you can honestly say, "No, I do not get it. I cannot see where coming from my head has not solved a single problem. I cannot see where I treat myself and others badly when coming from my head and not my Heart." If you can honestly say that . . . then don't worry . . . the rock will *personally* send you another Hitler so that you can get it. All at no extra charge to you.

If you are not in right relationship with the purpose and creation of all physical life, how can you possibly create a life worth living? You have come here to taste, touch, smell, see, and experience the contents of your wave. Yet you never realize the difference between what you *are* versus what you are here to get over. You are *asleep,* caught in an unconscious slavery agreement with the ego, and the disease of duality. When you do not know what you *are* or how to end your suffering and limitation, how will you ever be happy? You will be another lonely wave on this rock, reincarnating and recycling until you *do* get it.

We must wake up to the truth that everything is mind. Physical reality is most definitely *not* what we have been thinking and believing it to be. Physical reality is the mirror, the mirage, the reflection. The real you is inside. Invisible and intangible.

Solomon and Asmodeus

There is a story, from the Jewish tradition, of Solomon and Asmodeus. This story, like the story of Jesus and Judas, illustrates the spiritual danger of ignoring Divine Correspondence. The real menace is our loyalty to thinking and believing physical reality is real unto itself. This keeps us living in the froth at the top of the wave. This keeps our love, our attention, trapped at the most superficial level of understanding and wisdom.

The story of Solomon and Asmodeus is the story of two great Kings. Solomon is the legendary King of Israel. Solomon is the son of David, who killed Goliath with a slingshot, became King and married Bathsheba, the mother of Solomon. Solomon, also according to legend, was made the wisest man who ever lived, as a gift from God to King David at the time of Solomon's conception. Nice pedigree huh!

In addition to Solomon being a great and wise King, he

was also an extremely powerful mystic. As a matter of fact, when people at the time of Christ referred to Jesus as "The son of David," what they meant was not since Solomon, the son of David, has there been a person who displayed such dominion over the spiritual, as well as the physical worlds.

Asmodeus is the king of the demons. Asmodeus is hell's head honcho. Asmodeus is Satan, Lucifer, Beelzebub. He's the guy in the red suit with the horns, pitchfork and a tail.

There came a time in Solomon's life, when he sought to contain Asmodeus for the purpose of extracting some information from him. This was nothing new for Solomon. As an accomplished mystic, he had bound many demonic spirits in jars and cast them into the sea forever. But Asmodeus was going to be different. He was definitely the biggest, most slippery fish in the pond.

So, Solomon went about creating an ingenious trap to capture Asmodeus. (One of the many perks that come with being the smartest guy on the rock, not to mention the best dressed.) Just as predicted, the ingenious plan outsmarted Asmodeus, and he is brought to Solomon's court in heavy chains and considerable bondage.

Solomon spent many hours, many days questioning Asmodeus. Solomon arrogantly challenged the length, depth, and breath of Asmodeus' understanding of humanity. During one of these many lengthy talks, Asmodeus revealed the information Solomon wanted when he originally captured him. But Solomon does not release Asmodeus. He continually brings Asmodeus bound and chained to court both to pontificate at him, as well as question him.

One day Solomon goes too far with Asmodeus. The King of the demons confronts Solomon (paraphrasing, again), "You know, Solly, we both work for the same boss. So, dude, you better have a damn good reason for keeping me from doing my divine duty. What exactly do you want from me?"

Solomon has been doing some pretty heavy chest beating in front of Asmodeus for months now. It's easy to be cocky when your enemy stands humbled before you, bound up and chained. Solomon responds by continuing to goad Asmodeus, "You know Asmodeus, 'Mr. highest of the lows' just exactly how powerful can you be if you and your entire pitiful party of petty perverts could be tricked by yours truly?"

Asmodeus counters with, "Sure, it is easy to be Mr. Big, the stud monkey, when I'm tied up and you hold all the cards. What do you say we even the playing field. Release me, and I'll show you just how powerful I can be. Are you ready to put up or shut up, little daddy's boy?"

Will Solomon swallow hook, line, and sinker Asmodeus' bait? Or will Solomon rise above the bait, and use Asmodeus to learn about the nature of limitation, and its addictive hold on every living being?

Solomon, suddenly, responds to Asmodeus with the question all of mind is begging to know the answer to. Solomon asks Asmodeus to show him the hold he has on the human mind. Solomon is asking for the universal Toto to pull back the curtain so that we can see who is pretending to be the Wizard of Oz.

Asmodeus, never at a lack for a good come back, negotiates with Solomon. "I'll tell you what," Asmodeus offers Solomon, "if you untie and unbind me, I will not stop at just telling you what my hold is on the human mind, I will go you one further. If you untie me, let me go, and give me your sacred ring, the one with the Star of David on it. You know the ring I'm talking about. It is the one God gave you to do all that far out, cool, and groovy mystic stuff with. You know what I'm talking about, Solly, the ring that lets you bind my people in jars and cast them down to the lowest place. Yeah, that's the ring! You know the one that came in the Heavenly cereal box? That one! If you will just let me loose and give me your 'power ranger' signet ring, I will not only tell you what my secret is, I will show you in an up close and personal fashion what my hold is on humanity."

Talk about *"Let's Make A Deal!"* Does Solomon go for what is in the box, and keep Asmodeus safely contained in chains in the dungeon, bringing him up only at his own convenience? Or does Solomon go for what is behind curtain number two, and risk everything in the name of ending all suffering? Or does Solomon stumble over his own arrogance and trade in everything for the "booby prize"? What would you do? It is a great moment. We can only imagine what divine emotional visitors must have been beckoned and touched upon Solomon's nervous system in those critical moments. This is Solomon's Gethsemane. Will he drink from this cup, and if so, how?

Solomon, with great insolence, orders the guards to set the prisoner free. Solomon removes the ring and hands it over to Asmodeus. Like Gollum from Tolken's *Hobbit*, Asmodeus greedily shoves the Star of David ring, his "precioussss," on his right index finger. In a moment

Asmodeus is transformed into a giant black bird. With one huge black shiny wing touching Heaven, and the other monstrously large black wing touching the Earth, Asmodeus grabs Solomon in his mouth, and spits him out thousands of miles away from where he started only a moment ago standing in his court.

Now Solomon finds himself completely and utterly lost, thousands of miles from Jerusalem, wandering alone in the desert. His clothes are ripped and tattered from the journey. His presence, his demeanor, his outward behavior suddenly appears erratic and strange. Solomon wanders the desert shouting "I am the King of Israel. I am the King of Israel!" Needless to say, anyone passing by simply assumed that the homeless guy who likes to shout, "I am the King of Israel" over and over again, is just another freak from *People's Park* in Berkeley.

Legend has it that Solomon wandered lost, aimlessly, in the desert for seven long years. Asmodeus' little "I'll not only tell you, I'll show you" trick lasted seven long hot sand and dust filled years. It is suspected that these tribulations happened during the years in which Solomon grew into his greatest and finest wisdom. Theological historians suspect that it was during these years that Solomon wrote his contribution to the *Bible.* Or what we in the modern world suspect was his contribution. It is during this time Solomon discovered what it is to be in the present moment with an open Heart. It is here in the desert that Solomon discovers that everything else is ... simply ... vanity. Good thing we are timeless as God consciousness beings, or little trips like this could be really annoying.

Meanwhile back in Jerusalem, after Asmodeus has spit

Solomon out of his big bird mouth, he then assumes the appearance, the body, the face, the clothes, the status, the bank account of Solomon. Since he had no permission to use Solomon's ring, and he wished to prevent Solomon from regaining it, Asmodeus removes the "power ranger" Star of David ring, and throws it into the sea. In this instance, Asmodeus, like so many of us, forgot that he was not in control of everything. Heaven has its own plans. Asmodeus then assumes the temporal role of everything we think and believe we are. Why? Because Asmodeus knows he is safe hiding behind the illusion of what we think and believe. Asmodeus knows that unenlightened beings do not question or look beyond what they think and believe. Asmodeus knows that no one will recognize that he is not the real king, because he is going to come dressed up as everything we think and believe a real king is.

Indeed no one does realize that the true king is wandering lost in the desert, unrecognized, unheard, un-acknowledged. No one does become aware of the reality that they are serving a false king. No one does wake up to the truth that they are giving all of their attention to an illusion; they are only serving what they think and believe is real. Everyone gets caught up in the physical packaging part of duality. After all, isn't that what makes a king? The money, the specter, the clothes. (not to mention the babes!) For seven long years Asmodeus rules in Solomon's place, and no one is the wiser for it.

Meanwhile back in the desert, Solomon is still exiled to a state of confusion and loss of recognition. A few years into his exile he comes to a city where he happens to encounter the king's daughter, Princess Naamah. They meet, and by a miracle of Heaven, the princess falls in love with the homeless guy from Berkeley, and they marry. It is not hard to imagine that the king is not real thrilled with his daughter's choice of suitors. So in anger, the king banishes both Solomon and his daughter from the city.

Little does the banishing king realize that through the miracle of this marriage will come the gift of Christ consciousness. The union of Princess Naamah and King Solomon is the beginning of a new lineage. This marriage represents uniting wisdom of the head with the Heart.

The upside to our story is that at least Solomon now has someone to wander around the desert with. After years of struggling, Solomon's wife buys a fish with their last coin, and takes it home to clean (nice to know some things never change). Naamah calls out to Solomon, who comes running, and there in the belly of the fish he finds the Star of David ring Asmodeus had discarded in the sea! Solomon puts on the ring, and immediately his presence, his memory, and his demeanor return to normal. Solomon takes Naamah and heads for Jerusalem.

Meanwhile back at the ranch, Asmodeus is still sitting pretty on the throne completely uncontested. Solomon returns and makes his way to the court. (Bear in mind that he is still deeply in need of personal hygiene and a fashion consultant). Yet nothing in the temporal world can touch or tarnish this moment. Let us see what happens when the wisest man who ever lived responds to Asmodeus by being with *what is* in the present moment with an open Heart.

Solomon still adorned in his homeless garb of the past seven years pushes open the doors and enters the courtroom. There is the false king, in all his glory, sitting in his wrongful place. There is Solomon, the true king returned. Solomon is now self-witnessing what Asmodeus' hold is on the human mind. Solomon is witnessing what exiles our true nature to a barren place where it is not recognized or heard. Solomon is realizing how we put the false king of what we think and believe on the throne of our attention and then serve it loyally and endlessly.

Just as self-witnessing roasts the seeds of karma, the instant that the true king returns and confronts the false king, the illusion disappears. It has no choice! It is not real! Only love is real! The moment Solomon self-witnessed the hold Asmodeus has on us, Asmodeus returned to his rightful hideously ugly form and image. It was only then that all of the people could clearly, honestly *see* whom they had been serving all these years. After Asmodeus disappears, Solomon just walks up to the throne and sits down as if he had never left. He is not concerned with the temporal. He lets nothing hold him from his rightful place!

But our story does not end here. Solomon always posted a guard by his bedroom door at night. The legend has it that Solomon felt that there was always a need for an aspect of mind to be constantly watching for the possible return of Asmodeus. Solomon felt that it is essential to never go completely asleep. Always keep some part of awareness posted. Awake. Watching. Witnessing. Being with *what is* in the present moment with an open Heart. For that is truly the most powerful choice available to each of us in creating an Asmodeus free existence.

The beauty of the story of the life of Solomon is that it is the story of every person. We have all been arrogant.

We have all stumbled and lost our way as a result of the limited thinking. We have all forgotten the true king, and become confused by the "king of crap," which is of course what we think and believe. But not anymore, right!

there is only the One, there is always infinite abundance

Chapter Four

Mastery of the Human Experience

We need everything that is showing up in our lives: everything happening in the exterior world and everything going on within us. All of this exists solely for the divinely guided purpose of our enlightenment. We need the *whole* of our life in order to complete our visit here. There is nothing about effective and efficient that God consciousness fails to understand. After all, Heaven invented taking care of business.

Swedenborg writes that everything in the physical world corresponds to something in the spiritual realm. That is why it exists. This allows us as spiritual beings to have a physically tangible experience of self-manifesting in the form of what we are seeing, feeling, smelling, touching, and interacting with. In this way, we can wake up to the truth of what we are giving our love to. Swedenborg says that in order to reach enlightenment, we need to practice *right relationship* with everything that is showing up, everything on the planet in our lifetime. What is showing up is the contents of the wave we are here to realize. This goes back to the universal law that God consciousness cannot create a learning experience of itself it did not need; just a little perk that comes with being God.

A spiritual teacher was asked by one of his students,

"What then would be the right relationship with the hydrogen and atom bombs?" The teacher responded to the student, "Why, you accept it as *what is* given you in this life, of course." The physical bombs correspond to inequity in the spiritual realm. When we are not choosing to be equitable, we are dividing ourselves against ourselves; inner, spiritual fission, so to speak. We are a house divided against itself. Being unfair or inequitable is incredibly, spiritually destructive. And, because of Divine Correspondence, that is exactly how it manifests itself in the physical world as "the bomb." Splitting the atom is how the projection of inequity and inner self-violence appears in the exterior world. When this bias exists in our minds, unrealized, it is projected out into time and space so that we may experience it, realize it, and finally transcend it. Brings a whole new meaning to "bombs away" don't it?

The reason inequity still exists as unresolved in the physical and spiritual worlds, is because we are extremely loyal and well practiced at *resisting* the perfection of *what is* in every present moment. We align our Ruling Love with not accepting *what is* from the head, instead of embracing Heaven's liberating gifts with gratitude from the Heart. We practice resisting the perfection of *what is* through our judging and criticizing of everything, and we are not accepting the perfection of our own mind and the lessons we agreed to. We are asleep in the disease of duality giving all of our attention to thoughts and beliefs, memories and stories about why something is not right, not as it should be, not perfect, not acceptable. We did not come here to practice disliking and disenfranchising ourselves. We did not come here to practice *doing* things to our mind. If that were the purpose we would all incarnate in a giant "adult store" instead of the planet Earth, where vibrators would be used as a religious means to enlightenment. Instead of having our way with ourselves, we came here to fully accept ourselves. We came here for the sole purpose of directly experiencing the perfection of mind and all of the divine food sent us.

When we develop some practice of accepting *what is* in the present moment with an open Heart, we let go of our habit, our addiction to criticizing everything in our lives. We cannot be accepting the whole of our life and be criticizing a portion of it at the same time. We are either accepting *what is* as it is given from the Heart, or we are having thoughts and beliefs about it in our heads. We cannot be living and responding to life from both the head and the Heart at the same time. We are designed to live in the Heart and to let that wisdom instruct the head as to how it best needs to respond to *what is*. Acceptance happens in the Heart, not the head. There will be no mastery of the human experience without an acceptance for the whole of life in the present moment with an open Heart.

Personal Mastery

There is a wide difference between personal mastery and mastery of the human experience. Personal mastery involves working with your thought and belief system: cleaning it up sufficiently so that you can stop sabotaging yourself long enough to learn to like yourself. This is an essential step in the practice of learning about yourself and others.

Personal mastery is the process that allows you to choose a more positive story. It involves awakening to the negative stories you torture yourself with inside the privacy of your own head:

"I could have lived with or without_____.
(FILL IN THE BLANK)

"I hate myself and my life because_____.
(FILL IN THE BLANK)

"I would be much happier if_____
never happened."
(FILL IN THE BLANK)

The list of choices to fill in the blank is probably way too long to list here. Personal mastery involves cleaning up the ego-based information enough to make it user friendly to the wave.

If you are presently practicing at the personal mastery level, which is an absolutely necessary step on the way to mastery of the human experience, you are still taking all of the divine food of life very personally. *This is one of the most profound ways in which you can honestly answer the question of whether you are at personal mastery level or mastery of the human experience level.* With personal mastery there is still an individual, wrapped in the disease of duality. There is still an ego-formed personality, to take life personally. If you are at personal mastery level, you are still not *seeing* the *big* picture.

In practicing the mastery of the human experience, all sabotaging thoughts and beliefs would receive zero attention from you. You would not be giving any attention to thoughts or beliefs, about what life and its constantly changing situations mean, in relationship to your power, value, purpose, or love-ability. Instead, you would just be with *what is* in the present moment with an open Heart. You would know that you are indivisible from love. You would be manifesting a complete action: surrendering to loving and trusting your way through life. This is the action that brings you everything you need to know to solve *all* of your eternal problems: Who am I? Why am I here? What is the meaning and purpose of my life and relationships? What is my value? What is my power? What is my worth?

Beyond Personal Mastery

Mastery of the human experience is far beyond personal mastery. In mastery of the human experience you grow beyond the use of and dependence upon ego-based information for understanding any eternal problem. Mastery of the human experience involves watching what you are doing with your attention. It involves knowing that you have two forms of consciousness, and knowing which form of consciousness to give to resolve either a temporal, or eternal problem. Mastery of the human experience means you are only giving attention to thoughts and beliefs 5% of your day. The remaining 95% of the time you are in the present moment with an open Heart, loving and trusting your way through life without a thought or belief about what it all means.

With mastery of the human experience you practice identifying self with love, not identifying self with what you think and believe it is. With mastery of the human experience, practice living the truth that there are no individuals. Duality is the ugly perceptual disease we are all here to resolve. With mastery of the human experience, practice realizing yourself not as an individual, but rather as a doorway. Each wave is a doorway to either Heaven or hell, depending on what you are giving your attention to. Anything that comes, goes and changes in the temporal world cannot be true self. True self is eternal and unchanging. True self is nothing emotional, mental, experiential, or physical. Why? Because all these things are subject to frequent change. True self is the voice of nature's self-corrective guiding intelligence. If there is suffering, examine where mind has given energy, attention and love inappropriately to identification with something temporal, or using temporal consciousness to solve something eternal. *This is the basis of all suffering.*

Mastery of the human experience is realizing that self does not exist in the way we think and believe we do. We decide with our free will and our Ruling Love whether we love being a doorway to acceptance, love, tolerance, understanding and patience, or whether we love being a doorway to worry, manipulation, control, and bad faith in life. Existentialism at its finest. We decide! How? *Because you are what you love and you love whatever you are giving your attention to right now.* You would be best served to get used to hearing this. It is going to be the song of the *Sirens*, calling to you throughout this book to dock your ship on the shore of enlightenment. Unlike the *Sirens* of Jason and the Argonauts, this song will cause you to become more sane and present, not less.

You, as spirit, have been given a physical body and a physical world to practice in until you master the human experience. Mastery of the human experience is completed when mind contains no memories, impressions, or stories of how life and its many relationships are incomplete, lacking, not quite right, or not full. Instead every intention, every action, all speech, and all of perception is governed by the guiding wisdom of the love for the whole of life. Mastery of the human experience means living a practiced acceptance for the whole of life. In turn this means having an equal, even and whole response of acceptance, gratitude, and openness to all of life unconditionally, and to all of life's divinely sent food without effort, insecurity or fear.

> **Karmic Patterns**
> All suffering, all limitation occurs when mind is caught in the disease of duality: giving all attention and love to the ego, to fear-based information that is constantly changing. The ego responds to all of the stimuli of life in three basic karmic patterns:
>
> 1. Contraction
> 2. Re-creation
> 3. Stagnation

In the mastery of the human experience, these are universal negative forces. These are the three sisters that live on the isle of Medusa, that will turn you to stone if you give them your attention (insert sound of snakes hissing and evil laughter here).

Contraction

The first karmic pattern is contraction. In the evolution of the soul, you have two choices. You can either expand into the truth or contract back into illusion.

If we are solving an eternal problem, a relationship problem, the first thing to do is surrender attention to the practice of self-witnessing. This action brings expansion intelligence into the wave. We are now able to expand our consciousness deeper into the wave. We can now expand into realizing more of the unconsciousness territory within the wave. Since full and complete realization is the name of game, in order to get off the rock and move on, being One with the movement of expansion consciousness is critical for the liberation of the wave.

Eternal consciousness is One with expansion intelligence. It is the nature of a fully realized mind. Eternal consciousness recognizes only the movement of the One in all things. When aligned with the truth, a wave also becomes aligned with the fearlessness that is required to expand consciousness completely into any and all unrealized areas of the wave. The ego, on the other hand, due to the disease of duality, perceives threats and dangers that could come in from the outside. Due to the conflict and fear re-created by the story of duality, the ego contracts every time - a limited response from a limited form of consciousness. What a surprise! Not!!

When we try to solve an eternal problem using temporal consciousness, by thinking and believing, we immediately begin to contract. The information we are receiving from temporal consciousness is inherently limited and will only take us to an unhappy place. Let's face it. If it is an unhappy place, it is also not a very expansive feeling place either.

Contraction energy comes into mind when we give our attention to the wrong form of consciousness to solve a problem. This cause and effect is nature's way of helping us to realize what we are doing with our love. The contraction energy, what we have also been calling an incomplete action, is not happening because it is a personal attack from God. Life's challenges are not designed for us to take personally, nor are the challenges there to defend the lie of why we feel we have no value, power, or worth. The contraction is happening because of the law. What law is that you ask? *You are what you love, and you love whatever you are giving your attention to.*

Contraction is what happens when fear moves into the wave. Contraction can be felt and experienced in the body as panic or anxiety attack, a headache, a heart attack, an allergy of any kind, a pain that suddenly comes and goes, asthma or other breathing ailments where the person cannot inhale easily or completely. The list of symptoms is pretty much covered by any remedy advertised in television commercials.

Contraction affects perception in a very diseased and negative way. It costs us expansion intelligence in our ability to *see* self as the One everywhere. Contraction robs the wave of the truth to *see* that everything is perfect and as it should be. Expansion intelligence recognizes that *what is* only comes from One source: divine love and wisdom.

Contraction happens when we practice responding to life with a charge of criticism, mistrust, bad faith, or cynicism. Ladies, after a date, if you did not get a call the next day, do you contract? Gentlemen, if the lady in your life is inviting you to the feeling place, do you expand with joy, or do you contract into the lie "talking about my feelings is nothing I do well." Of course it isn't. No one can be good at anything they do not practice.

Just before opening the bills, do you contract into stories of *not enough,* or do you expand into infinite abundance? When you open your checkbook, or look at your on-line stock market portfolio, do you contract into "life goes out of its way to personally screw me every chance it gets," or "life is so hard, unfair, cruel and then you die."

When you are walking down the street and you encounter a homeless person, do you expand into the knowledge that this person is not his/her hair, bank account, or personal hygiene habits? Like Solomon, during his homeless guy from Berkeley phase, or like every God creature here, we are all wrongly being measured and judged by what we are here to transcend. Do you expand into the truth and witness the real person, or do you define mind by the very illusion it has come here to destroy? Do you trust *what is* as Heaven's gift, or do you contract into the hell, the limited place of what you think and believe it all means?

Re-Creation

The second karmic pattern is re-creation. Healthy eternal or God consciousness is creative. God created the Heavens and the Earth. **Healthy God consciousness is famous for creating something from nothing.** Unhealthy or unrealized God consciousness re-creates. Instead of creating a new expansive, playful, passionate, life-sustaining response to the stuff we are here to get over, unrealized beings are re-creating their same old limitations and suffering, over and over again ad infinitum.

What breaks the cycle of re-creation? Creating a new response or new experience. *No one can be creating a new response to life and be re-creating the same old story at the same time.* Re-creation is another limited response from a limited form of consciousness. Re-creation is another way to say incomplete action. Creativity is unlimited. Therefore it requires an unlimited form of intelligence. Creativity intelligence contains everything we need to end re-creation, incomplete action, and create a new response to the stuff we are here to get over. That new response is called a complete action.

Without exception everyone on the rock is either creating a new response to the stuff we are here to separate from, or re-creating what we have come to dismantle. Every unrealized wave is doing this. We could find a case in point in the life of every human being that has ever or will ever spend time on the rock. The perfect example of this pattern comes from the life of film director Roman Polanski. Again, because this is a universal movement, we could use anyone. Polanski's life just happens to illustrate the point with the drama of a Hollywood movie that simply cannot be missed.

Roman was born in France, where he and his family were safe from the tide of hatred against the Jewish people that was growing in Europe at that time. While still a child, for reasons unknown, Roman's father moved the family back to Poland. Soon afterwards they were rounded up and forced to live within the confined walls of a "Jewish ghetto." Roman grew up watching the Nazis at work. He grew up watching one group of people justifying the lie of why they terrorized another group of people, because the Nazis felt they were superior to everyone else, and therefore entitled.

Roman was very close to his mother, as most children are. Roman's mother was pregnant while the family was still imprisoned within the ghetto. The Nazis came for the women first. When Roman's mother was taken off to the camps, she was eight going on nine months pregnant. Roman never saw his beloved mother ever again.

She would die at the nightmarishly evil hands of the Nazis, while Roman was far away, unaware and unable to change the insidious fate of the most important woman in his life.

Fast-forward into the future. Roman is an adult and very happily married to the breathtakingly beautiful actress Sharon Tate. Roman and Sharon are expecting their first child. They have bought a home together and have set up a nursery. During the final months of the pregnancy Roman is filming in England. Sharon has stayed with Roman until she is eight going on nine months pregnant. At that time she returns to America to prepare for the child's birth. Roman remains far away finishing his contractual agreement as director. One night Sharon is home entertaining some of her dearest friends when, without warning, the malicious hands of the Charles Manson family reach into the living room of Roman and Sharon's home. Sharon and her unborn child are senselessly and violently murdered.

Twice in one lifetime this man has horribly, beyond tragically, lost the most important, most loved women in his world. Both times it happened when he was far away, completely unsuspecting of the hideousness that was to befall these innocent women. Both times the women were eight going on nine months pregnant, and both times the people committing the murders came straight from the lowest level of hell. Coincidence? As Swedenborg liked to say, there are no coincidences. There is no luck of the draw or throw of the dice. Everything is determined by either the unresolved force of re-creation, or by the liberating power of creativity.

What is so compelling about Polanski's life in this example is that his life truly underscores the enormous chokehold re-creation has on us. It does not matter what the stuff is. If it is not resolved, it will be re-created until a new response is created. Even if the universe has to provide a cast of characters that looks like the most unlikely and repellent collection of perpetrators that ever lived in order for us to *get it,* then so *be it.* Re-creation is why we feel that we have unremittingly been ground into the lowest possible place by life and its experiences. It shall be forever thus, until the wave creates a new response: one of feeling empowered, restored and healed by life and its experiences.

The best way to practice being in right relationship with creativity intelligence, is to practice giving attention to anything creative. Anything! Practice making something from nothing like gardening, painting, sewing, carpentry, any crafts, writing, raising animal companions, surfing, making your friends laugh, surprising someone with a picnic, or trip to the beach. Do anything different. What you do is not nearly as important as simply being engaged in the creative process itself. You cannot master anything that you have not practiced. For thousands of years many spiritual healers have recognized that **creativity heals fear.** That is some pretty powerful Mojo!

Swedenborg did not invent Divine Correspondence. He simply coined the phrase that best allows us to understand the principle in motion. American Indian spiritualism understands the concept of Divine Correspondence. One example of that would be the Divine Correspondence of animal spirits. The rabbit in native shamanism represents either fear or creativity. So, if a person were walking in the woods and a rabbit crossed their path that person would understand the event as showing that either fear was crossing their path in life or creativity was intersecting their soul. How would the person know if it was fear or creativity? They would know by what they were giving their attention to at the moment of manifestation. We either create a new response to life or re-create our old crap, and another name for re-creation is fear. Understand that the flip side of fear is creativity.

Never again laugh at grandpa for doing his paint by numbers clown picture. Here is where the beauty of Divine Correspondence comes in. In the mundane physical world, it is just a clown, paint by numbers. In the spiritual realm, grandpa has found a natural anti-depressant, without any physical side effects or internal organ toxicity stress. So next Christmas, give grandpa the paint by numbers of Elvis on black velvet and watch him heal himself as only God consciousness can.

Stagnation

The third karmic pattern of stagnation is energy within the wave that does not move and is not living. Once stagnation enters the wave, it no longer has the energy it needs to expand or grow beyond what is causing pain or limitation. Paralyzed energy cannot create a new response to life. You will never be able to accept the whole of life if your love is stuck in stagnation. No wave can free itself when it is held in the tyranny of consciousness that paralyzes the flow of truth, thus the saying, "The truth shall set you free." If you are looking at something and it is not setting your mind free, then you have not seen the truth of it. Why? We know a tree by its fruits. If you are looking at something and the story of duality is not being shattered, you are getting your navigating information from the ego, from the voice of limitation itself. Our job on the planet Earth is to practice not stepping in the ego's paralyzing shit!

Where can unrealized waves be found standing motionless in the ego's stagnant shit? Everywhere. Stagnation is the stuff in our lives that does not go away. Ever know anyone who for years hated parents, ex-partners, teachers, neighbors, even fellow drivers on the road? Ever know someone who for years expressed unresolved emotions towards others, whether or not they even saw the other offending person, or whether or not this other offending person was even still alive?

Ever know a person who constantly asked "Why me?" over and over again like a broken recording in response to everything that has ever happened to them? Ever know anyone stuck in the story that they do not have enough time, love, money and opportunity? Ever know someone who would consistently rather be right than happy? Ever see a person swallow their truth repeatedly so that they could *save* the feelings of others? If the answer was *yes* to one or more of these questions, you're looking at a wave paralyzed by the karmic action of giving attention to stagnation.

Remember we have a nervous system to keep us *real* about what we are doing with our love. Has anyone's physical body presently or in the past experienced kidney stones, arthritis, trauma of any kind, being overweight, cataracts, fused bones or vertebrae, blood clots, congestion of any kind, anything stiff, rigid or inflexible? What the wave is really experiencing is stagnation in mind that has manifested itself physically. That way we may become conscious of what the unconscious part of the wave is doing with its attention. That is the natural course of events. The stuff we are here to get over is designed to show up in this Earthly place so that we may feel it, and by feeling it, become fully conscious.

Stagnation shows up in any wave's emotional body as being stubborn, fixated or obsessed with something or someone, grief stricken or overwhelmed by a sense of loss, abandonment or depression. Stagnation appears as any situation, condition or relationship that the wave is not growing beyond.

There comes a point where contraction, re-creation and stagnation all become one, as they feed and support each other in a negative symbiotic way. First the wave contracts as a response to its own mind out of ignorance, set into motion by the disease of duality. Then, if the wave does not create a new response to *what is* at this time, it will be destined to re-create some neurotic response. What un-balanced response will the wave re-create? Whatever sick and troubled lie we have trained the ego we will give our attention to, of course. Once a wave gets to this point of loyalty to re-creation, that action will then solidify stag-nation. And voila! After the dust and destructive debris settles, we have the three karmic stages of suffering, pain and ultimately death.

Fragmentation vs. Wholeness

Giving attention to the ego to solve our eternal problems re-creates self-fragmentation. A wave that is fragmented is not whole. If your mind is not completely whole right now, then it is fragmented. All unenlightened beings are fragmented. It is a side effect of giving attention to the ego when it is not appropriate to do so. If we are giving attention to love, which is a complete action, then our wave would be made whole. If we give attention to the most limiting form of intelligence around, the ego, we are re-creating an incomplete action, and the wave will remain fragmented.

When we are not practicing the art of self-witnessing, the disease of duality steps in, courtesy of the ego's thought and belief agenda. This further fragments the mind with the charge and story of subject/object orientation. Duality tells mind, the wave, that there is no reality of wholeness occurring anywhere. I am over here. You are over there. We are separate, not related, not interconnected or Divinely Corresponding to one another. We are not whole; we are not the One.

The disease of duality shatters mind's relationship with wholeness intelligence right from the start. The ego and duality are inseparable. The ego cannot exist outside of the atmosphere of duality, because all ego information is based on duality. Who is more powerful here? Who is less powerful? Whenever comparison happens someone will always come out *better than,* and someone will always come out *less than.* This cycle of mind experiencing itself as *more than* or *less than* becomes self-perpetuating and entrenched in re-creation. Without *less than, better than* does not exist and visa versa. They endlessly continue to re-create each other, because they need each other in order to exist.

Those who dare, dare not compare. – Argisle

What does it mean to really love wholeness intelligence? Loving wholeness intelligence is to be One with the knowledge that *everything* is food that has come to bring liberation to mind. Loving wholeness intelligence does not fragment spirit's relationship with itself, like having thoughts and beliefs about itself. It is a complete action that heals all fragmentation of mind, all duality. It is the action of unconditionally accepting the whole of life, not just the parts we like, not just what feels good to us, or goes our way, but the whole of it. Loving wholeness intelligence is to be One with equability in mind, action, and speech. Loving wholeness intelligence is to be aligned with the knowledge there is only the One: One moment, One life, One happiness.

Beyond compromise is cooperation – Argisle

It is only when mind has shattered the illusion of identifying with duality that the wave creates an ending to the re-creation of playing either a victim or a perpetrator role. What victim and perpetrator both have in common is that they are limited states of being, therefore governed and run by a limited form of consciousness. Both require the charge of duality in order to exist. Outside of duality there is no victim and no perpetrator; there is only the One.

A Definition of "Sin" You Won't Hear in Church

Sin does not mean what most people, for thousands of years, have been thinking and believing it means. The word *sin* simply means *fragmentation*. Sin is a wave that has been fragmented by the inappropriate use of temporal consciousness for solving eternal problems. Sin involves organizing our wave to support giving attention to the ego, duality, and limitation. That is all.

The Bible asks the question of the ages, "Who has not sinned?" It does not mean that you or anyone else is an intrinsically bad or evil person. What it means is who has not had a thought or belief about themselves and others?

All unrealized beings are defining themselves by their thoughts and beliefs. The definition of an unrealized mind is that we are giving attention to the inappropriate form of consciousness to solve a problem. It is not good. It is not bad. It is just what unrealized beings do. It is the ability to practice recognizing it, forgiving it, and surrendering our attention back to Ultimate Truth as a response to the whole of life that transforms us into realized beings. We would be better served loving and trusting ourselves, thus ending the cycle of fragmentation, and making ourselves whole again. Every wave that ever has been here has come with thoughts and beliefs to surrender, because that is why the Earth was created. Here we, as spirit, have a place to go to, and practice ending this horrible addiction to giving our attention to anything that lives in hell, that lives in a place of limitation.

Once we understand that to sin is to be in relationship with mind in a manner that supports duality, the ego, as the senior movement of mind, then we can see sin appear even in places where it has been previously hidden, covertly camouflaged by the ego. If I am writing a check to a church or a charity, and my mind is organized according to duality, then I'm probably thinking and believing what a great person I am. I'm helping out people who would be nowhere without me. The problem is that I'm relating to this event in subject/object. I am the great person over here being so generous with those over there that are not as good as me: superior/inferior. I am re-creating a fragmenting relationship with mind. This is the way the ego hides a "sinful" or fragmenting relationship with mind:

behind the guise of being a really great person doing a really great thing.

The opposite holds true as well. There can be two people who love, care and respect each other in an equitable fashion that reflects the love of Heaven. But if these two people are of the same sex, or different religions, races, or ethnic backgrounds, the ego of others will judge them as *sinful* or *evil*. Sin has nothing to do with morality. Moral or immoral, it does not matter. It is self-evident to see that many cruelties and much suffering has been committed in the name of each. What does matter is what they both have in common. They are both a collection of thoughts and beliefs that vary in description and intensity of charge from person to person. As Oscar Wilde once said, "There is no such thing as a moral or an immoral book. Books are well written or badly written. That is all."

As spiritual beings having a human experience, we must organize our wave to increase receptivity to the Oneness of spirit by giving our attention to love, acceptance, patience, tolerance, and flexibility. This is the intelligence required to end the conflicts in our lives. We will never solve any eternal relationship problems by giving our attention to what the ego has told us to think and belief about morality or immorality. We can only resolve these problems by showing up in the moment from an open Heart.

If giving our attention to what we think and believe moral and immoral is really worked, Jesus would never have been on trial and killed for the immoral blasphemy of declaring, "The Father and I are One." Socrates would not have been arrested and convicted of the immoral charge of corrupting the youth. (Yes, Madonna, it is nice to know *that* lie has been around long before you showed up. You didn't invent it, honey, you just accessorized it and put it to music video better than anyone else.) If thoughts and beliefs about moral and immoral were useful, the literary genius Oscar Wilde would not be considered the most tragic figure of the Victorian Age, but yet he is.

Although Wilde lived his life with saint-like generosity towards others, he was found guilty of being immoral because he loved another man. The English court took away his legal ownership of all his possessions, his home, and all of his writings including *Picture of Dorian Gray,* and *The Importance of Being Earnest.* The courts also stripped Oscar of his right to be a father. After the trial Oscar was never able to see his two beloved sons again. His prison sentence is the story of a cruel and unusual punishment that nearly killed him. Oscar did survive prison, only to die in extreme poverty due to the immoral stamp placed upon him by the English court. Unfeeling cruelty is the "reward" for thinking and believing the moral way.

Loving wholeness intelligence means organizing the wave to recognize, heal and transform fragmentation, duality, and limitation in the mind. Only by unconditionally loving the whole of life, by giving attention exclusively to Ultimate Truth to solve all eternal problems, by loving and accepting ourselves and others with an open Heart in the present moment without a thought or belief, are we really living a life free of unhappiness, free of all self-inflicted violence, free of all *sin.*

Inner Air Pollution

Ayurvedic psychology says that energetically, thoughts and beliefs are like tiny, jagged, sharp pieces of glass-like particles that hang in the air in the same way dust particles hang in the air. Like dust particles, we breath these energetic thought and belief particles in and out. When we inhale, the oxygen particles go into the lungs. The thoughts and belief particles go into the brain.

This explains how people can realize the same thought at the same time, without any direct verbal communication, even across a large room. They are all breathing in and out the same thought and belief particles. This also explains why you sometimes get a strange feeling when talking with someone, even though the other person is not saying anything offensive. As long as the other person is thinking offensive or harmful thoughts towards you, you will be breathing in those same thoughts and beliefs. On some level in mind, you will know this person is not quite right, but you do not know exactly why.

When a spiritual being has reached, or is close to the end of the human experience, Ayurvedic psychology indicates that the accumulated thoughts and beliefs begin to unravel. They fill the space around the dead or dying body with these tiny energetic thought/belief sharp glass-like particles. Everyone near or close by, like driving by the site of a traffic accident, will breath in and out these highly charged, fragmenting particles. This phenomenon is also the "bad" or "creepy" feelings people get when they enter a place where lots of people have died or have shared a deeply traumatizing event. When the particles of mind are released in such a manner, they could stay hanging, charged in the ether in that same space for hundreds, even thousands of years, depending on how intense the charge was when the initial energetic impression was made.

This Ayurvedic understanding of thoughts as sharp glass-like particles allows us to see the truly limiting nature of thoughts and beliefs, and how they keep fragmenting wholeness within the wave.

A mind that focuses on and loves Ultimate Truth is the only protection there is from breathing in and out the fragmenting energy of the thoughts and belief particles that float in the air. Eternal consciousness is intrinsic to wholeness. Love is the wholeness making "Midas touch." Everything love touches turns into love, bringing real love and understanding into your experience of grief and loss, or whatever is limiting you. No other force in the universe has this power to make mind whole. This is why love rules. This is also why it is essential that we practice giving our attention exclusively to truth. It is in the action of surrendering consciousness to love that the ultimate action of wholeness occurs. It is a complete action that heals and transforms the wave into Oneness with the ocean.

Recognizing The Shit From The Shin 'Ola

The human experience is where we master letting go of the waste portion of the program. So do not be surprised when the shit hits the fan, because it will. Never let the ego tell you that you are a failure because of a divorce, bankruptcy, car accident, even rape or any experience that happens here on the rock. It does not matter. Remind the ego that none of it matters because only the stuff we are here to get over shows up on the rock, that is what it is for.

As Swedenborg says, "Remember you are nothing limited, nothing physical, nothing in duality". What that
means is what you really are does not even show up here.
Only what you are here to get over shows up. Why you
might ask is that the case? How else could we learn to
recognize the shit from the shin ola!

The rock is where spirits come to practice making separation from the flushable portion of the program. Like
other beings, you are just dumping as much of the *crap* as
you can. Make that discard pile as high as possible while
you are here. Establishing permanent separation from
anything that distracts your love from Heaven's love is
to fulfill the higher purpose of why you came here. As
God consciousness, you cannot create an experience you
do not need. Therefore, everything that happens here is
working for you. It is providing you with the means to
enlightenment. That sounds like the definition of success
not failure.

One of the larger paradoxes concerning unrealized waves
is the extreme attachment and fascination with the very
stuff that we have come here to put down. When did
worry ever "add one inch to your stature or one day to
your life?," as Jesus liked to say. Worry has never solved
a single problem. It has done unmeasurable damage to
our perception of *what is* as not even close to perfect. Yet
we reach for the worry drug over and over again as if it
were the solution instead of the contaminant. We relate
to worry as if it were the healing instead of the disease.
We depend on worry as if it were some great gift, instead
of recognizing it for what it is.

> *Worry is what we do, when we don't know what to do.*
> *– Argisle*

Another way we hold on to the disposable is by holding on to clutter in our lives. Disorder in the physical world has a Divine Correspondence in the spiritual world, of course, or it would not exist. In the interior realm disarray and clutter Corresponds to the confusion and uncertainty that is re-created in the mind by giving attention to thinking and believing our way through life. If the house is packed, the garage is crammed and the car is a rolling trash can, then it is accurate to say the wave is filled with the toxic e-coli of what the ego invests in as real and true. Clearly the wave is not filled with the spaciousness of truth.

What exactly are we holding on to when we cannot seem to empty our lives of the past and the irrelevant? We are holding on to some emotional, physiological, perceptual and experiential food that has long since gone stale and is now seriously dead. There is a direct relationship with *being here now,* and being clutter free. The more baggage you carry with you, the more burdened you will become. The more burdened your life feels, the harder it is to *be here now, available to a higher love focus.*

Even the financial guru, goddess Suzie Orman, denounces paperwork clutter as one of the chief causes behind loss of income as well as deterioration of clarity into one's present financial status. Be it pack rat or exterior pollution of any kind, it all equals confusion and loss, no matter where it appears, or how it camouflages itself in the physical world.

The upside to Divine Correspondence is that it does keep us honest about what we still need to be rid of. If the house looks as if it has been stuffed to the rafters, then we are looking at a wave that has no room for life. We are looking at a wave so completely filled up with the ego's agenda that there is no room for anything living to thrive and grow. When mind has been converted into the ego's personal outhouse, then filled to maximum capacity, there will be no flexibility, no compassion, no patience, no joy, no fun, no Heaven. Why? Because there will be no space for it.

The good news is that we always have the power to clean our interior house according to what we are giving our attention to. We must re-train the ego to receive from us only a dialog of trust and good faith in love and life. This is how we successfully practice the mastery of the human experience.

The Body Does Not Lie

The physical body is another form of expression, or reflection of how our wave is organized. Unlike the ego, the body does not lie to us. According to Ayurveda, **breathing is how the body thinks, and thinking is how the brain breathes.** When we are visited by anger or fear, the body's breathing will change. This change reflects that the body's thinking has changed as well. It is only when the body's breathing has returned to a more normal pattern that we begin to feel calmer. When the breathing has returned to a more normal place, the body's thinking has returned from a more agitated place. So, of course, we feel better. Any disturbance in the breath indicates the unrealized portion of the wave is giving its love and attention to one or more of the ego's ultimate lies. This can only happen if the wave is caught asleep in the disease of duality.

This is why so many spiritual practices are intimate with

the process of monitoring the breath. Due to Divine Correspondence, to watch the breath is to witness what you are doing with your love and attention. Being aware of the breath is to be in the present moment. You cannot breath in past time. You cannot breath in the future. Breathing happens in the now, in each present moment. When the breath becomes disturbed, somewhere in the wave you are giving attention to something limiting, something other than Ultimate Truth.

Because the brain breathes by thinking, it will chatter endlessly. The inner cranium will always be running a constant commentary about everything. In Eastern traditions this is referred to as "the barking dog" of mind. That is OK. It is a good thing that the brain is breathing. Breathing is the preferred action for all living things. When the chattering is going on, however, it is critical that we, in the moment, know who is talking to us. Are we listening to love or the ego? Who we are giving our attention to? We will always have to watch our mind while we are here. If we don't, as the brain breathes, we will confuse its chatter with real directional information, thus remaining caught in the trap of the ego and duality. *This is the simple reason for the suffering of unrealized beings.*

If we do not know that we have two forms of consciousness and that the brain is breathing (moving the thought and belief particles in and out, just as the lungs are breathing the air particles in and out), we will end up giving all of our love to this flow of mental breathing. We will end up giving our attention to thoughts and beliefs as the charge of the ego directs them. Using this limited information to solve our eternal problems will only lead us to various levels of hell. Hell, thoughts, beliefs and the

ego, are all limited forms of consciousness that only produce limited results. This is what they have in common.
We must master giving our attention to trusting love
and making that action of trust the senior voice over the
brain's breathing. This is what the mastery of the human
experience is all about.

Eastern traditions talk about a student leaving his teacher
for a new land. The student asks the teacher, "When I get
to this new land, how will I know a true teacher from
a false one?" The teacher says, "Ask them if they have a
technique for stilling the mind. If they say, 'yes,' you will
know they are a false teacher." If the brain isn't moving,
it isn't breathing, and that it isn't a good thing for a living brain.

Emotions as Divine Visitors

Emotions are really a universal force that we shall refer to
as divine visitors. Emotions, as divine visitors, invite our
awareness into a honest process of fully realizing exactly
what self re-created stories of limitation we are here to
get over. These stories are what we are presently giving
our attention to on both a conscious and unconscious
level. This is a very good thing too, as the ego loves to
repeatedly lie to us about what we have gotten over, and
what we have not gotten over. Our emotions, however,
will always honestly reflect what we are doing with our
love and attention. It is where we are putting our attention that will determine which divine emotional visitor
is going to be *touching* our nervous system at any given
moment.

If you give your attention to a limited quality of consciousness, like worry, then a limited emotional visitor

such as *stressed out* will come calling. Give your attention to a higher quality of consciousness, like Ultimate Truth, and an unlimited emotional visitor such as *fully supported and fearless* will touch the nervous system. This is nature's self-corrective guidance system to help us get in touch with what we are doing with our love, and to see where our attention goes in the face of the on-going dialog of limitation-on-parade re-created by the ego.

Ayurvedic psychology beautifully explains that emotions are a universal force and why we have them. We are going to define a universal force as something that existed on the planet before you showed up, as well as something all life forms on the planet experience such as air, fire, water and Earth. In the West, we have a tendency to think of and relate to emotions as if they were deeply personal possessions. "This is my anger, my pain, my grief. Nobody else can understand or know the agony I'm going through." We have a tendency to identify, define and understand ourselves through the filter of experienced emotions. "Oh, I'm just an impatient person, that is just who I am." "OK, so I am an angry, irritated person today. Got a problem with that?"

We think and believe we are our emotions, which gets reflected in our language about our lives and ourselves. We do not have this misunderstanding with the universal force of air. We do not take in a breath of air and, without letting it out, run around telling everyone, "This is my air! Hear me, my air! You just don't get it. It's my air!" However, we do this consistently with our emotions.

All divine visitors are healers, perfect food sent from Heaven for the liberation of mind. Anger is a purgative when we are in right relationship with it. It purges whatever is contaminating our life. Jesus purged the Temple of dishonesty, inequality, and *not enough* when he truthfully expressed his anger about the moneychangers. He literally purified the space by purging the contaminating relationship right out of the Temple. Jesus models for us a perfect relationship with all divine visitors. No unenlightened beings embody a relationship of such clarity.

When we are not in right relationship with anger, instead of purging that which is not truthful and life sustaining, we are merely maintaining the tyranny of the ego. We are giving our attention to misplaced wisdom, to thoughts and beliefs, which in turn invites the divine visitors of mistrust, misunderstanding and misinterpretation of divine wisdom deeper into the wave. **We cannot be giving our attention to the truth and to the ego at the same time.** Right relationship is giving attention to the truth, which in turn burns off illusion. Truth does not drive illusion deeper into the wave. That is the ego's limited job.

Why do certain limiting emotions like worry seem to visit us more consistently and frequently than un-limiting emotions, like carefree? The emotions that visit you are the emotions you are beckoning, according to what you are giving your attention to. If I am giving my attention to temporal consciousness to solve an eternal problem, what I'm really doing is inviting the divine visitors of frustration, disappointment, struggle, hopelessness, abandonment, and of course everybody's favorite, re-creation of unhappiness. These divine visitors go directly into the wave and into the nervous system. Why is that you ask? *Because you are what you love, and you love whatever you are giving your attention to.* (Who didn't see that one coming?)

When the divine visitor of anger comes, instead of saying, "I'm angry! Back off," we might want to re-examine our relationship with how we language our reality. Here we have an opportunity to express ourselves in a manner that more accurately reflects the truth, like, "Anger is presently visiting the body's nervous system, so why don't we talk later when calm and clear are visiting." It is much harder to take the visit personally if we are in right relationship with what is really happening.

Emotions, according to Ayurvedic psychology, are a completely different entity than we have been taught to think and believe they are. Again, this Eastern approach describes emotions as a universal force. There is nothing personal about our emotions, nor does anything useful come from relating to emotions as a personal event. Ayurvedic psychology says, "Don't take our word for it, you can prove it to yourself." Ask yourself if anger was on the planet before you personally showed up? Was fear? Insecurity? Rage? If it was here before you arrived, like air, water, and fire, it is not a personal force. It is a universal force. We all experience it. We all experience anger. We all experience fear. We all experience elation. We all get the whole of the universal experience.

Like emotions, experiences also appeared on the planet Earth long before you did. That means there is nothing personal in any of the experiences you are going through. People were re-creating thoughts and beliefs long before your butt hit tangible turf. Illness, pain, pleasure, social and economic status, death, birth, life. There is absolutely nothing personal in the lot of them. If you are not experiencing life as *beyond personal,* then you are experiencing the stuff you are here to get over. Just so you know the difference.

If we are identifying with our emotions as what we are, will our mind then be organized in such a fashion that it will allow us to create separation from that emotion? The answer is no. When you identify with being the emotion instead of identifying with being the awareness that self-witnesses the emotion, then you create a cul-de-sac in the mind. This traps the emotion in the wave. According to Ayurveda, the average person holds the pain of depression, anger and fear indefinitely through the action of personally identifying with temporal emotions. This, of course, keeps the ego fat and happy, sucking down its favorite food of unhappiness, fresh, right out of the tap of our mind and nervous system.

When we inappropriately give attention to the ego, we are giving attention to duality. This in turn invokes limited negative divine visitors into our life and wave. The purpose of the negative divine visitors touching our wave is so that we may realize what we are doing with our love. Why is that you ask again? *Because you are what you love, and you love whatever you are giving your attention to.* These negative emotional visitors facilitate the much-needed action of us *feeling* the truth of that statement.

(Have you got it yet? You will, we all will.)

Swedenborg reminded us that if we want to realize the contents of our wave, we must turn inward and look at what we are *feeling*. This is how we become truthful and self-realizing about what the unconsciousness portion of the wave is giving its attention to. Let's face it, we are dealing with the unconscious. How can we see what we are unconscious of? How can we see the invisible? It shows up on our feeling radar as our emotional truth. If I'm feeling worried or anxiety riddled, then the wave is giving its attention to the ego. The ego is telling the wave there is not enough: not enough time, not enough money, not enough love, not enough everything. The ego will make up anything. That is how it stays alive.

Our job is to be in right relationship with the self-reflective vehicle that the human experience is: to witness what mind is really doing with its attention. In this physical arena of the rock, we cannot fake what we are feeling, because we have a nervous system to give us immediate and honest feedback about what we are doing with our love. Spirit loves whatever it is giving its attention to. If you are giving attention to limitation, you will find yourself living in hell, because hell loves limitation. If you are practicing giving attention to beyond duality, beyond limitation, beyond thinking and believing, to just being with *what is* in the present moment with an open Heart, then you will find yourself in Heaven, because that is what Heaven loves.

Swedenborg points out that as spirit, we are beyond the physical. We are beyond the limited. We are beyond duality. So what we really are does not even show up here. Since we are here to experience mind through the physical, the limited world of duality, *only the stuff we are here to get over* shows up here. Notice in Swedenborg's wisdom there is no advice that urges us to take any of this stuff personally. Swedenborg only supports us in letting go and growing beyond what we can, while we can.

What me worry? – A. E. Newman

TRUST

Mastery of the human experience
is a journey of trust.

❋ Trusting that we are God consciousness.
❋ Trusting that the divine food sent us is
exactly what we need, when we need it.
❋ Trusting that we cannot make a mistake.
❋ Trusting that others cannot make a mistake.
❋ Trusting that we, as eternal consciousness,
are creating exactly what we need on the
path to realizing we are love.
❋ Trusting in our lives.
❋ Trusting in ourselves as God consciousness.
❋ Trusting in others as God consciousness.
❋ Trusting that divine love and wisdom are
running the whole show.
❋ Trusting that only divine love and wisdom
are real.
❋ Trusting that I am beyond all this, therefore
there will be an ending to all temporal
suffering.
❋ Trusting that I am senior to the divine food
sent me (emotions, experiences, anything
temporal), and that I can digest all of it to
my benefit.
❋ Trusting I can take the divine nutrients to a
deeper level.
❋ Trusting I am fully capable of recognizing
what to hold on to and what to let go of.

All relationship issues are eternal problems, because if nothing else, you will always be in relationship with yourself. That will never change. So after we have used thoughts and words to solve the temporal problems for filling out that 1040 form and sending it off to the IRS, we no longer need to have a thought or belief about it. If the IRS should send us something back, be it a refund check or a more challenging communication, we only love and accept it in the present moment. We accept the experience as whole, complete, perfect, lacking in nothing. We only give thanks for the perfect divine food that is sent to us. We only focus on the truth to solve this relationship problem. There is only the One. There is always infinite abundance. We trust that if we needed to be experiencing something different with the IRS in order to reach enlightenment, we would be.

We trust that we are eternal and therefore senior to anything in the physical world. Moreover, that the physical world was created for the convenience of our liberation. We fully accept what is given without a thought or belief, because we know it is working for us. It is bringing us enlightenment because Heaven creates everything that way. Therefore, we whole-Heartedly accept all of life unconditionally, for the whole of it is our enlightenment.

We trust and witness that life is perfectly reflecting exactly the inner relationship that we most need to self-realize, as well as to end our self re-created suffering. We respond with love and trust to all of life, because we know that everything that is coming to us is our own mind for self-realization. We know that there is only one serving relationship to have with our own mind: to love, to trust, and to accept it unconditionally. There is no big, bad IRS that could get us from the outside and take away our happiness and power. There is only an unrealized relationship with mind manifesting itself in the physical world for the purpose of spirit realizing itself through the process of experiencing itself.

Patience

Just as George Harrison was one of the greatest, yet most under appreciated guitar players of all time, so it is with the mind's relationship with patience. Patience is the most under appreciated voice in the orchestra comprising the whole of life. According to Buddhism, if you want to understand how much of your unrealized mind is giving its attention to any story of limitation, just examine **the three great karmic mirrors that are reflecting this reality back to you.**

The first is family. How much loyalty to patience (or impatience) does your family live on a regular basis? **The second is nation or country.** How patient or impatient is America as a whole? Are Americans famous for their tolerance or patience? Do most Americans "vapor lock" if they have to stand in line for more than ten minutes? Road rage and air rage cannot be the actions of a mind possessed by patience. A mind that loves patience does not worship immediate gratification. How much does America love immediate gratification? Look no further than you own nervous system to answer that question.

The third great karmic mirror is global. Examine the present global ether you find yourself in historically. Is this a time where the world at large is One with patience and tolerance for the other guy, the other country, the other market forces?

Heart disease and heart related problems like heart attacks kill an inordinate number of Americans every year. Chinese Medicine and Ayurveda show there is a powerful connection between the divine visitors of patience and impatience, and the physical heart organ in your body. According to the Eastern healing approach, certain organs in our bodies digest certain emotions. The heart is about patience, with patience defined as being One with the truth, that there is always infinite abundance. This means there is always enough time, love, money, opportunity. Now ask yourself, honestly, when would it serve you to not be One with the truth that there is always enough.

Chinese Medicine and Ayurveda want us to understand that when we organize our mind, our wave, with the notion that there is not enough, we are giving our attention to impatience. We are committing an act of self-violence against the heart. These great healing traditions say that when we give attention to impatience, this action is equal to reaching into the chest, pulling out the heart and "bitch slapping" it, or drop kicking it across the room. Heart breaking isn't? Literally. These Eastern sciences beg us to consider if giving our attention to impatience about *anything* is worth that level of unconscious self-inflicted violence?

The following article appeared in the Health section of the Oct. 23, 2003, Houston Chronicle:

Impatience Tied to High Blood Pressure

Do you honk your horn the minute the light turns green? Fume when someone's late, or a meeting runs over? Stress out when caught in a checkout line? You may want to have your blood pressure checked.

A large study that followed more than 3,300 young adults for 15 years found that those who were impatient or hostile faced a higher long-term risk of developing high blood pressure, independent of other risk factors.

And the more impatient and hostile they were, the study found, the greater the risk.

It attempts to tease out the unhealthy effects of psychosocial factors associated with the so-called type A personality, and it is apparently the first to pinpoint impatience as an independent risk factor for high blood pressure.

Patience is the magical spiritual energy that brings together many dynamic aspects of life. If there are unrealized dreams, parts of life we love but cannot seem to humanifest in our lives, then what is keeping all these dynamic forces from coming together as One, is a lack of patience. If there is an inner dialog running about *shoulds* ("I should have done this," or "it should have been done like that.") All *shoulds* are held together in the wave by impatience, and lack of acceptance. Do not fool yourself. There are many people *shoulding* all over themselves, and you could be one of them. Impatience is the exact opposite movement in mind as trust and acceptance. If we are impatient, we are not accepting the perfect divine food that is sent to us. We are not trusting eternal consciousness. Neither position is very serving in ending suffering or in creating a life worth living.

Impatience is the ego asserting its agenda as senior to love. Impatience is spirit loving the story that things are all screwed up. Life is not acceptable as it is. Impatience rejects the whole of life, and is aligned with all the same things hell loves.

When spirit practices identifying with beyond duality, with beyond limitation, with loving the whole of life and not taking the movement of life so personally, then letting go of impatience becomes easy. There is no way spirit could be experiencing impatience without taking life way too personally. There is no way spirit could be taking life way too personally, unless it is also unconsciously caught asleep in the disease of duality. Without duality there would be no *you* to take anything personally. There would be no subject/object experience. There would be only a realization of the One. When the divine visitor of impatience is touching the nervous system, it is spirit's divine opportunity to witness attachment to the ultimate lies re-created by the ego. In witnessing the illusory lies, you are simultaneously freeing yourself from the tyranny of the ego, because what is holding the lies in place is spirit remaining unconscious to its presence. ***Simply becoming conscious of the lies changes everything. You do not have consciousness you are consciousness.*** Consciousness is the name of the game. Once you become conscious of the shit you are standing in, you are then free to move to a *shit free* space. If you remain unconscious to the reality that you are actually standing in the ego's excrement, how will you realize the need to move elsewhere?

To the exact same degree that impatience is violence against the heart organ, patience strengthens, heals and makes the heart organ whole. To live a life of patience is to live from an expansive core of love, acceptance, and trust intelligence. To be One with patience is to be One with the infinite eternal present moment with an open Heart, without a thought or belief about what it all means. We just trust that all of life is perfect, because we know everything is sent by Heaven. To be inseparable from patience is to be inseparable from Ultimate Truth. To live as indivisible from patience is to live as indivisible from the love and wisdom of Heaven. Clearly, practicing patience is its own reward in the mastery of the human experience.

Self Witnessing - The Ultimate in Voyeurism

The mastery of self-witnessing and the mastery of the human experience are the same movement of mind. A wave that is watching the mind with realized attention is a wave that knows which voice is talking at any given moment. It is a wave that knows the voice of the temporal from the voice of the eternal. Realized attention also knows how much awareness to give each form of consciousness and when to give it. We should be giving about 5% of our waking day attention to the ego, to thoughts or words, to solve temporal problems in the temporal world. The remaining 95% of the time we are just showing up from the Heart and paying attention to *what is* from a place of innocence.

When I'm balancing my checkbook, deciding what clothes to wear, finding out who has the best price on car insurance, or trying to fill out that 1040 form, only then will I give attention to what I think. The rest of the time I am not giving any attention to what I think or belief. Don't get me wrong. The thoughts, thinking and words are going off all the time in the brain because the brain is breathing, and breathing is always the preferred action for something living to do. But I am not giving the movement of mental breathing and chatter my attention. Instead, I am focusing inward on what information the feeling body is giving me about how the wave is organized. Did the wave invoke and invite a limited or unlimited divine visitor? This will tell me honestly what I am doing with my love. In this way, I aim to become fully self-realizing in an arena I cannot fake.

The truly critical question is *how am I feeling in this moment as a response to the stimulus of life?* Is what I am feeling consciously becoming One in each moment with acceptance consciousness? Am I accepting that this moment feels awkward, embarrassing, painful, fearful, angry or worried? Am I identifying with the temporal portion of the program, or is temporal identification going on through the vehicle of thoughts and beliefs, and the dis-ease of duality? Am I thinking, "I am this fear? I am this worry? I am this limiting experience?" We came here to practice separation from limitation. We did not come here to defend and justify it or to build a monument to it with our attention.

Mastery of the human experience requires us to love consciously witnessing the movement of mind for the purpose of dismantling all unconscious re-created suffering. Why? *Because you are what you love, and you love whatever you are giving your attention to.* (You should be able to recite that in your sleep by now.) Being its own self-evident reward, giving attention to love as a means of ending all limitation and suffering is to share the love of Heaven.

However, the ego has a way of camouflaging its attachment to suffering in all unrealized waves. Through an elaborate process of thoughts and beliefs, the ego identifies with the story that our personal suffering is deeply complex and especially difficult. That our personal suffering comes in the most state-of-the-art destruction-resistant packaging. Heard this before? "Life, happiness and abundance works for everybody, except me. I have to live under a dark cloud, a curse, while everyone else gets a life worth living." Sounds like "fast food" for the ego. A "quickie" of unhappiness to keep the inner critic securely engorged. This is *not* a complete action. Playing games with the ego is not what we came here to do. We came here to take happiness into our own hands. That is a complete action. Not to mention deeply satisfying (wink, wink, nudge, nudge).

How is any wave, that is giving attention to a pathetic story of limitation, ever going to witness the simple truth of what is really holding together all of the suffering in mind? When mind's suffering cannot be ended because the ego based story is that this action is too hard, too painful, or impossible to accomplish, then self-reflective life on Earth will manifest that for you over and over again until you can see this is your unconscious story. Until you consciously *get it* and consciously *get real* about what you are choosing to love, you are going to be stuck with it. Hence the hideously ugly power of re-creation. And on the day you consciously *get it,* you are simultaneously consciously getting *real* about what you are choosing to love, and that is a complete action; that is what you came here to do.

Mastery of the human experience is also mastery of the fine art of relationship. The level of mastery you have developed with your own wave is reflected back as the level of mastery you have developed with all of your exterior relationships. Jesus had the relationship with others that he did, because he had that same equal healing, love of wholeness, and raising up from limitation relationship with his own mind. How Jesus treated others is an exact reflection of how Jesus organized and treated his own wave. Jesus did not judge, did not lie, did not cheat, did not have a thought or belief about himself or others. Jesus did not harm anyone in any way. Jesus only had wholeness-producing relationships with others. This is the entire contents of Jesus' wave: there is only the One, there is always infinite abundance.

Just like Jesus, how we treat others is really a mirrored reflection of what is going on in our own wave. The story we have about others is really the story we have about ourselves. If we are judging others as inferior, that is our story about ourselves. If we are experiencing conflict and struggle with others, then that is the relationship that we have with our own mind, with our own wave.

Here is the reality of Ultimate Truth: because there is only the One, what is done to another is also what is done to oneself. Jesus is always talking about loving your neighbors and your enemies as you would love yourself, because he realizes Divine Correspondence. Jesus knows that if you unconditionally practice loving all your exterior relationships, you will be healing, transforming and liberating your wave. Why? Because they are One. How you treat others is what your journey of enlightenment is going to look and feel like. You are here to practice treating others lovingly, patiently, and with joy. You are here to see everyone as perfect, equal, and beyond judgment. And you *have* to have that same loving, patient, joyful, fully trusting relationship with your own wave. Remember eternal consciousness cannot create an experience it does not need on our journey to enlightenment.

The converse also holds true. If you treat others with

judgment, superior or inferior (it does not matter, judgment is judgment), a lack of compassion, a lack of generosity, a lack of sensitivity to other's pain, or to the life challenges of others, then the relationship you have with your own wave lacks compassion, generosity and sensitivity to the dismantling of your own pain and life challenges. So if you are looking with a cold eye at the unhappiness of others, you are really looking at your own indifference to your own unhappiness. If that indifference remains unconsciousness, spirit will re-create it over and over again. Becoming conscious is the name of the real game here on the rock.

There is only the One. There is only One life and One happiness. All realized beings know the only useful and serving way to be in relationship with the whole of life is to willingly, lovingly, and unconditionally support the life and happiness of the One. Unrealized beings only have thoughts for their own life, for their own happiness. The truth of reality is, however, that there is no life, there is no happiness separate from the One.

Mastery of the human experience goes to those who witness the fragmentation in mind and will wholeness in response. Mastery of the human experience goes to those who witness *what is* and willingly choose to lovingly surrender their attention to Ultimate Truth that there is only the One. There is always infinite abundance. Thus, spirit transforms the contents of the wave into truth, into love. Truth and love are One; for there is only the One. This is mastery of the human experience. This is mastery of the interior practice of attending to God consciousness until it is fully realized.

Mastery of the human experience is remembrance of the

knowledge that nothing in the temporal world is worth the thoughts, beliefs, time, energy, and attention we give to it. No one has found a better way to express the mastery of the human experience than Oscar Wilde when he said, *"I have put my genius into my life; I have only put my talent into my works."*

There is only One — there is always infinite abundance

Chapter Five

Forgiveness & Equability

Forgiveness, like acceptance is vastly misunderstood as a form of divine intelligence. Most of us here on the planet Earth, really resent forgiveness. At the very least we hold a rather rigid grudge against what we think it is. We do not understand what real forgiveness is, what it means, or how it relates to our true nature. Real forgiveness is an inner movement of growth, not an intellectual posturing, but rather an authentic force that moves us beyond what has hurt us. Anytime we are running our understanding of an eternal quality such as forgiveness through the limited filter of thoughts and beliefs, the answer we get from the ego will always, always, always rob us of the very truth we are seeking. We cannot achieve unlimited results and understanding using a limited intelligence. Limited will rob us of infinite every time.

If our thoughts and beliefs were going to help us, as we have pointed out earlier, they would have by now. Our challenge is to put down the thinking and believing habituation and to consciously recognize the difference between what we know best, versus the best information that we know. Ego-based information is simply what we are most familiar with; the thing we know the best. It is not the best that we can know. Being in the present moment with *what is* with an open Heart is the best thing we know (wink, wink, nudge, nudge . . . sound familiar?).

Resistance to Forgiveness

Our ego-based stories and charges about forgiveness are very similar to those about acceptance. The ego, being the non-creative beast that it is, uses the same old lies over and over again without end. One of the lies that we have trained the ego to tell us is," I cannot forgive (accept) this person. If I do, then I alone will be the one to go through all of the suffering. The perpetrator walks off, unaccountable and unpunished, as if nothing happened. It is not fair. It is not just. Why should I be the one who has to swallow all the pain and say, 'OK, I forgive you' while you get away with your actions? By doing that, I'm getting screwed a second time!" Is it any wonder, with a lie like this, that we resist forgiveness, or that we will only move towards it if we are dragged kicking and screaming?

The only thing more karmicly painful than listening to this crap, is listening to the ego without realizing the paralyzing grasp it has on our wave. If we are that unconscious in witnessing mind, then we do not know who is speaking to us. Thus the ego has the means to diminish the flow of eternal consciousness into our wave, into our field of attention, and we don't even recognize it is happening. The ego has distracted us yet again into giving our awareness to something else that is limiting and incomplete. Why? Because that is what we have trained it to do.

The ego is working to convince us that there is not enough forgiveness intelligence in our wave. When the ego gets our attention with a story about how we just cannot forgive ourselves or someone else, then what has really happened, on a more profound level, is that the ego has convinced us that we do not have the power to grow and expand beyond its tyranny. The ego has now planted that covert message in our thoughts and beliefs that we are incapable of forgiveness. Diminishing our Oneness with forgiveness intelligence is the same as diminishing our Oneness with growth and expansion intelligence. So once again the ego has re-exerted its oppressive limitations over the wave.

Most people assume the greatest resistance to forgiveness comes from outside of them: the wrongdoer was not arrested, punished or held accountable for his/her actions. We confuse forgiveness with our interactions with others. We have an attachment to an outcome - punishment, revenge, or even death. Unless this result occurs, we will not grow beyond what has hurt us; we will not have closure. This is what we *think and believe* should happen and if it does not, we feel betrayed by life.

Resistance to forgiveness is held together in the unconscious portion of the wave. The lie is that all of life, relationships, money, love, time - all of it - is forever going to be such a struggle, it is all going to be eternally difficult; life is nothing more than a ceaseless cycle of never ending hardship. As the bumper sticker wisdom advertises, "Life is a bitch and then you die." When the inner voice tells us we are separate from love, we are deliberately turning our awareness away from the eternal, with nothing less than absolute disdain and contempt for it. Our attention goes to this fear-based information. We unconsciously perceive our unhappiness as senior to our real self, and there is nothing useful or honest in that. Especially when we consider that unhappiness is the stuff we are here to let go of, wipe off, flush away, and leave behind. Not the stuff we are here to put up on a "throne" and forever serve.

Yet when we are resisting forgiveness, we are giving attention to criticism of *what is* and of the present moment. We are caught asleep in the disease of duality, the ego telling us what our value, power, and lovability is. We have trained the ego to respond to *what is* with thoughts and beliefs, instead of responding with eternal consciousness: love, acceptance, forgiveness, and patience. Our job is to *realize* where *we* are resisting eternal consciousness.

Why do we resist forgiveness? Why do we resist growing beyond the things we are here to get over and leave behind? Why do we invest in remaining unhappy, stuck in pain, and victimized? Because we have not yet *realized* the whole of our wave, we have not realized how loyal the unconsciousness mind is to revisiting hell. That is why we are here. The point, process and purpose of all created life is to complete the action of full frontal self-realization.

When you understand how much your unrealized wave loves, and therefore invites in struggle, difficulty, effort, and hardship, reflect back on your life, playing out your unresolved stories. Just exactly how much struggle, difficulty, effort and hardship do you observe? If you witness a lot of struggle, difficulty, effort and hardship present in your life . . . then guess what? You love struggle, difficulty, effort, and hardship! You are in bed and having a wild orgy with the emotionally, furiously, frenetically, frenzing foursome, and you are the last one to find out who has been screwing who?! (That would be you on the bottom.) It brings a whole new meaning to pornographic visualization, doesn't it?

The unresolved loyalty given to struggle, difficulty, effort, and hardship drives unhappiness and worry deeper into the wave. When happiness decreases, worry and struggle increases. Unhappiness and worry paralyze the flow of truth from the field of our attention. The truth being that there is only the One, and there is always infinite abundance. We cannot be giving attention to a story about how hindered and oppressed we are, while at the same time be giving attention to the truth. We cannot be aligned with infinite abundance, and at the same time be aligned with depression and affliction.

We cannot serve two masters. Is it any wonder that when we organize our wave to giving attention to how encumbered every aspect of life is, that we feel terribly unsupported and heavily burdened. We do not feel that we have a life worth living. We do not feel that we are sharing a similar reality to Jesus when he says, "My way is easy, my burden is light."

Resistance to forgiveness intelligence, as the solution to our problems, weakens our relationship with being whole. Why? Because enlightenment and wholeness of mind is achieved by growing and expanding the wave until it is fully, wholly realized. Without growth and expansion, wholeness is going nowhere and becomes fragmented and stagnated, and this is clearly not a healthy state for your or any one else's God consciousness.

The good news is that you will discover happiness again the moment you are willing to put down the long-standing thoughts and beliefs about forgiveness, and make yourself available for being with *what is* in the present moment with an open Heart. When we do this, we can finally make contact with forgiveness, and allow the intelligence to move us to a place beyond what has paralyzed and hurt us in the past. For without accepting and forgiving the whole of our lives, there is no possible way that we can receive the evolutionary benefit from the whole of our lives.

Forgiveness the Real Thing

Now that we have investigated the illusion of what is not forgiveness, let us examine and explore forgiveness independent of what we think and believe. To facilitate a completely original, fresh experience and understanding of forgiveness, let us identify it with something new: growth. Let's define forgiveness as an agreement that all beings involved have an equal opportunity to choose to grow and expand beyond what has hurt them, regardless of an outcome, and regardless of whatever circumstances caused the suffering.

Forgiveness is spirit expanding and deepening consciousness into the wave It is the action of spirit shattering the stagnant grip of the ego and duality. Forgiveness is spirit fully realizing love is the senior intelligence to any experience, emotion, or thought. Forgiveness is the mastery of the eternal over the temporal; freely choosing to expand and grow beyond all limitation as a natural response to whatever life deals you.

As you can tell, forgiveness is an eternal quality. Eternal qualities are always the ultimate in spiritual fashion accessories, but you may be asking, "Just how does this information relate to me? Tell me what I need to do when some asshole idiot cuts across three lanes of traffic and almost hits me, just to make that exit ramp off the freeway. How should I react to that?" This is a great question. How do we respond to road rage? Or to people who cannot count, who are standing in the ten items or less line, at the grocery store while holding twenty or more items?

How do we respond to these or to the other generic insensitivities? Do we ...

1. Pull out a fire arm and ask them, "Well punk, do you feel lucky?"

2. Scream and yell, throwing an "adult" level temper tantrum?

3. Hold in all your feelings until you make the explosion of Mount Saint Helens look like a pimple?

4. Review the offensive situation over and over again, without any regard to a healthy sense of proportion or balance in your life?

5. Conclude that everyone else on the planet is a fricking moron but you, and that your destiny is to fight off being relentlessly "corn-holed" by the world's dregs.

Or would it be more useful to experience these situations as we want to experience *all* the gifts handed to us from Heaven; as yet another perfect opportunity to practice witnessing mind in motion, instead of *seeing* only the ego's myopic agenda. We want equality in every aspect of our lives. We want to receive the evolution of our soul with an equal and even mind. We want to increase our mastery of perceiving everything that happens here as perfect and working solely for God consciousness.

No matter what unfolds in the temporal world, engage with it as an opportunity to practice the following:

1. I am looking at my own mind. My unresolved stories are being mirrored back for the purpose of self-witnessing; that is why we are all here. There is obviously a lesson here for me, or this event would not have been allowed to occur.

2. Surrender to the perfection of *what is*. Everything and everyone is working for collective awakened God consciousness. Remind yourself that this experience has come for your benefit or it would not be allowed to exist. Thank everyone involved for the opportunity to master freeing your mind, because if you could do it without them, they would not have appeared in your life. Remind yourself that everyone, including Asmodeus, works for love, because only love is real. An attitude of gratitude is the perfect spiritual fashion accessory for every occasion.

3. Be here now from your Heart and choose to grow beyond. When I witness the rude car driver or the person pretending to not know they have more items then they do when standing in the express lane, I am really looking at my own stories of *not enough*. I am looking at how the stories of *not enough time or not enough opportunity* are effecting my movement through life. And, if I am not witnessing the limiting story re-creating the problem, then I am caught asleep in the disease of duality, thinking and believing my way through life.

Forgiveness is the process by which we learn to eliminate the waste from our lives. Letting go of the *crap* is a necessary step in healthy expansion, and practicing forgiveness is how a wave keeps spiritually fit and healthy. In essence, forgiveness is the means by which spirit is able to *get over and let go* of the useless, the futile and the worthless. We make a conscious decision *not* to let the temporal world rob us of a life worth living. Understand that we are never going to have a quality life if we simultaneously hold onto the stuff we have come here to perma-banish from mind.

The stuff we are here to get over is always going to show up. The stuff others are here to get over is always going to show up. That is why the physical world was created. We must make our peace with this action and focus our attention on loving and growing beyond it.

Only when aligned with the truth, can we see forgiveness for the truly dynamic healing force that it really is. From this place of clarity and right understanding of forgiveness, it is extremely serving for each of us to ask ourselves honestly, when does it ever serve us to not be receptive to the flow of forgiveness consciousness? When would it ever serve us to not grow and expand beyond all the pain, limitation, suffering and unhappiness?

When we recognize forgiveness for what it really is, then we can freely give it to ourselves, as well as honestly pass it on to others. Forgiveness is the wisdom that says, "I'm eternal consciousness. I am senior to the movement of all temporal forces here. Everything here is working for mind. I can be with *what is* in this moment and grow and expand beyond the temporal influences of pain and limitation. I am the portion of the program that witnesses what holds together the drama. I am not the drama that I am witnessing. I have come here to make separation from the limited. I am the *Flame of Pure Awareness* that ends the re-creation of all suffering!"

Equability

Forgiveness intelligence as well as acceptance intelligence is strengthened by equability. It is infinitely easier to accept and forgive when you realize that you are looking at your own mind. Living a life that is governed by the intelligence of divine equability means there is no one superior or inferior to anyone. There is no one who is more or less lovable, or deserving of love than anyone else. There are no life forms on the planet that are a waste of time, love, or attention. We are here to realize *what is,* is an exterior reflection of the interior relationships we have with our own mind. And it is for the complete acceptance and integration of these relationships that you have come to the rock, and you cannot accomplish this end without making everyone and everything else equally God. Why is that the only way? Because there is only the One! It is an inescapable truth.

Equability means removing all duality from perception, from relationships and from our way in life. Divine equability means that we give all aspects of the wave unconditional love, unconditional truth. We see and relate to every other life form as an extension of our own mind. It means there is no you; there is no me. We equally relate to ourselves and every other life form as the One.

Equability requires a practice of neutrality in dealing with duality, on the inside as well as the outside. Internalized neutrality is responding to pleasure, pain, happiness and inconvenience with an even or equal mind. No attachments to an outcome, no judgments, no thoughts or beliefs about good or bad. No matter what happens in the temporal realm, we accept that everything that comes to us is divine food from Heaven. Only what we need to evolve into an awakened being is sent us. And, it is given to us only when we need it. Exteriorized neutrality would be responding to everything as if it were the One. You would see every living thing as a manifestation of the One in all its infinite glory. You would be as honest, loving, playful and patient with yourself and others, as you would be to God, because in your mind there would be no distinction between God and the manifested world within and without you. You would be seeing everything in the outer world as God consciousness in motion reaching enlightenment the fastest most efficient way possible, because it does not have the power to be anything else.

There is an old story about a wise man. This wise man had a farm and a son. One day the wise man found a horse. All of the wise man's neighbors told him how fortunate and lucky he was to have found such a fine horse. The wise man simply smiled without a thought or belief about good or bad. Soon afterwards the horse stepped on the son's foot and broke it. All the neighbors told the wise man what a terrible thing this was that his son's foot should be broken. The wise man simply smiled again not having a thought or belief about lucky or unlucky. Shortly thereafter, a conflict broke out in a nearby village and all the able young fighting men were taken off, drafted into battle, and killed. But not the wise man's son, for his foot was broken and he could not walk or stand.

The point of the story is that life is not what we think and believe that it is. The most serving position for us to be in, is to relate equally to everything as the divine and perfect food that it is. After all there is nothing about efficient and effective that Heaven fails to understand. As the rock group ZZ Top likes to say about Jesus, "Taking care of business *is* His name!"

Bob Dylan has already pointed out, with great back up vocals I might add, that, "Your gonna have to serve somebody. It may be the devil (the ego) or it may be the Lord, (eternal consciousness) but your gonna have to serve somebody." It is sooooo true. You do not have consciousness, you *are* consciousness; therefore you are going to have to give your consciousness to *something* as you move through life. You're gonna have to give your attention to either temporal or eternal, since you have problems in both realms to resolve. Do you know whom you're serving on a moment-to-moment basis? Is your attention in service of equability? You'll know if you are because you'll know the equability tree by its fruits. Are you in a fair and honest relationship with yourself and others? Seeing yourself and others as perfect right now, unconditionally? If so, then you are also sharing what Heaven loves, and you cannot find yourself in better company than that.

So what are some practical steps to developing equability in our wave? First creating a new response to relationship, one that is based on mutual love and respect, instead of superior/inferior is what ultimately strengthens equability.

Here are some other perceptual yoga postures that strengthen equability as well:

1. Show up in the present moment with an open Heart.

2. Live beyond thinking and believing all your relationships to death. Feel what is happening, feel your truth, imagine how others might be feeling. Come from your Heart, not your head.

3. Embrace each moment with gratitude acepting it for the perfect food it is.

4. See every event and person as here for the sole purpose of liberating God consciousness.

Furthermore, equability is nurtured and sustained by the self-witnessing process, which brings about a resolution to all duality, all re-creation patterns and all suffering, because self-witnessing is a complete action. The fruitional intelligence of this power and magnitude requires giving attention to Ultimate Truth, without exception, for solving all eternal problems. Our spiritual equability muscles are built up by the practice of consciously choosing eternal consciousness over temporal, consciously choosing to feel the truth in our Heart instead of having thoughts and beliefs about it in our head. Equability is rejuvenated by a positive, unwavering, unconditional love for the happiness of all living beings in this and in every eternal present moment. Equability is what Jesus is asking for when he instructs us to, "Love our enemies."

Karma, cause and effect, the law that what goes around comes around, works perfectly every time because of the law of divine equability. Everything is mind. If you reach out and hurt someone, it will come back around and *you* will experience that pain. The bottom line here is that you've just bitch slapped your own mind! It does not get any more equal than that. If you hit yourself, you are going to have to feel it. That is the purpose behind a feeling human body. Keeps ya' real, don't it!? After all, what good is the truth that we are all One if we do not get the physically embodied opportunity to live it and *feel* it. So, imagine. On a higher level ex-president Bill Clinton was actually telling the truth when he said, "I feel your pain." He probably did, and plenty of it too!

The same principle of equality holds true for a positive action. When we live equability, we are aligning the wave with a universal force of healing Oneness. We are giving the wave unification intelligence. When we practice loving our wave, healing and unifying it, *we are going to feel it.* To live equability is to align the wave with Jesus' highest and greatest teachings, "Love each other, as I have loved you," "The Father and I are One," and "Whatever you have done to the least of my brethren, you have also done to me." No one can say it quite like the brilliant word musician Oscar Wilde. This quote is from one of his last works: *De Profundis.* In it he writes:

. . . If you want an inscription to read at dawn and at night-time and for pleasure or for pain, write up on the wall of your house in letters for the sun to gild and the moon to silver **whatever happens to another happens to oneself,** *and should anyone ask you what such an inscription can possibly mean you can answer that it means 'Lord Christ's heart and Shakespeare's brain'.*

Buddhism and Christianity would like every spiritual being to understand that if the organization of their wave does not honor divine equability, they are living a life that is in opposition to the law of divine equability. The results will always be the same. Spirit, that wave resisting equability, will never know happiness or a life worth living. It is impossible to create a successful life and successful relationships going against the divine law of equability. The law of divine Oneness governs all of life. How could any wave create anything that is honestly successful when they have separated themselves from the Source of all life? Are you looking for the perfect spiritual-human-alchemical formula for taking the contraction out of mind, to enable you to expand equally and infinitely? It is equability intelligence.

Buddhism talks about divine laws that must be observed. Every spirit, without exception, must be in right relationship with these laws in order to create a life worth living. Christianity has the same laws, more commonly referred to as the teachings of Jesus. Buddhism and Christianity share the divine law of equability. Each person, each spirit must organize the wave to love divine equability. Every person, every spirit must define themselves and others as eternal consciousness, as pure love and nothing else.

If you follow Buddhism, the practice is to see yourself as One with awakened Buddha consciousness. The purpose of Buddhism is to make your wave and the movement of a fully-realized, fully-awakened love One. If you follow Christianity, then the practice is to see yourself, your wave, as One with Christ consciousness. When you practice either Buddhism or Christianity, or both, the point is to begin to relate to yourself as a vessel of divine love, and nothing else. The next step, in both traditions, is to practice *seeing* every other being on the planet as either Buddha or Christ consciousness as well. It does not matter who you choose. You can even use both, as if they were One. (wink, wink, nudge, nudge). It all depends on what works for you, as it is essentially all the same. There is really only the One, and the divine law of equability governs all of life, no matter what tradition you align your wave with.

Equability perceives happiness as the purpose of all shared life. Equability is the divine intelligence that manifests itself as the realization of every spirit's highest dreams: that we shall all finally live in peace together. Equability is the divine intelligence that makes whole all fragmentation, limitation, suffering and duality in mind. Equability heals the concept of an individual self that bad hurtful things have happened to, and replaces it with a memory of the One. Equability aligns the wave with Ultimate Truth unconditionally, because equability is the intelligence that allows us to *see* and *feel* the truth that there is only the One.

Equability removes the neurotic story from the nervous system, that there are others out there with the power to take away our value, power and happiness. Equability levels the psychological and emotional playing fields, because finally no one is greater than, and no one is less than. Equability will ultimately require the surrender of any story that we *didn't do it right,* and that we are *not good enough.* We cannot be equally God and equally inferior to God at the same time. Equability heals as well as answers the question, "Am I finally deserving and worthy enough now?" The answer equability heals our mind with is, "You do not have love, you are love. Deserving and worthy were never an issue (except to the ego). You have always been and will always be divine, eternal love and nothing else." Without equability, we would not be able to align ourselves with the truth, we do not have love, we are love. Equability does this because this intelligence trusts loving the perception of the One in the movement of all things.

In order to organize our wave to be in ever increasing receptivity to equability, let us explore some living examples of it. What we do know about loving equability is that this action is One with an intelligence that heals and transforms all rigidly held ego fear-based information in mind. When we remember to live as One with equability, our life becomes so potent, so commanding it could only be told, realized, on the level of a Martin Luther King Jr., a Ghandi, or King's inspiration Rosa Parks and his contemporary, Cesar Chavez. Equability clearly shines forth as the senior intelligence of Dr. King's wave. It was the power and force of this Ruling Love, his deep abiding affection for equability intelligence, that began to move the South to desegregate. Dr. King knew, beyond a thought or belief, that love based on the law of divine equability was, is, and always will be the only energy supremely invincible enough to free up the South's contractive grip on the long held inequitable lies, cruelties, and atrocities that have dominated that portion of mind for so long. That is why Dr. King *knew* he would go about making changes against impossible odds through peaceful, non-violent means.

Television's primary enlightened being, (besides, Oprah, of course!) was Edward R. Morrow. In the late 1950's, on Thanksgiving Day, he broadcast an unparalleled masterpiece, *Harvest of Shame*. This early black and white television documentary chronicles the shame, horror, and stagnant cruelty that have plagued the lives of the people who work the thankless task of bringing the food of plenty to our homes and tables.

Morrow exposed a national shame: American inequality. There are laws on how to treat, feed, transport, and house farm animals that are more humane than the laws governing and protecting the extremely hardworking human beings that harvest our food from the fields. Cesar Chavez appeared as the human incarnation to Morrow's prayer, that as a nation, as a people, we would awaken our love, our devotion to equability, as a way in life unconditionally. For without it, none of us are successful.

Cesar Chavez devoted his entire life to championing, in a tireless, profoundly loyal and peacefully fashion, for the equality of all migrant farm workers. Chavez' love for equality was responsible for the greatest conscious movement of reform ever to be brought to the people we most depended on for our food. Yet, ironically, our version of reciprocity is to treat these hardworking, backbreaking supporters of a lifestyle we all enjoy, as the most profoundly disenfranchised group of people in our culture.

No nation will ever be successful that allows anybody, especially those who sustain our bountiful way of life, to be treated as disposable. Without Dr. King Jr., without Cesar Chavez, America would not be successful. Without those who advocate for equability, America would be just another super bully, instead of striving to be a conscious contributor.

More global examples of equability in action are Mother Teresa and Princess Diana. These women lived and shared their love from an uncompromising place of divine equability. Hence the incredible power of their lives to heal the world and set it free, even long after their human experience has ended. There is no greater definition of an auspicious life then a life that continues to give and to support others, long after the individual has shed the mortal coil.

The Dalai Lama and the Tibetan people have tirelessly spent their lifetime working for equability. Nothing inspires the need to bring equability to a global forefront like another country invading, killing, and torturing everyone they can get their hands on. Buddhism, like the Dalai Lama, is a living example of the power, of *seeing* equal love everywhere, unconditionally. For as God knows, the Dalai Lama and the Tibetan people have been given an arena to practice in, that they cannot fake, courtesy of the Chinese government.

Divine equability means every being does not have love. *Every being without exception is love.* That means everyone, not just the people we like, not just the people we find non-challenging and acceptable. This includes everyone: the lying, cheating husbands and boyfriends, or wives and girlfriends as the case may be. This includes people in your life that are abusive on some level. Everyone from the crack whores who walk the streets, to the business moguls who treat the world as if it were they own private ashtray, to the politicians we who sell out the very people they are supposed to represent. This includes your ex-spouses and ex-lovers, your parents and annoying neighbors, this includes your enemies and the people who would be happy to inflict harm every chance they get, because they have organized their wave in a pathological fashion.

The healing truth is to unconditionally perceive our wave, and everyone else's wave, as equally holy, equally sacred, equally God consciousness. This means showing up for yourself and others, just as you would for God. This means taking care of yourself and others, just as if you and they were God. This means being as honest with yourself and others, as you would be with God. This means being just as generous and patient with yourself and others, as you would be with God. The truth of the matter is we are all God, because there is only the One.

The following story illustrates how to begin to practice forgiveness and equability in the midst of the challenges of our everyday life. (Show 'em how it's done Gayle!)

Aba Gayle's Story

By all definitions I am a victim for I am the mother of a beautiful young daughter who was brutally murdered. But I have learned that there is another way to live and that I have a choice. I have chosen to stop being a victim. This has not been an easy road to travel!

My story began one early fall day in 1980 with a phone call. The voice at the other end of the line said, "Well, what do you think about Catherine being shot?" I quickly got off the phone and called the sheriff's department. Detective Landry came on the line. He was as kind and gentle as possible as he spoke these terrible words to me. "I'm sorry, but your daughter, Catherine, is dead. Your daughter was murdered. She was stabbed to death."

Something in my heart broke. My brain couldn't think. I had to remain calm. None of this day was real. Soon I would wake up and the nightmare would be over. But deep down inside, I knew it was real. I couldn't let anyone hug me, I was afraid I would break down. I couldn't cry, someone might hear me. I decided to take a shower and with the water running full blast, I screamed and screamed and screamed.

This was the start of a period of eight years I now call "my time of darkness." In order to survive in this life you just do what you have to do to keep your head above water. My method of survival was to be calm and not cause anyone any problems. I had no support system. I had no faith. I did not believe in God. I didn't have a minister, a priest or a rabbi, or anyone who could comfort me and help me. I had to remain strong to help everyone else. My husband announced that he didn't want to talk about Catherine anymore; he stated emphatically that he did not intend to mourn her the rest of his life. I found myself more and more isolated with no one to give me the love and encouragement I needed so badly. For a while, I could not even drive my car alone because, when I was alone, I would cry and I couldn't see the road.

On the surface, I carried on the false front. Had you known me at the time, you wouldn't have known about the dark, ugly cloud I carried around inside me. You would have thought I was getting along just fine. But, inside of me, a deep, dark rage began to boil. There was this awful, hideous darkness, and all I wanted was revenge for the death of my beloved child.

The District Attorney told me that the sheriff's department would find the person who murdered Catherine, put him on trial, get a guilty conviction, and make certain that the murderer would receive the death penalty. (Douglas Mickey was arrested, tried, convicted and sentenced to death in 1982.) I was assured that when that horrible villain was executed, I would be healed of my pain and all would be well again. And, because I didn't know any other way to believe, I thought that was true!

The Healing Begins

After eight long years of a passionate lust for revenge, I unknowingly began my first step toward healing. I began taking a course in meditation. After a time, I found myself able to sit quietly, to be still in my head, and to be in the present moment. For the first time in my life, I realized that I did not have to see, touch, or even hear something to know that it is real. I learned there is far more to this Universe than our senses perceive.

I found a beautiful little church in Auburn, CA. This church helped me change my life and find my God-self. I discovered the church's bookstore. Here I found books on Christianity, Buddhism, Hinduism, mythology and other books on the lives and teachings of the great religious and philosophical teachers who have come to this Earth for our enlightenment. I started reading and studying my way through that bookstore. I learned I am a beloved child of God; I am one with the Universe; and all of us are here to love each other, without exception. God is a loving God and there is no hell except that which we create in our own minds. I really "got it" that we are *all One in Spirit*.

It was while watching a video interview of a Jewish holocaust survivor that I got my first glimpse of the Healing Power of Forgiveness. He was able to forgive not only the German people, but the actual guards in the camps who had killed every member of his family. Something in me really clicked when I heard that testimony. I began to feel perhaps I could forgive the man who killed Catherine. A seed was planted in my heart.

After many hours of study, prayer, and discussions with

others, I thought that perhaps I could forgive the man who murdered Catherine. Perhaps, it would relieve my own frustration and suffering. That evening a friend suggested that I should let the murderer know of my intent. I was outraged! But as I drove home, I distinctly heard a voice. It said to me. **YOU MUST FORGIVE HIM AND YOU MUST LET HIM KNOW!**" This voice was so loud, so clear, and so persuasive that I didn't sleep at all that night. I was literally impelled to get out of bed at four am, to type a letter to the man who murdered Catherine. The letter follows:

Dear Mr. Mickey

Twelve years ago, I had a beautiful daughter named Catherine. She was a young woman of unusual talents and intelligence. She was slender and her skin glowed with health and vitality. She had long naturally wavy hair that framed her sparkling eyes and warm bright smile. She radiated love and joy!

Catherine was living with her friend, Eric, on a fifteen-acre pear ranch. Catherine's greatest love was her animals. She was raising two milk goats, her German shepherd with a new litter of ten puppies and an Arabian mare. She had tried to live with her father and his wife on their property (where there would be room for all her animals) but her stepmother's emotional illness made that impossible and she had just recently moved back with her friend Eric.

Two months after her 19th Birthday Catherine left her Earthly body and her spirit transitioned to her next stage of life. I know that Catherine is in a better place than we can ever know here on Earth. I did not know that when Catherine died. I knew that I had been robbed of my precious child and that she had been robbed of growing into womanhood and achieving all her potential. The violent way she left this Earth was impossible for me to understand. I was saddened beyond belief and felt that I would never be completely happy again. And indeed my loss of Catherine became the point of reference for my entire family. All family history was prefaced as happening either before or after Catherine's death.

I was very angry with you and wanted to see you punished to the limit of the law. You had done irreparable damage to my family and my dreams for the future.

After eight long years of grief and anger I started my journey of life. I met wonderful teachers and slowly began to learn about my God-self. I was surprised to find that I could forgive you. This does not mean that I think you are innocent or that you are blameless for what happened. What I learned is this: You are a divine child of God. You carry the Christ consciousness within you. You are surrounded by God's love even as you sit in your cell. There is no devil; there is only the goodness of God. The Christ in me sends blessings to the Christ in you.

Do not look to me to be a political or social advocate in your behalf. The law of the land will determine your fate. Do not waste your last days on Earth with remorse and fear. Death as we know it is really a new beginning. Hell does not exist except in our conscious minds.

I hope that this letter will help you to face your future. There is only love and good in the world regardless of how things may appear to you now. I am willing to write to you or visit you if you wish. I send blessings to you and to your children.

– Gayle, Mother of Catherine*

I remember the little click that the hinged mailbox made as I dropped in this letter. When I heard that "click," all the anger, all the rage, all the lust for revenge—-simply vanished in that instant. In its place I was filled with the most incredible feeling of Joy and Love and Peace. I was in a State of Grace. I knew in that Holy Instant I did not need to have anyone executed for me to be healed. I could now get on with my life!

It would not have mattered if Douglas Mickey responded to my letter. I had received a more profound answer. I had been healed by the simple act of *offering the gift* of forgiveness. However, I did get a letter back. I was totally amazed at the gentleness and kindness of the writer. Douglas wrote back with words of gratitude. He expressed remorse and sorrow for the crime; also stating that he fully understood how empty such words might sound. I could tell from reading his letter that he was intelligent and well read. He had obviously spent years studying for answers for himself. He wrote back, "The Christ in me most gratefully accepts and returns blessings of Divine Wisdom, Love and Charity to the Christ in you." He also said, "I would gladly give my life this instant if it would in any way change that terrible night."

Mickey enclosed a visiting form. It took 90 days to get permission from San Quentin to visit. When I arrived in the visiting room for death row inmates I looked around with surprise. I did not see a single monster in that room. It was filled with ordinary looking men. Everywhere I looked, I saw the face of God.

When Douglas came in, he said, "Gayle, you do the greatest honor by paying me this visit." We talked together for over three hours. I cried and he cried. We cried together.

We talked about Catherine. We talked about Douglas's mother and her death. We talked about his losses. I realized the night Catherine lost her life, Douglas also lost his future. I knew that if the State of California ever executes Douglas Mickey, they would be killing my friend.

I now refer to the time I spend visiting men on death row as my mini prison ministry. When asked by reporters if any of the men on death row have committed crimes, which are just too awful for me to still treat them with compassion, I respond, "I don't deal with their crime. I don't deal with that part of them. I deal with the God spirit within him or her. That is the truth of their being. It is the truth for every one of us.

I knew when I dropped the letter in the mailbox I must spend the rest of my life demonstrating that killing is not necessary and that violence only begets more violence. What I learned is healing and grace can be achieved by anyone under any circumstance through the miracle of forgiveness. This may have appeared to be a new paradigm to me as I began this healing journey, but it is actually the universal truth that has been given to all people through sacred teachings such as those expressed by Jesus, The Christ, the Buddha and other enlightened beings.

I know my daughter Catherine is happy I am honoring her with this work. She would not want me to go through life full of hate and rage. **Love and forgiveness is the way to make our world a kind and safe place.**

*Gayle's story has been edited for this publication. If you would like to read Gayle's story in its entirety, you will find it at http://www.forgivenessday.org/default.htm. Look under "Heros" for Aba Gayle. Thank you Gayle for you gracious sharing!

May we all have the strength and courage to integrate this wisdom into our experience of 9/11.

Chapter Six

Surrender & Neutrality

Surrender and neutrality are a little trickier to explore, as we are less familiar with them. We give them so little attention, so little love. Surrender and neutrality intelligence nurtures an unwavering wholeness of mind. They are the perfect antidotes for the ego's poisonous fragmenting lies. Strengthening surrender and neutrality intelligence liberates all unresolved charges and movements re-created by the ego in mind, in the wave. Pain re-created by the charge of duality cannot exist in the same wave that is giving its love to surrender and neutrality.

Another way of understanding surrender and neutrality is through the fine art of not taking anything in the temporal world personally. A wave that is neutral and has surrendered to eternal consciousness does not experience the disease of duality. Duality requires a sense of a separate *me* over here and a separate *you* over there. That scenario is absolutely necessary for spirit to be able to take anything that happens here personally. By definition, taking something personally requires that there be a *you* to take it personally, and an *other* around you to co-create the conflict.

Without realizing it, we have been operating unconsciously out of thoughts and beliefs about surrender, so this is good place to start.

What we have unconsciously concluded from the thought and belief process is that surrender is only used on two occasions:

1. Surrender is used in relationship to others when you have your foot on your adversaries' throat, and you are telling him/her to surrender like the dog they are. Under these conditions surrender is good. Under these conditions life is good; you are *greater than.*

2. The foot is now on your throat. You are now in the role of the person having to surrender to the force of others. Now surrender is bad. Surrender means you lose. Surrender now means you are a failure, a wussy, or a wimp. Once in the victim role, we will immediately find ourselves simultaneously *not good enough* and *separate from love,* as well as powerless to change the situation. Under these conditions life is not good; you are *less than.*

Surrender

Surrendering to *what is* happens in the Heart; that action does not happen in the head where the wave becomes contaminated by the ego's pontifications. The ego packages surrender as *not good enough* and *didn't do it right.* If that is not sufficient, the ego adds abandonment and rejection, as well as being separate from love and happiness. So like forgiveness and acceptance, we only go towards surrender kicking and screaming; not a pretty picture. However, embracing surrender is a necessary dance step we practice in order to not step in the ego's shit.

Surrender in its purest form is the conscious practice of remembering not to give illusion your attention. Surrender is a "core dump" of all temporal, limited, fear-based information. It is remembering to forget what you think and believe reality is. It is remembering that the illusion of the temporal world does not define your value, power and worth. Surrender is the practice of understanding reality through the Heart instead of the head. When you have surrendered the habit of responding to life from the head, you have freed your wave from the attachments of the ego, and you have returned to the present moment with an open Heart.

To see this, let us return to the story of the life of Jesus. Let's jump to the end of the story, to the relationship between Jesus and Pontius Pilate. Pilate believes he has his foot on Jesus' throat, but what is really happening is surrender in action, at its finest, doing its thing in all its radiant glory. Pilate is a Roman procurator in charge of keeping the law and the peace intact between the occupying Roman military presence and the local Jewish community. Pilate has heard of Jesus and his miracles. He knows Jesus is a man of peace and non-violence. Pilate's wife even had a dream foretelling of Pilate's meeting with Jesus. Her dream predicts that Jesus will be condemned to death, and that people all through time will blame Pilate for this tragic and unfair death. Pilate's wife implores him to let Jesus go immediately when the time comes for them to meet.

Fast forward to where Pilate is now face-to-face with Jesus. Pilate is keenly aware that the local Jewish religious authorities want Jesus dead. But why should Pilate kill Jesus just because someone else wants him dead? The Jewish religious authorities convince Pilate that Jesus is a political threat to the Romans as well and needs to be eliminated in order to meet with the Roman agenda of peace. Pilate remembers his wife's dream and tries to figure out a way around this dilemma. He decides to let the people of Jerusalem choose who will live, between Jesus and Barabbas, who has been arrested for murder. Pilate thinks and believes Jesus will naturally be the people's choice. Pilate hates the criminal Barabbas, as he has killed in cold blood many of his Roman soldiers. However, he is not worried that there is any real danger of having to release Barabbas. Pilate calls for the people to vote - Jesus or Barabbas. Pilate is horrified when he discovers the Jewish religious authorities have rigged this election. They have planted people everywhere to vote for Barabbas to go free.

Pilate has not yet sentenced anyone to die. He turns to Jesus and says, "I hold your life in my hands now." So Pilate thinks and believes he has his foot on Jesus' throat. He informs Jesus that if he will cooperate, Pilate will fix things and see to it that Jesus lives. Jesus, practiced at only giving his attention to the truth, informs Pilate (paraphrasing again) that everything is perfect right now, and that Pilate does not have the power to change that. Jesus has fully surrendered everything he thinks and believes. Jesus has surrendered the ego's agenda for real truth. Jesus has transformed the illusion, that the temporal world decides his fate, into the truth that whatever is happening in the temporal is exactly what he landed on the rock to be present for. He accepts this with an open Heart.

Jesus, because he has surrendered his attention only to the truth, cannot play the role of victim, even though the temporal world would cast him in this part. With this unwavering relationship with surrender, Jesus is beyond victim. Surrender has made Jesus like Teflon. Everything that is slung at him simply slides off. Nothing sticks! Jesus' physical body is killed, of course, but Jesus is not his body, and at no time does he confuse his eternal self with his temporal body.

Jesus is eternal, as are we. Jesus surrenders to the truth that he is immortal, and that Heaven decides when it is time to shed the mortal coil and return home. Pilate and the Jewish religious leaders were the vehicle Heaven used to accomplish this end. Nobody and nothing in the temporal determined it, and Jesus knows that! Surrender means aligning your attention with the truth that you can show up with an open Heart for everything that Heaven sends you. Surrender means letting go of what you think and believe is going on in order to fully understand reality. Jesus knows that his leaving the Earth in this horrible manner has nothing to do with his value, power and worth. He does not leave confused. Surrender puts you, as God consciousness, beyond whatever is happening to you in the illusory, temporal world.

If Pilate had surrendered, which he obviously did not, it would have looked quite different. Pilate would have caught himself asleep in the disease of duality. He would have stopped in his tracks, realizing that he is looking at sentencing his own mind to death; since we are all sharing the life of the One, because there is only the One. He would have said to Jesus, "I will not commit an action of violence or judgment against my own mind. I am not without sin, so I will not cast the first stone." Pilate would have then turned to the Jewish religious leaders and informed them in no uncertain terms that he will not be coerced into doing anything he knew not to be right. Period. End of sentence. Not open for negotiation. Do not even bother trying to go further with this!

As you have no doubt noticed, Jesus did not *win* in the typical way we think about *winning* as happening. Surrender does not have an attachment to any outcome. Surrender is not responding to *what is* from the mindset of how can I manipulate things to come out right. Surrendering illusion and aligning yourself with the truth does not mean that the painful challenges of spiritual development will simply stop and disappear from your life. To develop spiritually is the reason why we are all here. What it does mean is that you will now have the wisdom and compassion to feel yourself strengthened and liberated by these challenging events, instead of weakened and crushed by the movement and stresses of everyday life. It also means that you have stopped looking for eternal qualities like justice, fairness, value, power and worth to come to you through the temporal, the limited.

Now you may be saying, "Okay that is great for Jesus! Nice to know the Big Guy could do that without breaking a sweat, but what about an ordinary person like me?" Okay ordinary person, this enlightenment is for you. Next time you walk into your boss' office, surrender the made-up roles of *more powerful* and *less powerful* that you are playing. Show up fearless; speak the truth from your Heart. Your boss can only fire you if Heaven has determined it wants you somewhere else. Your boss has no power over you. Never did! Your boss does not decide your value, power and worth. Never did! Your boss can only make you feel inferior if you give your attention to the '*didn't do it right, not good enough*' lies re-created by the ego. If you surrender your attention to the truth, then you will witness the part of mind you are really *working for* being reflected back in the form of the illusory boss in the illusory world. In other words when you surrender to the truth that everything is perfect now, that everything you are experiencing is your inner condition made physical and exteriorized, then when you walk into your boss' office and witness an inner emotional dialog of worry running over your nervous system, you will no longer continue to project outwardly that your boss is a mean person who takes delight in raking you over the coals. Instead, what you will see is that you are actually witnessing the reality that your wave is supporting and working for *worry,* and indeed has been all along. The outer boss is merely the Divine Correspondence to the inner reality. The outer boss is simply representing the inner boss that you hired and continue to work for. As it is above, so it is below. As it is within, so it is without.

Your love is your true boss ... as you truly work for whatever you give your attention to.

If you ever have to go to court, remember the ex-business partner or spouse does not decide the outcome. The judge or jury does not decide the verdict. God knows lawyers do not decide anything. The most powerful force in the universe decides everything. Always has, always will. Heaven is sending you the perfect opportunity to practice surrendering your loyalty to thinking and believing. Heaven is hand-delivering to you the perfect invitation to be neutral to temporal gyrations, and to answer to the higher force, "I see your perfect gift, and I am grateful and I only recognize the power of divine love and wisdom in my life."

Only when we have surrendered all attachments to an outcome; only when we have mastered the practice of recognizing that everything in life comes to us from the One, for our benefit, or it would not be allowed to happen; only when we have practiced living a fearless life based on the truth that no one else and nothing else can threaten us, because nothing in the temporal world has any real power over our lives or our happiness; only then when we are aligned with the One are we in a position to receive the liberating gift Heaven is sending us, just as Jesus did!

> *Courage is not the lack of fear – It is acting in spite of it*
> *–Mark Twian*

Next time you go for a check up, if you should find yourself diagnosed with a terrible illness, stop! Surrender the habit of letting the ego interpret the present moment. Surrender your attention to the truth. You are not your body. You are not this diagnosis. The body was diagnosed, not *you!* The body is going through the disease process, not *you!* You need the "in body" experience of being diagnosed in order to practice not identifying with the body. You need the practice of not identifying your value, power and worth with temporal experiences and with the opinions of others. You need the practice of remembering, in an arena that you cannot fake, that *everything* that is coming to you is Heaven's perfect food that you need in order to free your mind, or it would not be happening.

When in great physical pain, stop, breathe and remember the body is going through this. Not you. You are the awareness that witnesses the movement of the temporal world. You are nothing physical or limited. You are beyond everything that you are witnessing. Surrender your self-identification with the body. Your awareness has an intimate relationship with the body, so you are intimately aware of what the body is going through. But you are not the body. The body loves you unconditionally. It will go through whatever you need to go through in the name of self-realization! You, as God consciousness, need the practice of remembering the difference between truth and illusion. You need the practice of right self-identification, in order to thank the body for its great love and offer it surrender and neutrality, instead of judgments and criticisms.

You can go through great mental, emotional, financial, as well as physical pain remembering, that you are senior to the experience. You came here to the rock just for this evolutionary gift, and you can be present for it in this moment with an open Heart. You can show up when in pain, surrendering all attachments to an outcome. You can show up and say,

> *Body you are going through this for me. Thank you, I trust you, body. I trust you have the wisdom you need to heal yourself. I trust the process I am going through in every present moment is bringing me enlightenment. I can choose to rant in rage at God, for having to feel the consequences of what I have been giving my love to. I can choose to make a monument to unhappiness and wrong self-identification with my attention. Or I can surrender my attention to the truth that I cannot create a learning experience I do not need. I can choose to practice surrendering crap in the head for the loving guidance of the Heart. I can continue to let the voice of limitation run my perception of reality and self, or I can surrender what I came here to get over and free my mind instead.*

I choose the latter.

Surrender is the exact opposite movement of mind from control and manipulation. Surrender does not have an attachment to any outcome. Surrender is not responding to *what is* from the mindset of "how can I manipulate this to make it come out right?" Surrender intelligence feels no need to control any person or situation. Surrender intelligence knows already that everything under the sun is the perfect food of Heaven, and therefore requires no alteration of any kind, only acceptance. Behavior guided by surrender intelligence is the precise opposite of passive-aggressive behavior. Surrender behavior is all about practicing separation from anything that prevents or diminishes us from being with *what is* in the present moment with an open Heart. Passive-aggressive behavior is all about duality and who controls whom; it is not about surrendering to the perfection of *what is* already there. Passive aggressive only recognizes the perfection of what the ego has controlled and manipulated. Nothing else.

In solving eternal problems, what is beyond compromise is cooperation, and **what is beyond cooperation is surrender.** Why? Because even with cooperation, that guidance is based on thoughts and beliefs. With surrender no one has any thoughts or beliefs about themselves, others or reality to get in the way of living the life of the One. Real authentic surrender, like forgiveness and acceptance, has nothing to do with spirit giving attention to controlling or manipulating or a less than or victim state. Once again, only the ego, a limited form of consciousness, could rob us of real surrender, an unlimited form of consciousness. Sensing a pattern here?

Surrender intelligence is a complete action of self-realization that ends the cycle of karma or incomplete action. Surrender intelligence is the fruitional action of self-witnessing. Surrender is inseparable from the intelligence of abundance, happiness, and the present moment. Surrender is eternal consciousness perceiving *what is,* not temporal consciousness, or the ego telling us *what we want it to be.*

What happens for example, when you are walking down the street and a homeless person asks you for money. If the first thing that you become aware of is your own empty checkbook, then it is useful to surrender to the reality that you are, because of Divine Correspondence, really witnessing your own stories of *not enough* as authored by the inner critic. Let's say in this same scenario upon looking at the homeless person and hearing their request you found yourself thinking, "Can't they get a job somewhere! They just are lazy and do not want to work," then it would be useful to surrender your projections of mind and witness your wave being possessed by *didn't do it right, not good enough* stories, again authored by the voice of limitation. The higher truth is that everything is perfect now, just as it should be. No one can create a learning experience that they do not need, and that all of us are beyond the stuff we are here to get over, now in this present moment, regardless of what the temporal world looks like. These are the truths we wish to remember when viewing a homeless person asking for money, or when viewing anything in the temporal world for that matter.

Surrender intelligence, when aligned with right use of will, creates a new response to *what is.* This union frees us from the tyranny of re-creation and ego-fear based information. Surrender is the integration of trust in true self, infinite possibilities, and unlimited abundance united as One. This unification forms a senior intelligence that is aligned with the wisdom needed to liberate us from the disease of duality. Ending duality is always a critical practice to develop while here in a body. We might even go so far as to say that ending duality is the entire point of still finding ourselves here in a body.

Surrender intelligence is not fear. Choosing to surrender to the perfection of *what is* from an open Heart is never a fear-based decision. Fear is held together in mind, in our wave by our habituation of thinking and believing our way through life. What happens just before the divine visitor of fear is beckoned? We give attention to a thought or belief about *what is*. This action of thinking and believing our way through life is how the wave beckons, invites over a visitor we all know and love very well . . . it is the invoking of the divine visitor of fear into the wave.

Another of the ego's favorite ways to sabotage spirit's relationship with surrender is to worry. Like waving a twenty-dollar bill in front of a topless dancer, all the ego has to do is pass worry in front of our field of attention. We then fall in line, and give a "lap dance" to our love of duality and the unresolved stories and memories of *unsupported* and *not enough*.

When we worry, the first thing that happens is unhappiness and stress increase their seniority in the wave. We will clearly feel this reflected back in the body's nervous system. The wave then becomes rigid and inflexible, constricting the influx of neutrality and surrender, since they are by nature very expansive and flexible forms of consciousness. No wave can be rigidly inflexible and expanding flexibly at the same time. No one can be re-creating worry while simultaneously creating a new response to worry. (You know, the serving two masters deal.) All worry stories are held together in the wave with the glue of the ego's lies. The principle lie in worry is *not enough:* love, time, money and opportunity for healthy supportive relationships in life. That is the ego's favorite fab four and "she does not love you, yeah, yeah, yeah!"

Worry is not able to exist simultaneously in a wave that loves surrender intelligence. Worry holds onto the waste with our attention. Surrender is the mastery of separating ourselves from the garbage; taking out the trash. Worry is trashed thinking, and its pathetic little mantra is, "Oh no! What is going to happen to me now? I'm so screwed! It's over, game over!" That is why we always *feel* so trashed after giving our attention to worry.

Our job is to re-train the ego so that we do not give our love to worry. We must teach the ego that our field of attention is immune to worry. No excuses, no exceptions. This is not negotiable. We can neutralize our wave's unconscious addiction to worry. Our most useful path to this end is to constantly focus on giving our attention to Ultimate Truth as an unstoppable inner devotion! As soon as we become aware of worry, our job is to tell the ego, "Excuse me, ego, but apparently you have not heard. There is only the One. There is always infinite abundance. So, ego, you have a choice. You can either become truth, or you can leave the wave, and don't let the foam hit you on the way out."

Giving more attention to surrender has a profoundly transformative effect on the seventh and sixth Chakras, where we organize our knowing and perception information. Surrender intelligence neutralizes "the impressions, the wounds" or samskaras re-created by giving attention to the ego, instead of to something higher. Surrender allows the wave to *see*, to *know*, to *relate* to all of life as the One; as the profoundly liberating, self-witnessing, divine gifts that we all are to one another. Surrender intelligence is One with happiness. According to the Eastern perspective, what surrender and happiness have in common is that they are both states of existence defined as being with *what is* in the present moment with an open Heart. If we are not surrendering, then we are not experiencing authentic happiness. Not what you were expecting? Yet it explains so flawlessly why so few of us here on the rock have any real relationship of lasting value with happiness.

Surrender intelligence is beyond catering to a co-dependent relationship with anything limited. Surrender is beyond thoughts and beliefs. Surrender is beyond fear. Surrender is beyond the grasp of anything that appears in the physical world. Surrender intelligence never relates to others as insignificant, unimportant, or as just taking up valuable space on the planet. It is aligned with the truth that nothing in the temporal world has any inherent power at all, because it is Heaven that determines the movement of all things. Surrender is inseparable from the divine law of equability. Surrender is the action of *seeing* everyone as equally God consciousness independent of the limited mental programming we are all here to get over. **Surrender is *seeing* everyone as we really are, as love, as God and nothing else.**

Neutrality Intelligence

Surrender and Neutrality intelligence have an interdependent relationship in which one empowers the other. If Surrender is weak and barely moving in a wave, neutrality intelligence is also weak and barely moving. The converse holds true as well. If surrender intelligence is vibrant, alive, radiant, fluid, and abundant in the wave, neutrality intelligence is also vibrant, alive, radiant, fluid, and abundant in the wave. Understand the relationship between surrender and neutrality intelligence as One. Whatever happens to one happens to the other.

The reason for this symbiotic relationship is because the more neutral you are to what you think, to the ego's chatter, the easier it is for you to surrender to the perfection of *what is*. Likewise if your wave is all charged up with stories and memories of events that did not work out the way you wanted them to, or if your wave is rigidly focused on how things *should be* or how things *better go,* then it will be very difficult to surrender to the higher reality that things are already perfect now.

Wholeness intelligence loves unconditionally perceiving *what is* with neutrality. **Acceptance intelligence** loves unconditionally perceiving *what is* with neutrality. **Equability intelligence** loves unconditionally perceiving *what is* with neutrality. **Wisdom** loves unconditionally perceiving *what is* with neutrality. For a neutral force, this intelligence sure gets around a lot. You can visualize neutrality as the "Glamorous bitch" like character (without the bitchiness) in a universal soap opera. Neutrality is already successfully in bed with any character that possesses any real power!

Neutrality is the finest "pain-free" fashion accessory a

spiritual being having a human experience can wear. A wave that loves neutrality intelligence is a wave beyond the grasp of judgment, criticism, and fear. Neutrality is One with a deep abiding trust that as spirit no one can create a learning experience that they do not need. Neutrality is a deep abiding trust that if anyone of us needs to be living, experiencing, or feeling something different, something other than what is happening, in order to reach enlightenment, we would be. Neutrality is relaxation and expansion that comes from trusting that divine love and wisdom is running the whole show. Only divine love and wisdom are real. Everything else is the illusion we are here to make separation from.

When we are neutral, we are in the correct position for self-witnessing. This is how we bring about an ending to every self re-created charge. With neutrality we can witness every positive and negative spin mind has projected as a result of listening to the ego telling us *what is*. Neutrality is like a pond of water without a ripple, without agitation. It is a place where self-reflection occurs naturally. **Neutrality is that space of peace where nothing inner or outer disturbs spirit from Oneness with Ultimate Truth.**

Everything in the temporal world is organized by charge: a positive or a negative. The planet Earth has a positively charged pole and negatively charged pole. All of the electromagnetic spectrum is governed by that charge. All thoughts and beliefs are constructed by a positive or a negative charge in perception. All things temporal require a positive and negative charge to hold them together, right down to the molecular structure of the temporal world itself. The ego, like duality, like thoughts and beliefs, does not exist outside of the atmosphere of positive and negative charges. *These four: the ego, duality, thoughts and beliefs; require a charge in order to exist* – a more than – less than, superior – inferior charge. What is beyond the charge of positive/negative, superior/inferior? Neutrality and Oneness, of course. All true and eternal things, beyond the ego, beyond duality, beyond limitation are inherently neutral and One.

When we listen endlessly to the ego's positive and negative judgments about *what is,* we are training ourselves to resist neutrality. Anytime a wave is organized in this manner, it will become very rigid, very heavy, and very difficult to shift. The wave finds itself focusing over and over again on the same stories and stresses, without being able to move on to the next useful or serving level of awareness.

A wave resisting neutrality, experiences awareness that does not shift, or does not shift easily. The symptoms of a wave resisting neutrality are: stubbornness, unforgiving, not growing and expanding, stagnation, unhappiness, tied up with worry, depression, obsessed and unable to make separation from focusing on the negative. These conditions are re-created by a dis-eased focus of awareness and can only be healed by spirit's practiced love for neutrality. The journey to enlightenment is the process of deprogramming our unconscious habit of giving our love to a positive/negative, good/bad, subject/object perception of *what is.*

Subject/object ego-trained perception is neutrality's greatest self re-created obstacle in mind. Subject/object perception stagnates the influx of neutrality intelligence in the wave. It has to, because subject/object perception is infused with positive and negative charges, and neutrality is by definition beyond a charge. *"Time to compost!"*

Taking things that occur in the temporal world personally is the covert incomplete action of the ego. It is what keeps us unconsciously giving attention to thinking and believing that we *are* the temporal world. We suffer only to the degree that we identify with being the movement of the temporal world. If we only identified with truth, with eternal consciousness, there would be no way we could ever be visited by the pain and suffering that comes from taking things in the temporal world personally. Ending pain and suffering can only come when we take awareness back from the disease of duality, and give that attention back to source, back to eternal consciousness, back to love.

The disease of duality, limitation and fear escalates the movement of suffering, unhappiness and hopelessness, making it top priority. This is how every unrealized wave is organized. Devotion to knowing all relationships, and the present moment as perfect, as the greatest invitation to Oneness with happiness, is how every *realized* wave is organized. Eternal is beyond duality, beyond the charge or movement of positive and negative. The glue of positive and negative charges holds the temporal together. Without duality, finite cannot exist. For a wave to shift from limited to unlimited, from finite to infinite, it must be rid of the charges; it must become neutral.

Remaining neutral to the ego's voice, and its never ending series of stupid human tricks is absolutely essential in shifting awareness from temporal to eternal. **When we practice seeing everything as governed by the wisdom of Heaven, this opens the door for neutrality.** The practice of aligning attention with trusting the perfection of Heaven's wisdom places us in the correct position for neutrality intelligence to enlighten and transform the wave. On Star Trek if Captain Picard (Pick-a-card, any card) wants to transport or shift his physical body from the ship to a planet's surface, he must align himself with the transporter energy. Awareness is like the transporter. It must be directly aligned as One with neutrality in order to make such a profound shift from one mode to another.

Awareness must become very intimate with neutrality intelligence in order to make the shift. You already know that the world is not what you think and believe it to be. Practice remaining neutral to the projections of mind in order to view the contents of the wave. Without neutrality intelligence, you are not self-witnessing. Without neutrality you are immersed in the charge of the crap we are here to get over. A wave is doing one of two things: either we are caught asleep in the disease of duality, or we are witnessing the movement of mind, realizing the One in all things. No wave can serve two masters. We are either making separation from the ego's voice and agenda, or we are defending it. We cannot do both at the same time.

Awareness directed towards neutrality frees the wave of duality, of subject/object perception and suffering. Awareness directed towards neutrality with great tolerance for *what is,* shatters all unresolved stories of *separate from love* and *unlovable* in the wave. Awareness that remains flexibly directed towards neutrality will destroy all unresolved memories and experiences of loneliness, isolation, as well as impressions of being cut off, invalidated, or ignored. Why? Because with neutrality we are re-united with Source. A wave that is one with neutrality, is One with the ocean.

When we are neutral we are beyond conflict, because we are beyond the friction of positive and negative. A wave that is neutral has surrendered to eternal consciousness for solving eternal problems and temporal consciousness for solving temporal problems. A wave that is neutral transcends the old adage that "it" takes two to tango, because a wave organized like this would know only the One. When a wave is One with the ocean it does not take the movement of life personally. It cannot, because it is One with life, and where there is the One, there is no disease of duality to personalize conflict.

Neutrality does not mean we are insensitive to the plight and the suffering of others. Neutrality is not an excuse for being emotionally shut down, dishonest or unavailable. Neutrality means we have cut the strings controlling the ego puppet. Neutrality means we dance to Heaven's music, and no longer to the ego's tyrannical break dance that looks a lot like performing a sexual act upon oneself, without any lubricant.

Try taking neutrality out with you on your next date. One of the many payoffs to neutrality, is that whether or not your dating experience feels like the one you would like to be experiencing, at least with neutrality, nothing about the relationship will bother you, frustrate you, or leave any lasting impression in your wave. Neutrality is the ultimate for inner wave "stain" removal. Just wash with neutrality, rinse with the truth and everything comes out sparking clean. Brings a whole new meaning to "wash n' wear," don't it?

Creativity and Patience

Just as surrender and neutrality are One and interrelated, so it is with creativity and patience intelligence. We can also understand creativity and patience intelligence as doing the same dance; mirrored movements of each other. Creativity and patience intelligence requires surrender and neutrality in order to perceive clearly that spirit is really One with eternal consciousness; the wave is really One with the ocean.

If creativity intelligence is going to create a new response to life, a requirement is that the wave must first surrender knowing through the diseased filter of thoughts and beliefs. The wave must instead align its attention with a knowing that comes from trusting that only love is real. If patience intelligence is going to resolve all of our *not enough* stories, we must first practice being neutral to the voice of limitation. We must practice being neutral to the inner narrative constantly reminding us of past pain and unavoidable future unhappiness.

An increasing influx of surrender and neutrality into a wave will always create greater happiness, joy, relaxation and grounding in the nervous system. Always! Creativity and patience intelligence will always diminish all unresolved re-creation patterns in the wave. Always! Creativity gives us the power to create a new response to all of the limitations we are here to put down. The upside to more patience in mind is that it keeps us One with the truth that there is always infinite abundance, and as God knows, there is no pain or suffering in that.

Creativity intelligence augments expansion, fearlessness and happiness by destroying the fear-based cycle of constricting re-creation. It is essential that we practice organizing our wave to love surrender and neutrality intelligence. We do this by solely giving attention to Ultimate Truth to solve our problems. Without surrender and neutrality, creativity and patience intelligence will simply stagnate in the wave. This leaves conditions ripe for the ego to distract us with more re-created stories of frustration, disappointment and apathy for the present moment. The shit hitting the fan will sound something like this, "See how hard you work to be patient and create a different response to life? And look. It never works. What did I tell you? Nothing ever changes."

It is not that being patient and creative do not work. There is a symbiotic relationship going on here. Surrender and neutrality are the tracks that transport the creativity and patience payload equally throughout the wave. Without the wheels the vehicle is going nowhere. Without surrendering our attention to the eternal, without remaining neutral to the unresolved projections going off in the head, without being with *what is* in the present moment with an open Heart, we are not growing. Without the feet, the heart and the head are going nowhere.

When neutrality is stopped in the wave by the restrictive nature of thoughts and beliefs, the influx of expansion, patience and creativity will also become contracted and limited. Why? No one can experience an empowered state of mind by giving attention to the voice of limitation. To end the contraction and turn it into expansion requires the illumination of the self-witnessing process. It requires *the Flame of Pure Awareness* burning off illusion and ignorance.

Creativity and neutrality work together through the magic of perception. When we create something from nothing (from the imagination), the nothing space that creativity comes through is neutrality intelligence; the inner space of infinite possibilities. When we want to create a new response to something we must first be in the present moment with an open Heart. This complete action aligns us with the neutrality needed to perceive the real problem and then the creativity intelligence required to end the re-creation cycle. Energy that is made up of a charge, positive or negative, is limited. Energy beyond charge is infinite. Therefore, if we want to create anything in the temporal world, a solution to a problem, a healthier more compassionate outlook on ourselves and the world, we must first be neutral as this space of neutrality is the birth canal of creativity.

Converse to creativity is the depleting cause and affect pattern of re-creation. In all unrealized waves, there is a tiring habit of perceiving the whole of life as not beneficial. We can recognize this in the inner dialog of the ego: "I could have lived very nicely without this event. I could have gone my entire life and never missed a thing if_____(*fill in the blank*) were never born, and I never had to experience them. I wish this would all just go away. I hate it. There is nothing beneficial in this experience."

Recognize any of that? Giving attention to the voice of limitation, the ego, arrests the influx of neutrality intelligence into the wave, while simultaneously re-creating unhappiness. This process in turn assures that the cycle of re-creation and unhappiness remains, as opposed to breaking that cycle with a movement of creativity and happiness. Remember the wave can only serve one master. The good news is that with your attention you get to empower which master it will be.

Creativity is spirit loving expansive right relationship with eternal consciousness. Creativity intelligence authentically destroys re-creation and suffering in our wave. Neutrality intelligence transports creativity throughout the wave. What supports neutrality in the movement of creativity throughout the wave? Awareness of self as eternal consciousness; awareness of self as the One; awareness of self as beyond duality, beyond the charge of positive or negative, beyond the insidious grip of *didn't do it right,* and *not good enough.*

Beyond Our Stories of Being Hurt, Wronged and Wounded

Creativity and neutrality also empower each other indirectly. We all lose a lot of energy whenever we are inappropriately giving attention to the ego. It actually requires a great deal of energy to re-create the crap. Remember when we talked about why we do not access the whole of our brains? It is because of the way we use our attention. We lose the energy needed to complete that action by manufacturing endless thoughts and beliefs about everything from; what your car *says* about your sexuality, to whether or not O.J. did it.

But that energy loss is only a part of the story. Once we have pissed away a God-sized portion of energy on fabricating positive and negative charges about everything under the sun, we add energetic injury-to-insult by holding ourselves hostage to these same self re-creating limiting thoughts. Oh, the gyrations we perform in the name of striving to attain *good enough.*

When a wave is neutral, that energy loss is stopped. Now the wave has a God-sized portion of energy available for creating a new response to life. All the energy, all the attention that had been going to worry, bad faith in life, mistrust of *what is* and the present moment, is now fully directed to supporting the wave in being with *what is* in the present moment with an open Heart, then, to witnessing mind reveal itself in pure innocence, which is a state of Heartfelt awareness, a state of being which is absent of any mental thought or belief awareness.

When the wave is aligned with neutrality, truth and gratitude, it is remembering that every relationship, every experience that touches us, is working to bring us enlightenment. We cannot create an experience we do not need. When the wave is in right relationship with neutrality and the truth, gratitude will flow freely as a natural by-product of what we are giving our attention to.

Creativity and neutrality support each other in our growth, in our inner expansion and in our feeling that we are One with a life worth living. Relating to self as One with Ultimate Truth integrates compassion and expansion intelligence, which in turn empowers us to love and accept *what is* with an open and honest Heart.

The Crocodile Hunter

Creativity and neutrality intelligence strengthen each other in the following manner: creativity loves happiness, the present moment, and perceiving all relationships in a playful way. In order for there to be creativity, we must first be neutral to the stories we are here to get over. The best example of this is Steve and Terry Irwin, otherwise known to millions of television viewers as *The Crocodile Hunter* and family. Here is a married couple that travels all over the world on behalf of crocodiles, venomous snakes, Gila monsters, spiders, mammals, fish, and various other reptiles and species. Terry, by the way, is as close to a modern day saint as they come. This woman jumps right into the mud and crocodile infested waters to support her partner in the most unusual and unique love story to hit television.

However this is not a love story involving just the Irwin family, this is a love story on the most inclusive and grandest of levels! This is the story of how Steve and Terry love every crocodile, every venomous snake, every spider and every creature equally; the warm, cute and fuzzy ones as well as the ugly, frightening and dangerous. They love them all! Steve and Terry have created a new response to the aspects of mind that have manifested in the exterior world as crocodiles, snakes, and spiders.

The exterior world is the inner contents of our wave physically revealed so that we may *see it* better. The new response Steve and Terry have created to this portion of their wave is unconditional love, acceptance and compassion for all, in every present moment. They are both aligned with the universal law for creating a successful life; they are completely accepting of *what is* in the present moment with an open Heart and see all life forms as valuable and loveable.

When Steve and Terry move into action to rescue, or to intervene on behalf of some fellow living creature on the planet, they are not being guided by thoughts and beliefs. Clearly they are being guided by their unconditional love, acceptance, patience, forgiveness, tolerance and compassion for *what is*. Anyone being guided by thoughts and beliefs would never go into the places or do the things that Steve and Terry do open-Heartedly and joyfully. While they are narrating their inner experiences to their television audience, they often speak of feeling Oneness with the moment, themselves and the animals as the senior movement of their wave. They do not speak of fear, anxiety or worry for their physical well being. Instead these feelings of love are the single focus of their attention; the senior movement of their unwavering devotion to love and *what is* in the present moment. This power allows them to create a profoundly fearless new response to all of life.

When Steve and Terry are out in the field, they are not filming animals from a safe and comfortable distance. We are talking about Steve jumping out of the safety of the boat right on top of a crocodile, or Steve single-handedly removing a twelve foot black mamba from a villager's home in remote Africa. Steve has also been known to jump from the protection of a boat into the ocean, armed only with his khaki colored clothing to release sharks that were trapped in a gill net. He has traded a knife for a small wild animal caught by some locals for lunch. When Steve offered the much more appealing knife, the locals happily traded, and Steve is off to the forest to release the frightened animal. He barely seems to notice when the little fur-covered fellow bites the hell out of his hand, for creating a new response to life is all in a day's work for the ever smiling, joy-filled *Crocodile Hunter* and family!

Steve and Terry speak unendingly of the beauty and love of every living thing on the planet. They model unconditional love for the whole of life. Even when animals large and small lick, bite, scratch, or even urinate on them while the cameras are rolling, they simply lovingly share the whole of life with the entire world. Steve and Terry have created a new loving, accepting, healing relationship with the portion of the wave that most of us continue to label as unlovable, ugly, evil, completely unacceptable and horrific. Most importantly, Steve and Terry are obviously incredibly happy as a result of their creating a new relationship with mind, with the portion of the wave that most of us find too challenging to love and accept. In the words of Dr. Phil, *"Judging by results . . ."* *these folks are doing something right and in a big way!*

Steve and Terry are clearly in the present moment as a result of their very creative life. No one is ever going to successfully wrestle with that many dangerous creatures and not be in the present moment. Their relationship with every living thing infuses them into the present moment via their consistent and abiding love for *what is.*

Steve and Terry have also clearly mastered what creativity loves most: to perceive all relationships in a playful manner. There is no way anyone could risk their life for a crocodile or a twelve foot black mamba, one of the world's most deadly snakes, then hold the creature up to the camera to talk about how gorgeous and bee-you-tee-ful it is, without perceiving that relationship as playful!

Truthfully, most of us would take our wave and move it in the totally opposite direction. Most of us would give all our attention to thoughts and beliefs about why these creatures that Steve and Terry love so much are ugly, disposable, *less than* and totally evil incarnations in our world. When we live in a world that is really our own mind being reflected back, labeling it as ugly, disposable, *less than* and evil is never going to be serving for anything other than increasing the seniority of unhappiness and fear in our wave. Judgment of ourselves and others is like war. "What's it good for? Absolutely nothing!"

War, war is such a bore – sweep it away and out the door –Argisle

There is no better living model for how creativity loves happiness, the present moment and perceiving all relationships in a playful way than the life and soul work of Steve and Terry Irwin. May we all learn from Steve and Terry to love the process of creating such a new and positive response to the whole of our lives. Most importantly may we all learn to love, as Steve and Terry have, to embrace the portion of our own wave that we have for so long labeled as unacceptable and non-lovable, while caught asleep in the disease of duality. And finally may we all learn to be as happy and freely sharing as the Irwins.

The action of self-witnessing is the wave shifting awareness from what the ego thinks and believes, which is limiting, to a whole and complete awareness of being with *what is* in the present moment with an open Heart. This is exactly what we were observing in the life of Steve and Terry Irwin that allows them to do the remarkable and fearless things that they do. This shift of awareness from thinking and believing to eternal consciousness is the awareness shift we are all here to practice and master. Steve and Terry Irwin teach others how to master this by giving their love and attention to the plight of the other life forms here on the planet. Every sacred tradition would agree with them that it is through the creation of loving relationships that we are best served in mastering the awareness shift from finite to infinite. This is why enlightened beings love and care for every living thing, unconditionally.

Surrender the habit of thinking and believing your way through life. We must practice remembering to get through life by shifting attention from the frontal lobe to Ultimate Truth. When we focus on the movement of the One in all things, this focus becomes our *Ruling Love* governing our perception. This use of awareness is a complete action that heals, transforms and liberates all neutrality in the wave from anywhere the flow is stagnant. Stagnant? Stagnant from what you ask? Could it be from the positive and negative charges building up from thoughts and beliefs clogging up the whole works? It always makes it harder to flush away the waste when the pipes are plugged up with duality, the sticky, smelly brain out-gassing of the ego. Call Ultimate Truth, the inner Roto-Rooter, right away, and away goes trouble down the drain. Looks like that is a snake of a different kind than the Irwins have mastered (Imagine the sounds of snakes and unclogged drains laughing here).

What we think and believe we are strengthens our attachment to the vicious cycle of suffering, fear, insecurity, worry and abandonment; a vicious cycle brought to you courtesy of the voice of limitation. To focus on self as eternal consciousness is to go against the ego, the greatest ingrained, unconsciously paralyzing lie of every unrealized wave. Without surrender we are in bondage to the slavery of thoughts and beliefs. Without neutrality we are bitterly dominated by the tyranny of the ego's limiting and brutal charges. Without surrender and neutrality we will never know the real value, power and worth of being with *what is* in the present moment with an open Heart. It is here, dreaming ourselves in a physical human experience, that we can practice full mastery: Oneness with surrender and neutrality. This is where we get to *feel* enlightenment happen. This is where we get to embody enlightenment. Perceiving *what is* as the perfect food of Heaven to transform the contents of our wave into unification with the One is the purpose and meaning behind why we as spirit are here.

Why So Many Souls?

When were you last really happy?
Let that experience ferment, bring it to
mind once in a while.

Surely in the genesis of that past moment,
when you danced, you would not have
wanted a constable to have knocked on
your door, or have said, "You just entered a
restricted ground."

Why are there so many stars and souls,
with no end in sight for them?

Because nothing can interrupt God when
He is having fun, Creating!

– By Meister Eckhart

Chapter Seven

Dreaming

There was the One, there is always infinite abundance

When the historical Buddha was alive, people would ask him if he was a God. The Buddha would smile and answer, "No, not the way you think and believe." The people would then ask, "Well are you a planet made human?" And the Buddha would smile and answer, "No, not the way you think and believe." "Well then are you half God, half human?" the people would ask. And the Buddha would just smile and say, "Not the way you think and believe, no." The people would ask, "Well then what are you?" And the Buddha would answer, "I'm awake. The only difference between you and me, my wave and your wave, is that I'm fully awake." When the Buddha used this phrase "fully awake" he is not referring to what we in the West consider as "awake."

According to Webster's dictionary, awake is *to rouse from sleep, to rouse from inactivity. Not asleep. Active; alert.* When the Buddha used this phrase *fully awake* he was not alluding to anything in the temporal world. He was referring to an inner state, a quality of mind. He was referring to having awakened fully from the deep sleep of duality. He was signifying the end of all subject/object toxicity in perception.

All unrealized waves are asleep, yet they still think and believe they are awake and are experiencing what is real unto itself. In actuality, all unrealized waves are projecting the illusory contents from the unconscious portion of their wave out upon life and the neutral, blank screen of reality, so that they may eventually *see* it. These unrealized waves are caught in the disease of duality. They are asleep, dreaming their life, and they are the last ones to know it.

Modern science has not been able to conclusively answer the question, "Why do we dream?" Modern science indicates that in fact every mammal dreams without exception. Even dolphins and whales sleep and dream. They just do it one brain hemisphere at a time so that they do not drown, being the air-breathing creatures that they are. Why do all mammals require some periodic REM rampage in the unconscious realm of dreamtime? REM stands for "rapid eye movement," the stage of sleep that signals dreamtime is visiting the wave. What modern science does know is that if a person is deprived of sleep, specifically the act of dreaming, the REM stage, the mind will begin to hallucinate. At first the hallucinations will be mild and harmless. Then, the self-created, interior illusions will become stronger, more fearful and terrifying both in intensity and duration. Finally the person either presumably goes mad, possibly seriously harming themselves and others, or they go to sleep, either voluntarily or forcible, and dream the incumbent insanity away. This is one of the reasons sleep depravation has been traditionally used as a form of torture by all people throughout human history.

People are perhaps best familiar with this concept from the movie, *They Shoot Horses Don't They.* The film is about the dance halls in America in the late 1920's and early 1930's, during the great depression era. These dance halls held marathons in order to generate more business and interest. People would come and participate for big prize money that went to the couple that could dance the longest. The dance halls would be filled with desperate people, in desperate times, going to desperate lengths to win desperately needed money. Some couples, out of fear of not enough money, would stay up for days, even weeks without sleeping or dreaming, in hopes of winning the big prize money. These people found themselves descending into the unrealized hell of their own mind until they were forced to sleep and dream it off. The unrequited, unresolved in our dreams will always require recycling; it is a part of the universal human experience without exception.

According to Swedenborg, we all dream at night because this is the time when higher order spirits, also known as angels, visit the wave. Swedenborg describes dreaming as our time to receive divine commentary on the quality of our love. This occurs when the angels project the divinely sent information up into the wave. Heaven speaks to us in a symbolic, primarily visual/feeling language; this is the language of the Heart, not the head. Dreams are Heaven reflecting back to us what we are doing with our love and attention.

Swedenborg also suggests that the reason we *need* to dream is because, as spirit, our mind will begin to unravel if we are disconnected from Source. Since the truth is there is only the One, if we become disconnected from the One, we fail to exist. At the very least, our illusory self, what we think and believe we are, would fail to exist. Without this quality of dreamtime connection and information healing our waves, we would begin to fall apart and disintegrate relatively quickly, because we do not exist independent from this divine connection. The wave does not exist independent of the Ocean. Without Source we do not exist at all.

Many ancient traditions use the same saying, *"As it is above, so it is below. As it is within, so it is without."* This saying was not only a favorite of Swedenborg's, but also an incredible accurate statement about life here on the rock. This adage will be our filter for understanding dreams as a higher communication, as another way of *seeing* Divine Correspondence. Dreams, like everything else here, are simply another reflection of how our wave is organized according to what we are giving our love to. No different than how the outer physical reality is a tangible manifestation that mirrors back how our inner spiritual perception is organized.

Lucid Dreaming

In dream work there is a disciplined technique known as lucid dreaming. Lucid dreaming occurs when the person, *while dreaming,* realizes that he/she is fully asleep and dreaming. People often have flashes or glimpses of lucidity during a dream. However, flashes and glimpses are only the most superficial understanding into the reality that what the dreamer is experiencing is really a dreaming state of mind. Lucid flashes and glimpses are not actually full-on lucid dreams. The thought, "Oh, this is just a dream. I'll just change it into something I like better" this example is only a lucid flash. It is still not the real thing.

The main difference between a lucid flash and a full-on

lucid dream is the length of time you remain clear about what reality you are presently experiencing. A full-on lucid dream is to actively know and recognize at all times that you are asleep and dreaming. You completely realize that your mind, the contents of your wave, is making up everything that you are experiencing for the duration of the dream, not just for an instant. The unconscious sector of the wave is manufacturing everything: how the dream looks, what happens, who shows up, and how it feels. The dream just looks and feels so incredibly real, just like waking reality! The only difference is that now you are lucid, awake to the reality that mind is the producer, scriptwriter, director, editor, the cast and the crew of every dreamtime production. Once again, *as it is above, so it is below. As it is within, so it is without.*

During a lucid dream you know that everything you are experiencing is pure dreamtime illusion. It is a world totally created and lived inside your own cranium. It has no basis in the physical world, other than it is really happening in your physical head, complete with real physical white and gray matter. When you become lucid in a dream, the door between the conscious and the unconscious portions of the wave now stands wide open, fully available. All you have to do is walk through it. Does it sound like the *Twilight Zone*? Wait till you get there! Lucid dreaming will make the *Twilight Zone* pale in comparison, although you just might run into Rod Serling, Oscar Wilde, Swedenborg or Joan of Arc there.

Why Practice Dream Work?

We practice lucid dreaming to establish a living relationship with waking up to the highest reality: that there is only the One. We are only dreaming this life, this world.

We are dreaming each other. We therefore need a practice that supports our waking up to the true nature of reality. In order to fully realize the whole of mind and its many relationships, lucid dreaming can be a useful technique for sneaking an honest glimpse into the contents of the dreaming wave. How do we really treat others and ourselves? How do we really feel about others and ourselves? How honest are we? Like Asmodeus spitting out Solomon in the middle of nowhere, lucid dreaming will take you to places where you can answer all these questions and more. Lucid dreaming is mind revealing itself for a heightened opportunity of self-witnessing to occur.

To practice lucid dreaming is to engage in a continual practice of remembering that reality is not what we think and believe it is. In order to practice lucid dreaming, you must first remember to practice letting go of thinking and believing you know what reality is. Instead you must learn to let reality tell you something about its self-evident nature, without projecting your temporal stories, labels, memories and charges upon it.

When you practice lucid dreaming you are also practicing waking up from the disease of duality. The reason why practicing waking up in dreamtime simultaneously works to wake you up from the disease of duality in the physical world is Divine Correspondence, and the truth behind the statement: *As it is above, so it is below. As it is within, so it is without.*

Self-witnessing counts no matter how or when we create it. We can witness the contents of the wave anytime: dream time, waking time, non-ordinary reality time, tea time, Greenwich Mean Time, Eastern Standard Time, lunch time, play time, it does not matter. As long as there is a witnessing of *what is* with an open Heart in the present moment that is all that matters. That is the magic that makes it all count. The truth is that all experiences and dimensions of time count equally, because there is only mind, there is nothing else. It is all One, because there is only the One.

Furthermore, as long as you find yourself in a body: dream body, physical body, imaginary body, coma body, plastic surgery body made of nothing but silicon and Teflon, it does not matter. As long as there is a body to facilitate consciousness we have lift-off. The packaging, make and model, organic or inorganic, are all equally irrelevant. The type and form of bodily accessory used to become self-aware really does not matter. As long as you find yourself in a body, self-witnessing is going to be the name of the "unconditional game." It is the only real game on the rock.

The only enemy there is, if there is one at all, is subject/object diseased perception itself; the illusion of subject/object re-created by duality. That is the hell portion of the physical world; the stuff nightmares are made of.

The perception of the One in all things is the Heaven portion of the physical world, and the lucid portion of lucid dreaming. The only way anyone can become or remain lucid is to be One with the remembrance that everything you see and experience is the contents of your own wave being reflected back for self-realization. What you are looking at, feeling, experiencing is nothing you think or believe it to be. You are getting a clear shot at seeing just how your wave is organized. How are the different intelligent aspects of your wave, such as neutrality and surrender, getting along? How is your wave's use of temporal and eternal consciousness getting along? Is your wave integrating itself or at odds with itself? Do the dream characters help each other, or are they in conflict with each other? Are some dream characters consistently stalking or chasing you or another dream character? If you ask a dream character for help and friendship, do they give you a fist and the finger, or do they extend a caring and compassionate open hand? Do you?

As Sogyal Rinpoche, author of *The Tibetan Book of Living and Dying* says it:

> *If we have a habit of thinking in a particular pattern, positive or negative, then these tendencies will be triggered and provoked very easily, and reoccur and go on recurring. With constant repetition our inclinations and habits become steadily more entrenched, and go on continuing, increasing and gathering power, even when we sleep. This how they come to determine our life, our death, and our rebirth.*

Becoming lucid while dreaming is only half the challenge. Remaining lucid is the other half. If lucid dreamers forget that what they are looking at is their own mind, or if they forget that they are in fact dreaming their present reality, then they will quickly become re-absorbed back into the dream. So if a dreamer forgets to remain clear about what reality he/she is experiencing, he/she will slip back into the dream and begin to think and believe that it is real. That's right folks, forgetting what voice is talking to you in dreamtime yields the same results as if it were happening in waking reality. Why is that? Indeed *as it is above, so it is below. As it is within, so it is without.* (This will not be the last time you will hear this little "spiritual jingle.")

It's A Remembering and Forgetting, Or A Lucid and Non-Lucid Thing

As Plato wrote in his most famous essay *The Cave*, all unrealized waves are like people chained to the back of a cave. The chained people are staring at shadows created by a fire behind them. The shadows dance and move about on the back of the cave wall. The chained people all think and believe that the shadows are real. Because some of them can even predict what the shadows will do, they are even more convinced that the shadows are real. It is only in the freeing of mind from the tyranny of what we think and believe that we are able to liberate ourselves from the chains that bind us to the back of the cave wall. It is only after we have delivered our love from the shadows, from the lying darkness of the ego's grasp and loosened the illusory bonds that shackle us, that we are finally able to live a real life in a real world, as the real force of love we are.

The key to being lucid and remaining lucid is that you do not give your attention, your love, to anything that re-enforces an unconscious, chained to the back of the cave position, with mind. Becoming and remaining lucid is how we make our big escape from the ignorant prison of the cave. Again the very definition of lucid is that you know when you are asleep and dreaming, and when you are not. When you are lucid you know the difference between what is a shadow on the back of the cave wall, and what is not. Take away that minute but very important detail and the result is what most people call regular dreaming or non-lucid dreaming. Non-lucid dreaming is going to be a commentary on a life lived inside the cave; lucid dreaming is the means and wisdom by which we break the bonds of what we think and believe, and free ourselves from the cave of the ego's limitation, forever.

Becoming and remaining lucid, ending the re-creation of subject/object perception is essential in both dreamtime and in the physical waking world. Why is that? It is due to the law *as it is above, so it is below. As it is within, so it is without.* What you do in your waking life, you will do in dreamtime. What you do in dreamtime, you are also doing in waking reality. According to Swedenborg it must be this way, because one is a commentary on the other. In this way dreaming becomes a self-corrective guidance system designed to keep us increasingly more honest about how we are living/dreaming our lives.

If you find yourself running away from something frightening in a dream, you may wake up, rub your eyes and comfort yourself with the age-old wisdom of "it was only a dream, it was just a dream." However, because the commentary of the dream applies to waking reality as well as dreaming reality, what is really being communicated is that you are running away from some conscious or unconscious anxiety. There is something unresolved in your life (and the ego is no doubt behind it) that you need to examine and heal, because it's coming out of the void and headed right for your charming ass.

But, please, don't take someone else's word for it. How can you be sure if you are really dealing with a state of internal denial? If you are having dreams of being chased, instead of having dreams of wild, sweaty, swinging from the rafters, jungle sex, then you are trying to tell yourself something! We dream about all manner of things. So, if we are not finding ourselves dreaming about mutually consenting orgasms, but instead if we find ourselves dreaming of being chased, stalked or hunted down by something, it would serve us well to ask ourselves, "What am I running away from?" Because in a dream, if I am not confronting the frightening image, or if I am not asking the image what I can do for it to heal it, then I am just running away from it. This would be a good time to honestly ask yourself, "So why am I avoiding honesty with myself? What is *that* all about?" Remember whatever you are doing in waking reality, you will do in your dreams. That means if you are running away from something in your dreams, then you are running away from something in your waking life. This "mirrored world reality thing" is designed to happen on purpose, so that you can become clear and honest about what you doing with your love. We all need the wholeness-making commentary from Source; that is why dreaming is a universal experience. Keep a dream journal. Notice patterns emerging?

Dreams are purely ethereal, made of purely spiritual interaction. Nothing in the dream realm is physical. Nothing is dense or solid, since there is no molecular structure to dreamtime. Everything is fluid, everything is mind made visual, not material. Dr. Stephen LaBerge at Stanford University's Sleep Research Center pioneered lucid dream work in the scientific world using modern technology. Dr. LaBerge has written many books on the nature of our ethereal dreams. He explains that dreams do not imprint on either the short or long-term memory at the time the dreamer is experiencing the dream.

This is why so many people insist that they do not dream at night. It is not that every person does not dream. Every person does in fact dream, but not every person remembers the dreams. That is the primary difference. In order to remember we must either review the dream several times over and over in our head, write or otherwise record the dream in some fashion, even telling another person about the nocturnal journey. All of these activities will imprint the dream details in our memory. The dream itself is so ethereal it does not imprint in memory, unless we do the imprinting while waking up into the physical world.

There is this phenomenon of reoccurring dreams. You dream something and then the next night or over a certain span of time you have the same dream over and over again. This type of dream is always a divine commentary on a recreation pattern your wave is stuck in. That is why you keep recreating the same dream over and over again. It is a commentary on a pattern you are repeating over and over again with your attention. These dreams, due to their repetitive nature, will eventually become imprinted on the short and then long term memory.

Even with the ethereal nature of dreams, there are some things that one cannot do in the dream world that one can only do in the physical world. Surprised? Most of us are only aware of the opposite: flying without any aid, perform brain surgery (well, we probably all could *do* it in waking reality, but we would have a hard time guaranteeing the results), sailing a 14th Century ship, ballroom dancing, wrestling crocodiles, climbing Mount Everest. However, there is actually an action that can be done in the physical world that cannot be done in the dream world: reading the same thing more than once.

In the physical world because of matter, we can write something down, read it, put it down, and come back seconds, minutes, hours, or years later, pick up that same written material and read it again. In the dream world, nothing is stable. Nothing is dense. Everything is fluid, constantly changing. There is no atomic structure to hold anything in place. In the dream world, if you write something down, you cannot read that same thing twice. The printed material will read differently, or it will become very blurry and unreadable. It could turn into another language, or hieroglyphic like symbols. In dreamtime there is no matter to maintain a static or semi-permanent reality that one can hold on to. It is a world of pure ether, pure space, pure projection of mind.

Dr. LaBerge, understanding this fluid realm, insightfully suggests to dream-workers that they use this little factoid as a means, or a trigger to become lucid in a dream. The idea is that if you are asleep and dreaming, but do not realize you are asleep and dreaming, you are experiencing the dream and thinking and believing it is real. This is the same as when you experience duality in life, and think and believe that you are awake, and that the physical world is real. You are still asleep, dreaming, projecting mind. How could you forget - *As it is above, so it is below; as it is within, so it is without.*

At some point in a dream, you may find that you cannot read something twice, as Dr. LaBerge points out this is the perfect opportunity to lucidly test your reality. If you cannot read any material more than once, let whatever reality you are experiencing tell you something about its self-evident nature, instead of you thinking and believing that you are awake and that you already know what reality is.

The way you would practice "testing reality" for its self-evident nature is as follows:

Stop, in the course of your day and read something. It does not have to be more than a word or two. Look away and focus completely on something else, a flower, the landscape, anything around you. Then go back and try to read the same one or two words again. See if those words are still printed there or did they change into something else right before your very eyes. If the words have changed then reality has told you something about its self-evident nature and that is that you are asleep, dreaming and nothing in this "reality" is static. It is all permeable and fluid. If the ability to read the words is duplicable, then "reality" has once again revealed to you something about its self-evident nature; you are experiencing waking reality, that this "reality" is static, it has a physically based structure to hold it together.

The truth of the matter is that unrealized waves do not know which reality they are experiencing. They cannot tell the difference between when they are asleep and dreaming, and when they are awake. That is the first bit of self-revealing information that dreams have come to show us: we do not realize that we are actually asleep. You can prove this to yourself. Dr. LaBerge points out in his books that if we could tell the difference between when we are awake and when we are asleep, as we are falling asleep at night, we would be consciously aware of the various stages of sleep as we pass through them, which of course, we are not.

If we could tell the difference between awake and asleep, as soon as we hit REM, we would realize it. We would be aware of descending through the last stage of sleep, and we would be aware of the fact that we are now entering into a full-blown dreamtime experience. As the dream was ending, we would become consciously aware of the fact that the dream was decaying. We would be aware of ascending through the various stages of sleep until we find ourselves once more in our physical rooms entering physical, waking consciousness. However, we are not consciously aware of this movement of mind. We are not lucidly in relationship with *what is.* This is the way it is for every unrealized wave caught asleep in the disease of duality.

It is very revealing about our waves, that on the most basic level we do not even know if we are asleep and dreaming, or if we are experiencing what we all commonly, and laughingly, refer to as waking reality. Shocked? This is why it is essential to wake up from the disease of duality, because if it is not ended in our wave, we go on forever ignorantly asleep to the true nature of reality. We are asleep at the wheel, without even knowing it, endlessly running into the same obstacles over and over again. An unrealized wave is like the line from a *ZZ Top* song, *"How could anyone be so unkind as to arrest a man for (dreaming) driving while blind?"*

What Happens In Our Brains When We Dream?

Dr. LaBerge, with the aid of modern technology, really ushered in a completely new understanding of dreaming. The scientific community was now able to open the door to dream research in a way that had been previously closed. In the past it had been very difficult to compare what happens in the brain when a person is asleep verses when they are awake. Someone would be brought into the sleep lab, and while they were awake, their brain would be measured while they performed different left and right brain activities, such as counting and then singing. If the researchers then wanted to know what happens in the brain during dreamtime, how would the researcher know when or even if the sleep subject was performing these activities while dreaming, so that the results of dreamtime verses waking time could then be measured and compared?

During the descent through the various stages of sleep until one reaches REM, the body turns off all the non-involuntary motor activity to protect the dreamer. That happens so that they do not get up and physically act out their dreams. Only the body brain connection from the eyes up does not turn off, as movement to that limited a region of the body cannot cause the dreamer any physical harm. Sleepwalking, however, is a totally different story. Sleepwalking is an abnormal condition where the hormones that are normally turned *off* to render the body completely inactive are left *on,* due to some great physiological stress that impairs the natural *turning off* process. Narcolepsy is also not normal.

The gift of lucid dreaming research is that the sleep subject can now give the researchers in the lab a series of predetermined eye movement signals to indicate just exactly when they were counting and when they were singing. Since eye movement is the only muscular movement that one can still control while asleep in REM, it made sense to use that ability to catch the attention of the researchers and capture the needed data. The sleep subject could now reach out and communicate with the researchers in the laboratory, directly from the dream and dream time itself. What Dr. LaBerge was able to scientifically document, is that what happens in the brain when we are awake and what happens in the brain when we are asleep, is one in the same reality.

As far as the nervous system and the brain are concerned,

there is no experiential difference between awake and asleep. There is no difference between the two realties. This explains why everyone at some time or another has awakened with a dream hangover, emotionally and psychologically still feeling the effects of the night before. Once again, *as it is above, so it is below. As it is within, so it is without.* Thanks to Dr. LaBerge and all the many others who have lucidly contributed, science has only just recently discovered a way to see, understand and even measure in dreamtime what the Aboriginal and other native people from around the world have been experiencing and exploring for centuries.

Why is practicing lucid dreaming so important in the journey to enlightenment? Because of the tremendous opportunity dreamtime offers us: the opportunity to de-brainwash our chronic habituation to temporal consciousness, the monkey on our back that we give all of our attention and love to. It is an essential step in self-honesty and de-brainwashing to admit that we do not know what reality is. If we did know the truth about what reality is, we would have solved all of our problems and ended all of our suffering a long time ago.

As Lily Tomlin in her one-woman show used to say, "Reality is nothing more than a collective hunch." When you authentically admit to yourself that you do not know what reality is, then and only then you can catch yourself dreaming and become lucid. When you think that you know what reality is, reality cannot show you that you are indeed actually asleep, because you are operating under the mistaken belief that you are already awake when you are not. No one can practice lucid dreaming without practicing *waking up* to self-awareness. Lucid dreaming requires a level of surrender and neutrality awareness that is needed in ending the ego's hold on the wave. That is why lucid dreaming and self-witnessing are actually One practice.

As previously mentioned, the first stage of practicing lucid dreaming occurs during waking reality. During the course of the day, pick up something and read it. Dr. LaBerge suggests keeping a piece of paper in your pockets that says, "Am I dreaming?" Give the reading material all of your attention. Again it can be something short like two or three words. Now look away at something else and focus on it. Give this new thing all of your attention. Now turn back and try to read the same short two or three words again, and see if you can read it twice. If you can read it twice, then you are most likely not dreaming. If you cannot read it twice, guess what? You've caught yourself in REM, dreaming.

The real trick is that you must perform this reading task with a completely neutral mindset about whether or not you are awake or asleep. You cannot perform this task while you are thinking and believing that you know what reality is. You cannot do this simple task if you are thinking and believing you already know you are really awake, and that this is stupid. If you test your reality that way when you are awake, then you will test your reality that way when you are asleep. You will assume you are awake, when you are not, just as you are presently assuming that you are awake when you are asleep, caught in the unconscious disease of duality. You will completely miss your chance to catch yourself asleep, and completely miss the opportunity to turn the state of unconscious awareness into a state of fully lucidly consciousness.

In both realties, awake and asleep, unrealized waves have already mastered the habit of assuming that they are awake when they are not. We must now learn to master letting reality tell us *what is,* without a thought or belief about it. It is only when a wave begins to practice not giving attention to thoughts and beliefs about *what is,* and breaks the habit of letting the ego run the show, that we are asking from a truly open Heart for reality to reveal something to us about its self-evident nature.

Any unrealized wave that practices neutrally observing reality by way of this quick little reading test five or more times a day, will after some time find themselves doing this same task in a dream. Eventually everything you habitually do in waking reality will appear in dreamtime, since one is a commentary on the other. Why? Indeed *as it is above, so it is below. As it is within, so it is without.* This simple technique is one of many Dr. LaBerge recommends in his books on lucid dreaming. It is very easy, very simple and very effective.

Neutrality Vs. Controlling

So, in order to become lucid, one must practice honestly embracing the truth that we do not know what reality is. The only thing we do know for sure about reality is that it is not what we have been thinking and believing it to be all these years. In order to remain lucid, we must learn to surrender attention unconditionally to the first law of Ultimate Truth: there is only the One. The dreamer must remember, "I'm dreaming this life and all of its experiences. Everything I am looking at, touching and interacting with is my own mind being reflected back. I am not the dream, which is merely the projection of mind. I am the observer of the dream, the projector of mind, and I am observing what I am doing with my love." Only through the conscious ending of duality does lucidity occur and remain present.

Another successful strategy that works in lucid dreaming, just like it does in waking reality, is neutrality. With neutrality we can witness the movement of mind, without taking the parade and the drama personally. With neutrality we can witness *what is* without contracting into the habit of thoughts and beliefs. In waking reality, neutrality is the relationship panacea for solving all conflict. Neutrality is the healer in waking reality, because you cannot turn your relationship challenges into another form and then send them off to Jupiter, like you can in a lucid dream.

The opposite of remaining neutral to *what is,* is the attempt at controlling and manipulating *what is.* This can happen in dreamtime just as it does in waking reality. If you are putting your attention to controlling and manipulating *what is* in waking reality, then you will be controlling and manipulating *what is* in dreamtime; they are both mirrored realties reflecting each other, and the one is always destined to be a commentary on the other.

Controlling and manipulating in either reality is an unhealthy, neurotic, fear-based response re-created by the ego and the disease of duality. If you find yourself enjoying lucid dreaming because you can control and manipulate everything in sight, then what the dream is here to show you is that you love controlling and manipulating your way through life. Controlling and manipulating is the ego asserting its story of bad faith in life and love as the senior movement of mind. Controlling and manipulating is a wave giving all love and attention to the ego's re-created story that things are not going to work out unless I force an outcome that I have decided is right.

What surrender and neutrality are to eternal consciousness, control and manipulation are to temporal consciousness. No one can organize their wave to love surrender and neutrality, and control and manipulation simultaneously. They are opposing movements of mind. They are mutually exclusive. One movement is unlimited; the other is limited. As we have already established, no wave can serve two masters at the same time, even if one only does exist in a dream. Just as Agent Smith from *The Matrix* only existed in virtual reality, so it is with the ego.

We cannot be trusting love and at the same time be feeling the need to re-arrange external furniture in the temporal world in order to solve an eternal problem. Trusting love is to know that what we are really witnessing is the organization of our wave's love, no matter what stupid human tricks the temporal world would like us to perform. This witnessing process requires acceptance and neutrality in order to see the internal made external for the purpose of practicing self-realization.

If any control or manipulation occurs while in witnessing mode, the process will suddenly stop. Duality will step in and possess the wave. Then the very predictable divine visitors we recognize as disappointment, abandonment and unhappiness arrive. This can be the only possible karmic result for a wave that unconsciously sabotages the self-realization process. Loving the process of self-witnessing is the meaning and purpose behind all of creation. There is no way anyone can sabotage self-witnessing without paying the price, which is, of course, a life worth living.

Control and manipulation means that you do not trust

that divine love and wisdom determines everything. Control and manipulation is the exact opposite of Deepak Chopra's Spiritual Law of Success *that everything is as it should be.* Control and manipulation screams that if *what is,* is not organized to my ego's liking, then I will act like a spoiled child, throw a tantrum, and change everything to my liking. Control and manipulation is a contractive energy and movement. A wave that loves controlling and manipulating cannot love Heaven. Heaven is One with expansion. No wave can serve both contraction and expansion at the same time. We either live in Heaven or in hell, by aligning ourselves with either expansion or contraction, depending on what we are doing with our love.

Controlling and manipulating, as a response to life, is never serving, unless you want to live in hell. Then it is just the right vehicle to enliven duality, fear and frustration. Yes indeed, mistrust and angst are all the favorite finger foods of the ego, ready for a party on the patio in hell. The successful mastery of both lucid and waking realities requires we resolve our fascination with control and manipulation. It requires we organize our wave to unconditionally love acceptance, surrender, neutrality and expansion. Only unrealized waves do not see or understand that the control and manipulation of another, is the control and manipulation of their own mind being reflected back to them. As a general rule, realized beings have already learned not to screw themselves. It comes naturally with the territory of being enlightened.

With lucid dreaming we have yet another opportunity to practice not identifying with our bodies as what we are. In a lucid dream we have a dream body, not a physical body. A dream body can do anything from fly to laugh at nuclear weapons we can stop with our bare hands. Dreamtime can become therapy time for reversing where the wave has identified with the temporal, instead of identifying exclusively with the eternal. Dreamtime is a non-physical arena where we can practice fearlessness. Our dream bodies are immortal. We are indestructible. Dream bodies survive all trauma like the most resilient cartoon characters, "cause everyone knows you can't kill a toon."

In dreamtime we directly experience the truth that we are not our bodies. We can dissolve the habituation to think and believe our way through life. We can instead reinforce the fine art of witnessing the mind project the fear-based information that we have come here to get over. In dreamtime we practice realizing that we are immortal and beyond the limited stories we are witnessing. And when the dream body dies, what we really experience is the opportunity to *wake up* to a greater reality.

Swedenborg's articulation of the truth is that you are what you love, and you love whatever you are giving your attention to. We are here on the Earth, in a body, to get real about what we love. Ayurvedic psychology says, because you are the *Flame of Pure Awareness,* whatever you give your attention to you are enlivening, infusing with "God Juice," because you are Pure Awareness itself. Therefore whatever you give your attention to, you have also made it your God. If you are thinking about that next cigarette all the time, then you have made that next cigarette your God. If you are giving your attention to money or worrying, then you are worshipping worry and the almighty dollar.

What Ayurvedic psychology is stating is that if you make

something limited and temporal your God, you will find it to be a very cruel God. The only appropriate use of "God Juice" is to return it to its rightful place. When we do this we are aligning our wave with God consciousness, infusing mind with pure love, which is beyond money, beyond denial, beyond the temporal and beyond the limited.

The path to enlightenment, the ending of all our suffering, ultimately requires that we consciously realize *what* we have been giving our attention to, *what* we have been making our God. In waking reality we have a nervous system and divine emotional visitors to help keep us real in this area. In dreamtime you can explore this in a truly unique fashion, because you can ask all the dream characters, or a tree, or a cloud for feedback. Remember in dreamtime we are not subject to the same laws that we are in waking reality. Visiting dreamtime is like visiting a Disney movie. We can talk with everything there: the animals, insects, birds, and plants, even rocks. In dreamtime everything is capable of communicating very effective and specific feedback.

Watch Out – You Might Get What You're After

In lucid dreaming you cannot predict how any dream character or image will respond to you. If you are looking for a journey into what the unconsciousness mind is making God, just ask your dream characters the following questions, "Who am I? Who are you? What do I love? What do you love? Then integrate all the acceptance, surrender and neutrality intelligence you possible can, because a big self-realizing meteor is coming out of the unconscious void, and headed right for your conscious mind. Smile big, 'cause that puts you right at ground zero'.

Swedenborg would like us all to remember that the Earth plane is where we have come to practice unconditionally giving our love and attention to Heaven, being One, being open and equitable, sharing and honest. It is only on the Earth plane that we can practice being unconditional. In the spiritual realm, all spirits can see the intention and truth of every other spiritual being, so the practice of being unconditional cannot be mastered there.

Only here can a spirit practice and master unconditional love, because of the process that life on Earth puts the wave through. Here, and only here, can you be lied to, cheated, ripped off, betrayed, fooled, swindled, hoodwinked, scammed, and never leave the comfort of your own home. So only here can you practice loving what Heaven loves, for no other reason than to love what Heaven loves. Only here could the person you love turn around and screw you seven ways to Sunday, and you never even see it coming. When you do not know how it is all going to come out in the final reel, you learn to love either breakthrough or breakdown; no one can love both at the same time. Out of sheer practice one will have to become senior over the other.

You are either expanding into a whole-Hearted *yes* response to whatever life and love asks of you, or you are contracting away from life and love, giving attention to the limited voice of the ego. It is only here that the consciousness rubber meets the unconditional road. It is critical that we organize our wave in such a manner that we love removing the obstacles and conditions that mind has placed on saying *yes* to life and love.

When you practice lucid or non-lucid dream-work, you are practicing removing obstacles by tapping into the unlimited realm of mind. The gifts you have for yourself there are beyond imagination; be willing to take the journey; be willing to practice conscious dream-work. Notice it is not called dream vacationing, or dream-non-conscious-participation. The practice of anything will always require some work on your part, even nose picking. Again, the rewards of dream-work practice are endless. Robert Louis Stevenson, the great writer most remembered for the classic pirate adventure *Treasure Island*, (arg matey), said that he got the inspiration for the stories he wrote from his dreams. When he described his relationship with his dreamtime, he said it was as if Brownies came in the night and told him the stories. He often said that he looked forward to his next dream when the characters within the story would tell him how it was going to all work out. Stevenson himself did not know what the characters real motivation was or how the story was going to end, until he dreamt it! Of the nocturnal tale spinning Brownies, or little people, Stevenson said, (they) "do half my work for me while I am fast asleep, and in all human likelihood do the rest for me as well when I am awake and fondly suppose I do it for myself."

Mozart said he heard the music we give him credit for writing, in his dreams. Of course, the acoustics are always infinitely better in dreamtime with inner digital sound and all. Albert Einstein was an enormous fan of dreamtime. He favored working his theories out in the flexible universe of dreamtime. There are numerous biblical as well as Buddhist accounts of people receiving special information from Heaven through the vehicle of dreamtime. Mohammad, the great prophet of Islam, wrote the *Koran* from visions revealed in dreamtime. If these people did not value dream-work, they would not have been such significant dream receivers. They were obviously, by results, very practiced at discerning a *non-ordinary* dream from an ordinary dream. Of course, practice does make perfect.

Dream-work is the cornerstone in the foundation of modern Freudian and Jungian psychology. Dreamtime is valued in this work as a profound and powerful means to understand and explore the mystery of mind. Many ordinary people have been sent premonition dreams to avoid airplane, train or sailing vessel trips that were destined for disaster. Dreams have been used and valued for healing and self-revelation purposes by the ancient Egyptians and Greeks to name but a few. It was not just the fancy colored coat that gave Joseph such a prominent position with Pharaoh. It was a combination of the fashionable crotch-less underwear he wore (The Egyptian clothes men wore always looked crotch-less to me.) and the remarkable God-given-talent for interpreting dreamtime messages. If practicing dream-work liberated Joseph from an Egyptian jail, imagine what it may do for you!

In his book, *The Tibetan Book of Living and Dying,* Sogyal Rinpoche describes the application of dream-work as preparation for the greatest adventure of all, the death bardo:

> *How your mind is in the sleep and dream state indicates how your mind will be in the corresponding bardo states; for example, the way in which you react to dreams, nightmares, and difficulties now shows how you might react after you die.*

> *This is why the yoga of sleep and dreams plays such an important part in the preparation for death. What a real practitioner seeks to do is to keep, unfailing and*

unbroken, his or her awareness of the nature of mind throughout day and night, and so use directly the different phases of sleep and dream to recognize and become familiar with what will happen in the bardos during and after death.

Instead of listening to our highest dreams, we are giving our loving to the re-creation of fear as our senior navigating intelligence when we meet the ego's conditions. Most of the time we are not honest, we fool ourselves about the fear, the insecurity that arises when we have not met the ego's conditions. Most of us convince ourselves that we need to be loyal to the ego's agenda, because we see it as actually being a practical plan of action. We do not understand that what we are calling a "plan of action," Heaven would call an "incomplete action." In truth, loving and trusting our way through life, without being a slave to the tyranny of what we think and believe, is the only action Heaven would call a "complete action." *Being* with *what is* in the present moment with an open Heart is the only agenda, strategy or plan we will ever need.

Loyalty to meeting egoistic conditions can appear as giving attention to any criticism of yourself or others that involves a dialog about how someone *did not do it right,* or is *not good enough.* Re-creation of loyalty to meeting the ego's conditions fragments and shatters the wave's relationship with the inherent Oneness of all created life. Why? Because loyalty to the ego's conditions is not in alignment with the truth that everything is already perfect right now. A wave cannot be aligned with meeting the ego's stipulations and be aligned with the inherent perfection of *what is* at the same time. A wave that loves the whole of life is loyal to remaining unconditional to *what is* and cannot be sabotaged by the ego's condescending dialog.

Lucid dreaming, like waking reality, offers us a pristine opportunity to unconditionally accept the movement of mind without a thought or belief. All we have to do is show up and witness *what is*. Dreamtime is highly unpredictable due to its fluid, non-material nature. Dreamtime offers us a heightened mastery in the learning of unconditional acceptance for the whole of life and mind. In this medium your nervous system experiences as real, dreamtime is going to put you through more, at a faster pace, than waking reality. Once again this truth is brought to you courtesy of the law: *As it is above, so it is below. As it is within, so it is without.* Repeat after me.

Most of the dreams experienced by an unrealized wave involve memories of unresolved conflicts, or commentaries on the diseased habituation of identifying with the temporal, the ego, instead of identifying with eternal love. If you are interested in realizing, healing and transcending all inappropriate identification with what is impermanent, then lucid or regular dreaming can provide you with all the juicy details the ego has been hiding from you. Remember any external unresolved conflict only exists because it is a mirror reflecting back an internal unresolved conflict, as the external world cannot exist without the internal state it is mirroring. *As it is above, so it is below. As it is within, so it is without.* Pleasant dreams, and don't forget to pass on a friendly "hug and hello" to any dream character you may encounter. After all, the wave you befriend will be your own!

258

There is always infinite abundance there to tap into, the One.

Chapter Eight

Inner Space: The Real Final Frontier

When we are children we imagine that God is a person. Sometimes we imagine God as a person sitting on a cloud far away in the Heavens. Swedenborg describes absolute realized God consciousness appearing in the spiritual realm as the form of a person in the sun of the highest level of Heaven. This is what he calls Celestial Heaven. Swedenborg, however, would not disagree with the Eastern traditions that speak of God as a quality of consciousness, not as a person in the way that we typically think of an individual person as existing.

Swedenborg and Space

Swedenborg's personal articulation of the quote; *"As it is above, so it is below. As it is within, so it is without"* can be understood by his explanation of Divine Correspondence. Basically, the idea of Divine Correspondence is that the physical world does not inherently exist by itself. The physical world exists merely as a mirrored manifestation of what it Corresponds to in the spiritual realm. It is reflecting a spiritual reality that pre-existed before the advent of the material world.

Swedenborg defines the mastery of both realms as a state of consciousness that realizes how to see the spiritual by looking at the physical. Divine Correspondence is not a mystery to an enlightened mind. Only unrealized waves think and believe the physical world, and all the things in it, exist not only independently of each other, but also independently of absolute truth. (Insert audible sound of knee slapping and angels laughing loudly here!)

The journey of enlightenment will always involve the mastery of both realms, inner and outer space. The truth is they are really One, because there is only the One. Outer space is really a metaphor for inner space. Outer space only exists because it Corresponds to the divine reality of inner space. Now this is truly the final frontier.

Swedenborg and Ayurvedic psychology have very different ways of saying the same thing about space. Swedenborg says that outer space exists as the seminary of Heaven. Every planet and every moon has a spiritual life form on it. However, only the planet Earth involves spiritual beings having a physical experience. Every other life form out there is having a purely spiritual experience. Only here does the spiritual rubber meet the physical road.

The distance between planet Earth and other planets and solar systems directly correlates to our Ruling Love. The closer the Ruling Love of other spiritual beings matches ours, the nearer in proximity they will appear. So essentially we share the same Ruling Love as the other spiritual beings in our solar system. It stands to reason; the closer the Ruling Love, the closer we manifest to each other in the physical world, so that we can see the Correspondence and become fully self-realizing.

In astrological terms, suppose a person has a strong influence of the planet Mercury in his/her chart. What that means in Divine Correspondence is that the person has organized his/her wave so that he/she profoundly loves the same or similar things that the spiritual beings on Mercury love. What the spiritual beings of Mercury love is what Swedenborg called "the froth on the surface of the wave." These spirits love thinking and believing as an endless form of mental masturbation. Giving their attention to intellectual pursuits, not as a clear means to an end, but as an end unto itself. They love living in their heads. Not to solve problems, as much as they love to cram their heads full of as much intellectual *crap* as they can possible get in there. That is their definition of what it means to be powerful, valuable, and important. Sound familiar? Talk about revenge of the nerds! The spirits of Mercury are mirroring back our unconscious habit of loving thinking and believing our way through life as a means to an end, instead of loving and trusting.

Why is it that so many people feel they are effected by Mercury retrograde? If your Ruling Love goes to temporal forms of understanding and communication instead of eternal forms of knowingness and sharing, then when the planet ruling that temporal love goes retrograde, so will your Ruling Love. Pretty sobering awareness.

Swedenborg wrote about his many journeys into the spiritual world, into the different levels of Heaven and hell. When he described traveling to another planet or even another solar system, in what we would understand as outer space, he would simultaneously be describing the journey he was making through the inner space of his body. So although Swedenborg might describe being in a certain spiritual location, like Heaven or hell, he would simultaneously describe where this consciousness space dwelt within his own body.

Chinese Medicine and Space

In Chinese medicine the planets in our solar system correspond to the internal organs in the human body. The liver corresponds to the planet Jupiter. The liver is the organ that controls both the physical and mental digestive functions of the body. Jupiter is the planet known as the "inner guru" or the "higher self." When we are using eternal consciousness to solve eternal problems, and temporal consciousness to solve temporal problems, the liver is able to completely and fully digest physical food. Physical food being a metaphor for the food that is the evolution of our soul. Fully digesting the soul food, as well as the physical food, means absorbing the energy from life that makes us stronger and more loving - taking those nutrients deeper into the tissues of the body, deeper into the wave.

In Chinese medicine, the spleen and pancreas are considered a paired organ, since they function as one. The spleen, stomach and pancreas are associated with the planet Earth. The stomach, in the physical world, digests whatever is deposited there. In the spiritual realm, these paired organs digest worry, anxiety, feelings, experiences, and memories of being unstable, unsupported, unbalanced and abandoned. When fully digested and the waste eliminated, these organs transform the limited states of being into unlimited states of being: feeling life is sweet, supporting, stable and completely balanced.

Just as Jupiter has an affect on us, so does the planet on which we reside. Imagine that! The Earth is associated with balanced and stable energy. Although the Earth is hurtling at an incredible speed, while simultaneously spinning around its axis, our experience is that it is not moving at all (unless you live in Earthquake country). Our perception of the Earth is one of balance and stability, unconditional love and sweetness. It does not matter who you are, from Charles Manson to Ghandi. The Earth has always provided an atmosphere for every living being here. The planet unconditionally grows food and flowers for anyone. Since we live on the planet Earth, not Jupiter, we should be walking around with an unconditionally loved, balanced, stable, sweetness of life, shit eating grin on our faces. We should be stoned on Earth energy, enjoying a God intoxicated buzz that would completely destroy any charges of worry, *less than, not enough,* anxiety, suffering or limitation. You name it we can bust it. Life is good. Or is it?

We squat 24-7 on the love rock, receiving endless Earth-energy. Yet we do not experience life as sweet. How could that be? Why are we not rocking around the clock in bliss? What seems to be the problem? It is because *you are what you love, and you love whatever you are giving your attention to.* (Never would have guessed that one.) Even if your butt is glued to the planet Earth, if you love giving attention to worry, anxiety, *not enough* or *less than,* then you will live in worry, anxiety, *not enough* or *less than.* You can filter out Earth's energetic influence by giving your attention to what erodes that energy. You always have to watch what you are doing with your attention when you are God consciousness. It just comes with the territory.

Heaven and hell do not co-exist in the same space. Even though Heaven has put you on the love rock to realize your wave, if you continue to give your attention to hell, then you will override everything else, and put yourself on an express elevator straight to hell. The law is that you do not exist independent from what you love. With your love you choose to be a doorway to either Heaven or hell. You choose to live on the love rock, or you choose to take up space in hell. It is up to you. What'll it be?

Ayurveda and Space

Ayurvedic psychology describes outer and inner space as One, just as Swedenborg personalized it in his spiritual journeys. According to Ayurvedic psychology, the inner space between atomic particles corresponds to the outer space between planets and solar systems. This Correspondence happens when we as spirit live in a world where everything is mind being reflected back for self-realization. This is where spirit lives the reality *as it is above, so it is below, as it is within, so it is without.* This is truly where we can *see* our wave as a microcosmic representation of a macrocosmic reality.

Eastern traditions go even further and say that what we really are as God consciousness, a physical being with a Divine Correspondence, is *that space* between all atoms, all electrons and protons. It is that way now and has been throughout all of time. This is what spirit really is! We are the context, the space, in which all of reality resides, the true Ether-net. As the rock band, *The Police*, reminds us, "we are the ghost in the machine." This is how we can be immortal. This is how we can really be beyond our bodies and experiences, dreaming our lives, our bodies and relationships. We really are the eternal space between the temporal atoms.

So how do the atoms take their instructions? It depends on how our inner space is charged. The particles configure themselves and relate to each other in the physical world based on the unresolved charges within the wave. We determine these charges by what we are giving our attention to.

If the nucleus of an atom could be enlarged to the size of a baseball, the electrons and protons that circle the nucleus would be more than a city block away. That is a lot of space! On a chemical level we are mostly water. On an atomic level we are mostly space: pure, simple, perfect nothing-ness. We really do not even exist at all, at least not in the way we typically think about existing. This space is true self. Hope you are not too surprised to discover that true self is nothing that you have been thinking and believing it to be.

On the physical level, outer space is mostly nothing. There are plenty of stars, planets, asteroids, dust, gases, even the debris left like satellites and empty jars of Tang. Still, even withstanding the entire contents of space, it is still mostly nothing . . . just empty space.

Unrealized waves do not look like outer space. They are packed full of temporal consciousness. There is very little to no space at all in the wave. In an earlier metaphor, the birth of Christ was a symbol for mind. Jesus, a higher form of consciousness, was born in a manger because that was the only space available. The rest of the space was filled up. No room at the Inn. Our job is to empty the wave of what we think and believe, so that our interior may be One with Source, One with pure space.

A Practical Ayurvedic Meditation For Spiritually Integrating Self As Space

This meditation can be done with the eyes open, focusing on either the left or right hand. Or it can also be done with the eyes closed focusing inwards using imaginary vision to *see* the heart organ in the chest just slightly off to the left side of the body.

With your eyes open, focus on the palm of either hand. Imagine your awareness is traveling deep within your palm. First just see the palm as it is. Then imagine going deeper into the tissue of the palm. Gradually go deeper into the muscular structure, then beyond that and into the bone tissue. Imagine going into a single cell in the bone marrow. Envision the atomic structure of the single cell of bone marrow. Travel into a single atom, going into the space between the nucleus and the surrounding electrons and protons. Continue to expand into the pure space between these atomic particles. Go deeper into the space. Give the space all of your attention. After a while you will see a light, a white light. This light is what you really are. This is the universal white light we all see in our death bardo. This is the *light of the Flame of Pure Awareness.* Feel free to hang out in this space as long as you would like.

Now gradually bring your attention to the identical process only in reverse. Come back to the atomic structure of a single cell of bone marrow. See a single cell of bone marrow tissue in the center of your palm. Imagine the bones, now the muscles, then the skin tissue, and finally the complete exterior of the palm in present time.

With eyes closed, imagine looking inward at the heart organ beating within your chest. Envision traveling into the muscle tissue of the beating heart. The human heart has four chambers. With your inner awareness, see into the tissue in the center of the heart, into the tissue that divides the four chambers. Focus on penetrating into the cell structure of the heart tissue. Look for a single cell. Go into that cell, into the atomic structure of a single cell. Imagine a single atom with a nucleus encircled by electrons. Travel into the space in between the center of the atom and the charges moving around it. Go deeper into the space. Give the space all of your attention. After a while, you will see a light, a white light. This light is what you really are. This is the universal white light we all see in our death bardo. This is the *light of the Flame of Pure Awareness.* Stay in the light for a while.

Gradually bring your attention to the identical process, only in reverse. Coming back to a single atom, moving back through the space in between the nucleus and surrounding satellites. See now a single cell of heart muscle tissue. Move back to the center of the heart and the four inner chambers. Imagine the heart beating inside the body. Slowly open your eyes and your Heart.

This meditation brings back the connection, the feeling, the memory of self as space into the present moment, and then re-enforces it as familiar. This meditation helps you to remember that you are really space, not the painful things that you keep identifying with. Remembering that you are space is absolutely essential in the practice of not taking the world personally or seriously. Being One with inner space is the source of all spiritual flexibility, neutrality and surrender, not to mention creativity. The practice of living unconditionally in the space is what we are here to master. When we live in the space, there is no pain, suffering, or unhappiness. When we live in the space, we are infinite. We know only the One.

To quote the spiritual teacher Deepak Chopra, *"The body is constantly eavesdropping in on what the brain thinks about it."* Then the body organizes its health around what we think and believe about ourselves. This way we become aware of giving our attention to something limited, instead of giving attention to love and surrendering to the practice of unconditionally accepting this and every present moment as perfect, whole, complete and lacking in nothing.

Just as the body is eavesdropping in on the brain, so are the atoms eavesdropping in on the thoughts and beliefs, the charges that influence the space in and around our bodies. What we experience as *self* is what Ayurvedic psychology calls the localized field of consciousness. This is what Swedenborg envisions when he refers to the wave. The atoms inside the space of the localized field of consciousness are constantly being directed by the charge of what we think and believe, so that we may witness how we have organized our love. Remember, everything in the physical world has only one purpose: *to help us get real and honest about what we are doing with our love.*

Everything in the physical world happens by energy agreement. All atoms will organize themselves according to the charge within the localized field of consciousness within the wave. If you have organized your wave to love worry, then there will be an alignment, an energy agreement, to manifest worry. The atoms within your localized field of consciousness will organize themselves in such a way as to re-create something in the physical world for you to worry about. This idea of energy agreements is discussed more thoroughly in **Chapter Ten.**

Any time mind loves worry, the atoms and subatomic particles will go out of their way to re-create something in the exterior world that will support the re-creation of the worry charge, until you *see* it and consciously choose to change the charge and create something different. Everything here on the rock is designed to go out of its way to reflect back to us what we are doing with our love. Until you realize how your wave is organized, and what part of that organization is not working for you, you will never be honest about the opportunity you have to choose a higher love. Indeed anyone who has sovereignty over his/her own mind has the power, at any given moment, to choose something more life sustaining, such as Ultimate Truth over illusion.

Swedenborg describes awareness or consciousness as self, space, a wave on the ocean. We are here to fully realize the contents of the wave, and to transform it into the ocean. For there is only the One. There is always infinite abundance. Ayurvedic psychology also describes awareness or consciousness as self, space. The journey from illusion is the movement out of the head and into the Heart. This will transform the experience of self as a localized field of consciousness into the realization of self as space, as the unified field of consciousness, unconditionally One with the ocean.

Deepak Chopra's statement about how the body organizes itself around what we think and believe means the highest choice that we could organize our body's intelligence around is space. Identifying with space is eternal consciousness - to not have a thought or belief about yourself, life or others. To identify with space is to be emptied of the unconscious loyalty to temporal awareness that clutters and pollutes the mind.

Jesus did not have a thought or belief about how we are going to live or get food and clothes. Remember Jesus asking us to consider the birds and flowers, as they do not have a thought or belief about their survival, and yet they are taken care of? The reality that they are getting fed and clothed, and the fact that they are not polluting their mind with toxic thinking have a direct relationship with each other. In the previous quote from Buddha, when asked about enlightenment, his response was, *"The only thing that comes between you and enlightenment, or anyone and enlightenment is polluted thinking."*

Jesus, Buddha and Socrates, all fully awakened beings, have completely transformed the localized field of consciousness into the unified field of consciousness. As Jesus phrased it over two thousand years ago, *"The Father and I are One."* Jesus, Buddha and Socrates did not have a thought or belief about anything eternal. The intelligence of an awakened being loves identifying with being the space between the atoms, and nothing physical, temporal or changeable.

That is why when the time came, Jesus, Buddha and Socrates did not fear or contract in the presence of the physical body dying. When their peers condemned Jesus and Socrates to death, they did not flinch. They were not disturbed in the least. They knew they were truly the space between the atoms, which can never die. Only beings that think and believe they are the atoms, the temporal portion of the program, can die. When you know you cannot die, witnessing others still caught asleep in the disease of duality issuing you a death penalty, is a moot point.

Identify with being the space between the atoms, electrons and protons. Allow all things in the temporal world to come and go, without a thought or belief about what it means. This is one of the many meanings behind Jesus' famous saying, "Be in the world, but not of it." Be the space between the atoms. Show up, be in the world, but do not identify with being the temporal. Do not be of it. Simply allow it to come and go and fulfill its purpose in manifesting on the Earth plane. The bottom line is that everything in the physical world is here for our viewing pleasure. It is all here for the sole purpose of our liberation, or it would not be allowed to exist or touch our nervous system.

Going deeper into Jesus' statement, "Be in the world but not of it," the world is physical, limited, and comprised of duality. You are not. You are Eternal. Be in the world because you need it to realize your wave, but do not identify with it. Do not be *of* the world. Being *of* the world is to give attention to duality, the temporal, and other limited forms of consciousness to solve eternal problems. The way of the world is to think and believe that the stuff we are here to grow beyond, is actually valuable, real, important and worth holding onto.

Enlightened beings love identifying with being the space between the atomic particles. This is the true nature of all miracles in the physical world. Depending on how the space is charged, we could have either water or wine. If we knew we were the space between the atoms, we could instruct the atoms to form into anything by creating that charge. We could pull fish and loaves from seeming nothing, or shatter the illusion of a physical death. All the charges in mind, unresolved or not, are the guiding force that determines how all of the physical world will play itself out.

If you are identifying with being this space, how could you possibly take anything that happens in the physical world personally? You could not because there would be no personal point of reference from which to take anything personally. You know you are really the space between everything, and there is nothing personal there. You could never be powerless or helpless, since you are really the context, the space, in which all of reality plays itself out. How could you ever play the role of victim, or *less than* ever again identifying only with pure space?

When you identify solely with the space, instead of with anything physical, you can then truly realize the inherent equability of all life. Equability translates into perceiving the fruitlessness of thinking and believing that anyone or anything can be better than or less than, more power-ful or less powerful, or more lovable or less lovable, than anyone or anything else. If we are all essentially space, then we are really all equal. We are all the One. When we grasp that we are really space, we can fully understand why it is that whatever is done to the least of us is done to all of us. We all ultimately live in the same place. All roads lead to space.

In an earlier reference to the spiritual MRI that could ex-pose the contents of a person's mind, it reveals that the entire contents of an enlightened being's mind, is Ulti-mate Truth: there is only the One, there is always infinite abundance. Well, the rest of mind is space. It is pure no-thing-ness, no subject/object perception, beyond charge, beyond duality, beyond limitation and beyond the physical.

Letting go of that which no longer serves us requires space. We need space to be able to open and release the ever-tightening grip our wave has had on duality. The wave requires space in order to breath. Where there is no breath, there is no life. Space is required in order for spirit to heal and realize itself as whole, complete, perfect, lacking in nothing. We do not have space, we *are* space. If we are not experiencing that space, then we are experiencing the garbage we are here to get over. Our job is to empty the space in the wave of whatever is not space. Of course, the first thing to empty from mind is the clutter re-created by thinking and believing our way through life. Take out the trash, have an art enema or third eye wipe. Our job is to replace the junk with the spaciousness of loving, accepting, forgiving and being unconditionally patient and flexible as a response to whatever life hands us.

Taoism speaks of space as being the intelligence that makes everything in life useful, and the energy which sustains all living relationships. It is the space within the vessel that makes it useful. It is the space between the walls, roof and floor of your home that sustains all the living relationships contained within. Without space nothing can live, or move, or function properly.

One of the stories in Taoism tells of a scholar who goes to visit a Tao master. The scholar informs the Tao master that he is there to learn. He would like to know everything the master knows. The Tao master offers to make some tea first. He places a teacup on the table before the sitting scholar. The Tao master proceeds to fill the cup with tea. The cup soon fills, then overflows on to the table and floor. The master simply continues to pour from the teapot. The scholar jumps up from the table angrily yelling at the master, "What are you doing? Stop pouring! Can you not see the cup is already filled? The master stops pouring, *"You"* he says, *"are just like this cup. You come to me already filled, and ask me to fill you."*

Expansion requires space in order to occur. If spirit desires to surrender in order to become One with the ocean, it must to be able to expand infinitely. If there is no space for expansion within the wave, then expansion will never happen.

If you want something in your life, be it friends, better health, more fun, time to enjoy the intimate relationships you have, it will not happen unless there is space for it. How could it? It would spill out on the floor just like the Tao master's tea. If you want friends, then you need to ask yourself if you are making yourself available for that to happen. If you spend all of your waking hours working, watching the stock market, staring at a computer screen, or attending endless meetings, then where is there space in your life for your desires? Forget what you do or do not have in the physical world. Without space, you cannot actualize anything useful. Why? Because you do not have space, you *are* space. Lack of space in the physical world always corresponds to a loss of self in the spiritual realm.

Creativity requires space and expansion in order to break re-creation. Re-creation, on the other hand, requires contraction and limitation in order to remain in place. Therefore you cannot be giving your attention to both limitation and space at the same time. You cannot be loving and serving both space and limitation. Space will always feel like Heaven. Space will feel like there is always enough. Space will always feel carefree and unburdened. Limitation will always feel like hell. Limitation will always feel like scarcity. Limitation will always feel unhappy, indebted, and enslaved. Like the old commercial that would ask, "It is ten at night. Do you know where your kids are?" Well, it is the present moment. Do you know where your wave is? Is it in a spacious place of enough, or is it in a limited place of not enough?

Examine your life for a moment. Is there any space to make the needed changes in your life? Is there the space to grow and be present unconditionally? Or is the space you need for growth and change cluttered with thoughts and beliefs about why expansion cannot happen? Is there the necessary space to be honest and loving with yourself? Or, have you backed yourself into a corner and rationalized, courtesy of the ego, all the reasons why you do not deserve to be loved and happy? Is there space to be fully present and available for the relationships in your life? Or do you constantly tell your children and other loved ones that you just do not have the time for them?

Are you realizing your highest dreams and aspirations? Or have you told yourself there are too many limiting responsibilities and duties to have the space for that now? Is there enough space in your life for happiness and a life worth living, or are you filled up with all the stuff you are here to practice not stepping in? Are you loyal and devoted to creating space in your life and mind, or are you married to the clutter and chaos of what you think and believe?

The commercials may ask you, "Got milk?" But without space, you've got no place to put the milk or digest it. So, the more important question we might be asking ourselves is, "Got space?"

Space and Permission Are The Same

Space on an energy level equals permission. If you examine your life and discover that you have organized your wave in such a fashion that there is no space for growth, change, or for unconditional love and acceptance of *what is*, then what you are really experiencing is a lack of permission in the wave. The ego, when running as the senior movement of mind, will never give permission for the eternal to supersede it. The limited master will never give permission to the unlimited master to take over. Our job is to fire the ego by not giving it our attention, to empower solely divine consciousness and the mastery of Heaven on Earth.

Heaven is a very spacious existence. Hell is a very limited, contracted existence. Healthy, life-sustaining use of imagination requires copious quantities of space in which to move about. Focusing on limitation and bad faith in life is like a black hole in our wave. It will suck all the light and space right out of the wave.

Nature creates timeless spaciousness. Yet the average unrealized person crowds their wave with fear and unhappiness, the ego's fast food. It is only when we take our focus off our pity party and move it to the ocean, or to the top of a mountain, that we begin to expand the spaciousness of our focus and therefore our life. Hence the truth, *you are what you love and you love whatever you are giving your attention to.*

The following is a true story about Mellen-Thomas Benedict's death experience. This is his story of self as inner space:

THE ROAD TO DEATH

In 1982 I died from terminal cancer. The condition I had was inoperable, and any kind of chemotherapy they could give me would just have made me more of a vegetable. I was given six to eight months to live. I had been an information freak in the 1970's, and I had become increasing despondent over the nuclear crisis, the ecology crisis, and so forth.

So, since I did not have a spiritual basis, I began to believe that nature had made a mistake, and that we were probably a cancerous organism on the planet. I saw no way that we could get out from all the problems we had created for ourselves and the planet. I perceived all humans as cancer, and that is what I got. That is what killed me. Be careful what your world view is. It can feed back on you, especially if it is a negative world view. I had a seriously negative one. That is what led me into my death.

Because I did not want to be surprised on the other side, I started reading various religions and philosophies. They were all very interesting, and gave hope that there was something on the other side.

I was facing the medical profession without any kind of insurance. My life savings went overnight in testing. Eventually I ended up in hospice care. I had my own personal hospice caretaker. I was very blessed by this angel who went through the last part of this with me. I lasted about eighteen months. I did not want to take a lot of drugs, since I wanted to be as conscious as possible. Then I experienced such pain that I had nothing but pain in my consciousness, luckily only for a few days at a time.

CHAPTER EIGHT – YOU ARE WHAT YOU LOVE

THE LIGHT OF GOD

I remember waking up one morning at home about 4:30 a.m., and I just knew that this was it. This was the day I was going to die. I woke up my hospice caretaker and told her. I had a private agreement with her that she would leave my dead body alone for six hours, since I had read that all kinds of interesting things happen when you die. I went back to sleep.

The next thing I remember is the beginning of a typical near-death experience. Suddenly I was fully aware and I was standing up, but my body was in the bed. There was this darkness around me. Being out of my body was even more vivid than ordinary experience. It was so vivid that I could see every room in the house, I could see the top of the house, I could see around the house, I could see under the house.

There was this Light shining. I turned toward the Light. The Light was very similar to what many other people have described in their near-death experiences. It was so magnificent. It is tangible; you can feel it. It is alluring. As I began to move toward the Light, I knew intuitively that if I went to the Light, I would be dead. So as I was moving toward the Light I said, "Please wait a minute, just hold on a second here. I want to think about this; I would like to talk to you before I go." To my surprise, the entire experience halted at that point. You are indeed in control of your near-death experience. You are not on a roller coaster ride. So my request was honored and I had some conversations with the Light. The Light kept changing into different figures, like Jesus, Buddha, Krishna, mandalas, archetypal images and signs. I asked the Light, "What is going on here? Please, Light, clarify yourself for me. I really want to know the reality of the situation." I cannot really say the exact words, because it was sort of telepathy.

The Light responded. The information transferred to me was that your beliefs shape the kind of feedback you are getting before the Light. If you were a Buddhist or Catholic or Fundamentalist, you get a feedback loop of your own stuff. You have a chance to look at it and examine it, but most people do not. As the Light revealed itself to me, I became aware that what I was really seeing was our Higher Self matrix.

The only thing I can tell you is that it turned into a matrix, a mandala of human souls, and what I saw was that what we call our Higher Self in each of us is a matrix. It's also a conduit to the Source; each one of us comes directly, as a direct experience from the Source. We all have a Higher Self, or an over-soul part of our being. It revealed itself to me in its truest energy form. The only way I really describe it is that the being of the Higher Self is more like a conduit. It did not look like that, but it is a communication to the Source that each and every one of us has. We are directly connected to the Source.

So the Light was showing me the Higher Self matrix. And it became very clear to me that all the Higher Selves are connected as one being, all humans are connected as one being, we are actually the same being, different aspects of the same being. It was the most beautiful thing I have ever seen. I just went into it and, it was just over-whelming. It was like all the love you've ever wanted, and it was the love that cures, heals, regenerates.

We're all snowflakes on our way to the big melt!
– Argisle

As I asked the Light to keep explaining, I understood what the Higher Self matrix is. We have a grid around the planet where all the Higher Selves are connected. This is like a great company, a next subtle level of energy around us, the spirit level, you might say. Then, after a couple of minutes, I asked for more clarification. I really wanted to know what the universe is about, and I was ready to go at that time. I said "I am ready take me." Then the Light turned into the most beautiful thing that I have ever seen: a mandala of human souls on this planet.

We are all prismatic refractions of the equation of civi-
lization. – Argisle

Now I came to this with my negative view of what happens on the planet. So as I asked the Light to keep clarifying for me, I saw in this magnificent mandala how beautiful we all are in our essence, our core. We are the most beautiful creations. The human soul, the human matrix that we all make together is absolutely fantastic, elegant, exotic, everything. I just cannot say enough about how it changed my opinion of human beings in that instant.

I said, "Oh, God, I did not know how beautiful we are." At any level, high or low, in whatever shape you are in, you are the most beautiful creation, you are. I was astonished to find that there was no evil in any soul. I said, "How can this be?" The answer was that no soul was inherently evil. The terrible things that happened to people might make them do evil things, but their souls were not evil. What all people seek, what sustains them, is love, the Light told me. What distorts people is a lack of love.

The revelations coming from the Light seemed to go on and on, and then I asked the Light, *"Does this mean that humankind will be saved?"* Then, like a trumpet blast with a shower of spiraling lights, the Great Light spoke, saying, "Remember this and never forget; you save, redeem and heal yourself. You always have. You always will. You were created with the power to do so from before the beginning of the world."

In that instant I realized even more. I realized that WE HAVE ALREADY BEEN SAVED, and we saved ourselves because we were designed to self-correct like the rest of God's universe. This is what the second coming is about. I thanked the Light of God with all my heart. The best thing I could come up with was these simple words of totally appreciation: *"Oh dear God, dear Universe, dear great Self, I love my Life."* The Light seemed to breathe me in even more deeply. It was as if the Light was completely absorbing me. The Love Light is, to this day, indescribable. I entered into another realm, more profound than the last, and became aware of something more, much more. It was an enormous stream of Light, vast and full, deep in the Heart of Life. I asked what it was, the Light responded, *"This is the RIVER OF LIFE. Drink of this manna/water to your heart's content."* So I did. I took one big drink and then another. To drink of Life Itself! I was in ecstasy.

Then the Light said, "You have a desire." The Light knew all about me, everything past, present and future. "Yes!" I whispered. I asked to see the rest of the Universe; beyond our solar system, beyond all human illusion. The Light then told me that I could go with the Stream. I did, and was carried through the Light at the end of the tunnel. I felt and heard a series of very soft sonic booms. What a rush!

Don't wait for light at the end of the tunnel, take your light with you always. – C.W. Washington

THE VOID OF NOTHINGNESS

Suddenly I seemed to be rocketing away from the planet on this stream of Life. I saw the Earth fly away. The solar system, in its entire splendor, whizzed by and disappeared. At faster than light speed, I flew through the center of the galaxy, absorbing more knowledge as I went. I learned that this galaxy and all, of the Universe, is bursting with many different varieties of LIFE. I saw many worlds. The good news is that we are not alone in this Universe!

As I rode this stream of consciousness through the center of the galaxy, the stream was expanding in awesome fractal waves of energy. The super clusters of galaxies with all their ancient wisdom flew by. At first I thought I was going somewhere; actually traveling. But then I realized that, as the stream was expanding, my own consciousness was also expanding to take in everything in the Universe! All creation passed by me. It was an unimaginable wonder! I Truly was a Wonder Child; a babe in Wonderland!

It seemed as if all the creations in the universe soared by me and vanished in a speck of Light. Almost immediately, a second Light appeared. It came from all sides, and was so different; a Light made up of more than every frequency in the Universe. I felt and heard several velvety sonic booms again. My consciousness, or being, was expanding to interface with the entire Holographic Universe and more.

As I passed into the second Light, the awareness came to me that I had just transcended the Truth. Those are the best words I have for it, but I will try to explain. As I passed into the second Light, I expanded beyond the First Light. I found myself in a profound stillness, beyond all silence. I could see or perceive FOREVER, beyond Infinity.

I was in the Void. I was in pre-creation, before the Big Bang. I had crossed over the beginning of time - the First Word - the First Vibration. I was in the Eye of Creation. I felt as if I was touching the Face of God. It was not a religious feeling. Simply I was at one with Absolute Life and Consciousness. When I say that I could see or perceive forever, I mean that I could experience all of creation generating itself. It was without beginning and without end. That's a mind-expanding thought, isn't it?

The images that even come close in human terms would be those created by supercomputers using fractal geometry equations. The ancients knew of this. They said Godhead periodically created new Universes by breathing out, and de-creating Universes by breathing in. These epochs were called Yugas. Modern science called this the Big Bang. I was in absolute, pure consciousness. I could see or perceive all the Big Bangs or Yugas creating and de-creating themselves. Instantly I entered into them all simultaneously. I saw that each and every little piece of creation has the power to create. It is very difficult to try to explain this. I am still speechless about this.

It took me years after I returned to assimilate any words at all for the Void experience. I can tell you this now; the Void is less than nothing, yet more than everything that is! The Void is absolute zero; chaos forming all possibilities. It is Absolute Consciousness; much more than even Universal Intelligence.

Where is the Void? I know. The Void is inside and outside everything. You, right now even while you live, are always inside and outside the Void simultaneously. You don't have to go anywhere or die to get there. The Void is the vacuum or nothingness between all physical manifestations. The SPACE between atoms and their components.

What the mystics call the Void is not a void. It is so full of energy, a different kind of energy that has created everything that we are. Everything since the Big Bang is vibration, from the first Word, which is the first vibration. The biblical "I am" really has a question mark after it. "I am - What am I?" So creation is God exploring God's Self through every way imaginable, in an ongoing, infinite exploration through every one of us. Through every piece of hair on your head, through every leaf on every tree, through every atom, God is exploring God's Self, the great "I am." I began to see that everything that is, is the Self, literally, your Self, my Self. Everything is the great Self. That is why God knows even when a leaf falls. That is possible because wherever you are is the center of the universe. Wherever any atom is, that is the center of the universe. There is God in that, and God in the Void. As I was exploring the Void and all the Yugas or creations, I was completely out of time and space as we know it. In this expanded state, I discovered that creation is about Absolute Pure Consciousness, or God, coming into the Experience of Life, as we know it. The Void itself is devoid of experience. It is pre-life, before the first vibration. Godhead is about more than Life and Death. Therefore there is even more than Life and Death to experience in the Universe! I was in the Void and I was aware of everything that has ever been created. Suddenly I wasn't me anymore. It was like I was looking out of God's eyes. I had become God. And suddenly I knew why every atom was, and I could see everything. The interesting point was that I went into the Void; I came back with this understanding that God is not there. God is here. That's what it is all about.

So this constant search of the human race to go and find God . . . God gave everything to us, everything is here - this is where it's at. And what we are into now is God's exploration of God through us. People are so busy trying to become God that they ought to realize that we are already God and God is becoming us. That's what it is really about. When I realized this, I was finished with the Void, and wanted to return to this creation, or Yuga. It just seemed like the natural thing to do. Then I suddenly came back through the second Light, or the Big Bang, hearing several more velvet booms. I rode the stream of consciousness back through all of creation, and what a ride it was! The super clusters of galaxies came through me with even more insights.

I passed through the center of our galaxy, which is a black hole. In its total energy configuration, the galaxy looked like a fantastic city of lights. All energy this side of the Big Bang is light. Every sub-atom, atom, star, planet, even consciousness itself is made of light and has a frequency and /or particle. Light is living stuff. Everything is made of light, even stones. So everything is alive. Everything is made from the Light of God; everything is very intelligent.

THE LIGHT OF LOVE

As I rode the stream on and on, I could eventually see a huge Light coming. I knew it was the First Light; the Higher Self Light Matrix of our solar system. Then the entire solar system appeared in the Light, accompanied by one of those velvet booms.

I saw that the solar system we live in is our larger, local body. This is our local body and we are much bigger than we imagine. I saw that the solar system is our body. I am a part of this, and the Earth is this great created being that we are, and we are the part of it that knows that it is. But we are only that part of it. We are not everything, but we are that part of it that knows that it is.

I could see all the energy that this solar system generates, and it is an incredible light show! I could hear the Music of the Spheres. Our solar system, as do all celestial bodies, generates a unique matrix of light, sound and vibratory energies. Advanced civilizations from the other star systems can spot life as we know it in the universe by the vibratory or energy matrix imprint. It is child's play. The Earth's Wonder Child (human beings) make an abundance of sound right now, like children playing in the backyard of the universe. I rode the stream directly in to the center of the Light. I felt embraced by the Light as it took me in with its breath again, followed by another soft sonic boom. I was in this great Light of Love with the stream of life flowing through me. I have to say again, it is the most loving, non-judgmental Light. It is the ideal parent for this Wonder Child.

"What now?" I wondered. The Light explained to me that there is no death; we are immortal beings. We have already been alive forever! I realized that we are part of a natural living system that recycles itself endlessly. I was never told that I had to come back. I just knew that I would. It was only natural, from what I had seen. I don't know how long I was with the Light, in human time. But there came a moment when I realized that all my questions had been answered and my return was near. When I say that all my questions were answered on the other side, I mean to say just that. All my questions have been answered. Every human has a different life and set of questions to explore. Some of our questions are Universal, but each of us is exploring this thing we call life in our own unique way. So is every other form of life, from mountains to every leaf on every tree. And that is very important to the rest of us in this Universe. Because it all contributes to the Big Picture, the fullness of Life.

We are literally God exploring God's Self in an infinite Dance of Life. Your uniqueness enhances all of Life. As I began my return to the life cycle, it never crossed my mind, nor was I told, that I would return to the same body. It just did not matter. I had complete trust in the Light and the Life process. As the stream merged with the great Light, I asked never to forget the revelations and the feelings of what I had learned on the other side. There was a "Yes." It felt like a kiss to my soul. Then I was taken back through the Light into the vibratory realm again. The whole process reversed, with even more information being given to me. I came back home, and I was given lessons on the mechanics of reincarnation. I was given answers to all those little questions I had: "How does this work? How does that work?" I knew that I would be reincarnated. The Earth is a great processor of energy, and individual consciousness evolves out of that into each one of us.

I thought of myself as a human for the first time, and I was happy to be that. From what I have seen, I would be happy to be an atom in this universe. An atom. So to be the human part of God . . . this is the most fantastic Blessing. It is a Blessing beyond our wildest estimation of what Blessing can be. For each and every one of us to be the human part of this experience is awesome, and magnificent. Each and every one of us, no matter where we are, screwed up or not, is a Blessing to the planet, right where we are.

So I went through the reincarnation process expecting to be a baby somewhere. But I was given a lesson on how individual identity and consciousness evolve. So I reincarnated back into this body. I was so surprised when I opened my eyes. I do not know why, because I understood it, but it was still such a surprise to be back in this body, back in my room with someone looking over me crying her eyes out. It was my hospice caretaker. She had given up an hour and a half after finding me dead. She was sure I was dead; all the signs of death were there - I was getting stiff.

We do not know how long I was dead, but we do know that it was an hour and a half since I was found. She honored my wish to have my newly dead body left alone for a few hours as much as she could. We had an amplified stethoscope and many ways of checking out the vital functions of the body to see what was happening. She can verify that I was really dead. It was not a near-death experience. I experienced death itself for at least an hour and a half. Then I awakened and saw the light outside. I tried to get up to go to it, but I fell out of the bed. She heard a loud "clunk," ran in and found me on the floor.

When I recovered, I was very surprised and yet very awed about what had happened to me. This world seemed more like a dream than that one. Within three days, I was feeling normal again, clearer, yet different than I ever felt in my life. My memory of the journey came back later. I could see nothing wrong with any human being I had ever seen. Before that I was really judgmental. I thought a lot of people were really screwed up, in fact I thought that everybody was screwed up but me. But I got clear on all that. About three months later a friend said I should get tested, so I went and got the scans and so forth. I remember the doctor at the clinic looking at the before and after scans, saying, "Well, there is nothing here now." I said, "Really, it must be a miracle?" He said, "No, these things happen, they are called spontaneous remission." He acted very unimpressed. But here was a miracle, and I was impressed, even if no one else was.

LESSONS HE LEARNED

The mystery of life has very little to do with intelligence. The universe is not an intellectual process at all. The intellect is helpful; it is brilliant, but right now that is all we process with, instead of our hearts and the wiser part of ourselves. Let us come to our senses.

The mind is like a child running around the universe, demanding this and thinking it created the world. But I asked the mind: "What did your mother have to do with this?" That is the next level of spiritual awareness. "Oh! my mother! All of a sudden you give up the ego, because you are not the only soul in the universe.

Since my return I have experienced the Light spontaneously, and I have learned how to get to that space almost any time in my meditation. Each one of you can also do this. You do not have to die first. You are wired for it already. The body is the most magnificent Light being there is. The body is a universe of incredible Light. Spirit is not pushing us to dissolve this body. This is not what is happening. Stop trying to become God. God is becoming you here.

The center of the Earth is this great transmuter of energy, just as you see in pictures of our Earth's magnetic field. That's our cycle; pulling reincarnated souls back in and through it again. A sign that you are reaching human level is that you are beginning to evolve an individual consciousness. Just being born a human, whether deformed or genius shows that you are on the path to developing an individual consciousness. That is in itself part of the group consciousness called humanity.

Individual identity is evolving like branches of a fractal; the group soul explores in our individuality. The different questions that each of us has are very important. This is how Godhead is exploring God's Self - through you. God is expanding itself through us. So ask your questions, do your searching. You will find your Self and you will find God in that Self, because it is only the Self. More than that, I began to see that each one of us humans is a soul mate. We are part of the same soul fractaling out in many creative directions, but still the same. Now I look at every human being that I ever see, and I see a soul mate, my soul mate, the one I have always been looking for. Beyond that, the greatest soul mate that you will ever have is yourself. We are both male and female. We experience this in the womb and we experience this in reincarnation states. If you are looking for that ultimate soul mate outside of yourself, you may never find it; it is not there.

Just as God is not "there." God is here. Don't look "out there" for God. Look here for God. Look through your Self. Start having the greatest love affair you ever had . . . with your Self. You will love everything out of that.

I had a descent into what you might call hell, and it was very surprising. I did not see satan or evil. My descent into hell was a descent into each person's customized human misery, ignorance and darkness of knowing. It seemed like a miserable eternity. But each of the millions of souls around me had a little Star of Light always available. But no one seemed to pay attention to it. They were so consumed with their own grief, trauma and misery. But, after what seemed an eternity, I started calling out to that Light, like a child calling to a parent for help.

Then the Light opened up and formed a tunnel that came right to me and insulated me from all that fear and pain. That is what hell really is. So what we are doing is learning to hold hands, to come together. The doors of hell are open now. We are going to link up, hold hands, and walk out of hell together. The Light came to me and turned into a huge golden angel. I said, "Are you the angel of death?" It expressed to me that it was my oversoul, my Higher Self matrix, a super-ancient part of ourselves. Then I was taken to the Light.

I went over to the other side with a lot of fears about toxic waste, nuclear missiles, the population explosion, the rainforest. I came back loving every single problem. I love nuclear waste. I love the mushroom cloud; this is the holiest mandala that we have manifested to date, as an archetype. More than any religion or philosophy on Earth, that terrible, wonderful cloud brought us together all of a sudden, to a new level of consciousness.

What happens when we dream? We are multi-dimensional beings. We can access that through lucid dreaming. In fact, this universe is God's dream. One of the things that I saw is that we humans are a speck on a planet that is a speck in a galaxy that is a speck. Those are giant systems out there, and we are in sort of an average system. But human beings are already legendary throughout the cosmos of consciousness.

One of the things that we are legendary for is dreaming. In fact, the whole cosmos has been looking for the meaning of life, the meaning of it all. And it was the little dreamer who came up with the best answer ever. We dreamed it up. So dreams are important. After dying and coming back, I really respect life and death. Soon we will be able to live as long as we want to live in this body. However, living forever in one body is not as creative as reincarnation, as transferring energy in this fantastic vortex of energy that we are in. We are actually going to see the wisdom of life and death, and enjoy it. As it is now, we have already been alive forever.

Mellen-Thomas Benedict's story is so powerful because, as we know, we do not have truth, we are truth; and the truth is, there is only the One. There is always infinite abundance. If we are the One, which we are because there is only the One, and we are infinite abundance, then how could we not have all the space we need for everything in our lives? The only way we could be lacking space, our true nature, is if we have robbed ourselves of it by giving our attention to filling ourselves up with the crap we are here to leave behind. Or as Benedict says it *"Be careful what your world view is."* If it sounds limiting, looks limiting, tastes limiting and smells limiting, just walk away from it!

Happy unconditional expansion to you, folks! As realizing, liberating and celebrating the collective inner space is a complete action, it is truly the final frontier!

Chapter Nine

Perception Is A Choice

There is but One, there is always infinite abundance

Perception is the magic carpet that either elevates us into Heaven or plummets us into hell. Perception is how we behold the divine in everything and everyone, or how the relentlessly tight grasp of hell demolishes us. Perception is a gift of free will from Heaven. Where we focus our attention determines whether we freely return perception to its rightful place, Heaven, or whether we surrender it to hell. We choose on a moment-to-moment basis.

We do not choose according to our experiences or what our parents may have taught us. Nor do we choose according to how much money we have. We choose according to our Ruling Love, because it is our Ruling Love that creates our experiences. It is what we are giving our attention to that determines the outcome of what we have learned here. It is what we do with our love that is our true wealth, security, and happiness.

To illustrate the power of perception, consider the story of two children who grew up with alcoholic parents. One child grew up to be a teetotaler. The other child grew up to be an alcoholic. When asked why they chose the path that they did, they both gave the same response, "With parents like that, what else could I be?"

Dr. Phil McGraw, on his television program, *The Dr. Phil Show*, uses an interesting technique while working with a guest. He directly addresses the person's perception of self. Dr. Phil will walk the person through a complete examination of their perception. One of his guests was re-creating great turmoil within the family due to deliberate, insensitive overspending of the family's financial resources. Dr. Phil walked this person through her perceptual trap. He explained to her that when she is driving around, and it hits her to go the mall and shop, she should stop and shift perception instead to something more life-sustaining, such as spending time with her kids and spouse, or going to the gym and doing something nice for her body. Dr. Phil explains that each person has sovereignty over his/her perception. So if life, relationships or anything else is not working for you, then you and only you can shift your perception to something that does work.

All of our suffering is held together by our perception, or mis-perception of self and *what is*. Right relationship with perception is an inner event. It happens in the Heart, not the head. Right relationship with perception has nothing to do with the body's physical visual ability. Perception based on what we think and believe, based on the projections of mind we are here to get over, is the basis of mis-perception or polluted thinking. Unrealized waves are coming from the head and not the Heart, so the perception of self and *what is* becomes highly distorted and extremely limiting. All unrealized waves perceive no hope, no possibility for growth, no good faith in life and love in their story about *what is*. That is why the wave is unrealized; it has not realized the true nature of mind and reality, and the perfect divinity of *what is*.

Once again, that is why the third rock from the Sun is here, so that we as spiritual creatures have a place to come to practice right relationship with perception. This is *the place* in the universe to come and practice realizing what you are doing with your attention, because this is where we *feel* it. Having to feel the quality of our perceptions is the lesson we came here for. Most of us re-create very confining, perceptual stories that keep us living narrow and severely restricted lives, compared to our potential as God conscious made manifest. Most of us live our perceptual lives within "the box" of duality. Perception is like a stamped envelope. We could perceptually live on the envelope that has the potential to go anywhere at anytime. But instead we choose perceptually to live on the stamp, and we let the "stamped perception" define our value, power and worth and tell us where we can go and when. How does one free oneself from a limiting perception that one is not even aware is holding them hostage?

The following is a delightful story about an old frog who lived in a dark well, who is visited by an old frog who lived in the ocean. This story is from Sogyal Rinpoche's book *The Tibetan Book of Living and Dying*:

"Where do you come from?" asked the frog in the well.
"From the great ocean," he replied.
"How big is your ocean?"
"It's gigantic."
"You mean about a quarter of the size of my well here?"
"Bigger."
"Bigger? You mean half as big?"
"No, even bigger."
"Is it . . . as big as this well?"
"There is no comparison."
"That's impossible! I've got to see this for myself."

They set off together. When the frog from the well saw the ocean, it was such a shock that his head just exploded into pieces.

We are just like the old well frog. We are so familiar with living in the dark hole of our perceptions - that we are the body, money, experiences, thoughts and emotions, all things limited - that when confronted with the truth that we are in fact love, that we are in fact God conscious-ness realizing itself, our head just explodes into a million pieces.

The good news is that it is not up to the government, it is not up to large corporations, it is not up to your family or co-workers to create a life worth living from the power of right relationship with perception. It is up to you. No one can eat for you. No one can sleep for you. No one can breathe for you. And no one can watch your mind for you. No one else can shift your perception from temporal to eternal, from lies to truth, except you. You re-created all your limiting perceptions. Therefore only you can create an ending to these limitations. It is up to you, and what you are freely giving your attention to on a moment-to-moment basis. No matter where you go or what you do, you cannot escape the truth: *you are what you love and you love whatever you are giving your attention to.*

Perception is as unique and imaginative as whatever you are giving your attention to and choose to love. You cannot change your life for the better without changing your out-dated illusions. You cannot change your outdated illusions without changing what you are giving your attention to. Perception . . . Change . . . Growth. They are all perceptual choices. The illusory perception tree produces only illu-sory fruit. You will find nothing life-sustaining there, only the un-ripe fruit of greater disappointment.

We have all experienced the magical healing qualities of perception. Everyone has met someone for the first time that initially did not appear very attractive. However, over time you see and share their Ruling Love, and you grow to deeply love the person as authentically beautiful. Historically speaking Quasimodo and the elephant-man are perfect examples of this.

You also know the opposite. You meet someone who appears in the temporal world to be very attractive. But over time you see their real Ruling Love. They are strongly loyal to hell and inflicting pain. When this happens, the initial illusory perception falls away and the other person is then seen for the true ugliness that they give their attention to. It is then that we honestly perceive the deformed nature of the other. It is the Ruling Love of each wave that ultimately determines our perception of ugly or beauty in ourselves, and everything and everyone around us.

You are your perception. Not just physically or mentally, but emotionally as well as metaphorically. **The ultimate goal of all self-witnessing, and the purpose behind all of created reality, is to master clear perception.** Divine intelligence has given us all free will in our use of perception. You choose your perception and you are One with your choice. Due to the divine law that *you are what you love and you love whatever you are giving your attention to*, everything in this world is going to continue to go out of its way to keep you honest about what you are doing with your love. Contemplate this the next time your perception informs you that you have no value, power or worth. Not exactly a program you want repeated on the "inner syndicated" airwaves.

To establish right divine relationship with perception, look back to Swedenborg. When he was alive, people would ask him, *"What do you do to be an such an actualized person?"* Swedenborg would tell them, *"It has nothing to do with doing. It is not a doing thing."* It is a remembering to give attention to truth, and forget everything else, it is a perceptual thing.

To *Be* or Not to *Be* in the Present Moment

The world at large values, even worships *doing.* The world perceives *doing* as the highest purpose of all created life. We reflect that perception back to ourselves in our language. We ask children, "What do you want to do when you grow up?" The first bit of information we get from people we meet for the first time is, "What do you do for a living?" We have a bad habit of measuring our happiness by what we can or cannot *do.* We perceive advancing age with great fear of all the things we may lose the ability to *do.* We as individuals, as a nation, as a planet, love giving endless attention to *doing* and the value of *doing.* Anyone who has ever spent more than five minutes in America knows that America worships productivity. In America if you do not work unrealistically hard at *doing* something, if you are not *producing,* you are dead weight. Goals and quotas are the name of the game, and your worth is only as good as the last thing you produced.

Being Simple – Simply Being. – Argisle

The Eastern perception of mind, Ayurvedic psychology and Taoism, suggest a completely different perception on *doing.* These masters suggest that *being* is a higher state of mind than *doing.* Being in the present moment with an open Heart is the very purpose and nature of mind

dreaming itself in a material arena. We are human beings not human doings. Nothing will ultimately work for
us until we surrender to *being* here now. These ancient
philosophies indicated that there is a way to stop all the
problems, limitations, struggles and suffering. There is a
way to simply end these in our lives. There is a way to create a final resolution to the on-going drama. How? *To be.*
The instant we are willing to be with *what is* in the present moment, we are in the feeling place, the Heart, not
the doing place, the head. This is a self-corrective place,
the place where the human and the divine become One.

Ayurveda and Taoism warn us that all of the most menac-
ing acts against life and love have happened in the name
of defending what we think and believe, and in the name
of *doing.* Why did Hitler do what he did? To become the
next world leader, of course! Why did Charles Manson
do what he did? To lead what he thought and believed
was the next Cultural Revolution. Why do large corporations squeeze the lifeblood out of their employees, and
then fire them when their bodies cannot keep up with the
pressure? Why do they replace these loyal workers with
someone half their age at half the salary? It is done in the
name of productivity - becoming more work efficient
and cost effective. That is all that matters. It is truly an
ugly attack on equability. This vicious cycle of ignorance
and pain will unendingly feed upon itself until the *doing*
perception is broken.

We have discussed at length the disease of duality. This
disease infects our perception. Once the disease enters
mind through the doorway of perception, it then immediately infects the frontal lobe with deep loyalty to
subject/object orientation. I am over here - the subject.
And everything not me is the object. A wave must be

giving attention to duality; it must love subject/object in order to have developed such a strong and abiding love for *doing*. In order to *do* there must be a *you* to start the action, and an object in order for the "doing" action to become complete. If there were no subject/object, no duality, there would be no love for *doing* or *doing to become*. Instead everything would simply be about *being* here now.

No wave can serve two masters. A wave cannot be giving attention to *being* and *doing* at the same time. The Eastern studies of mind say that *being* is One with eternal consciousness. *Doing* is one with the ego. The ego wants, needs to *do*. Without *doing* how could the ego tyrannize you with *not good enough* and *did not do it right? Doing* is how we define our value, power and worth. *Doing* is the camouflage we wear to distract us from how we are treating other people. After all, isn't getting the job done more important than how we treat others and ourselves in the process? *Doing* is the doorway to hell that comparison and judgment charge right through. We have trained the ego that we will rely on *doing* to define our identity. The ego will decide according to when and how the *doing* gets done what value, power and worth we are allowed to accept, if any. *Doing* gets more of our attention than sex. There is something just not right about that.

Doing to become is our very most beloved demon of destruction. If the purpose of life were *doing to become,* then every workaholic in the history of mankind would have reached enlightenment by now. But as we have all noticed, it does not happen that way. No one could produce enough temporal anything to evolve their way into an eternal place like Heaven. We did not come here to *do* things to our mind. We came here to *be* with our mind.

We did not come here to *do* things to our relationships. We came here to *be* with our relationships. It is in *being* with *what is* in the present moment with an open Heart that true enlightenment is realized. Jesus did not come to the planet to model *doing* for us. He came here to model being with *what is* in the present moment with an open Heart. He came here to model an inner space of complete innocence from any thought or belief.

In the life of the historical Buddha, when he left home, he scaled the walls of the palace leaving behind his wife, children and his parents, the King and Queen. The Buddha set forth upon a path of *full awakening*. The journey he set upon had nothing to do with *doing*. That is what he left behind. That is the false king he would not serve. This is the first thing he separated from his attention. The Buddha's path was about *being* fully awake, not *doing* to become fully awake. The famous Tibetan Buddhist master Sogyal Rinpoche says it like this, *"When you realize the nature of mind, layers of confusion peel away. You don't actually "become" a buddha, you simply cease, slowly to be deluded."*

Sure there are plenty of meditations to *do* to expand mind. Look at Buddhism with all those orange clad guys with shaved heads. Like Jimmy Durante use to say, "I got a million of 'em." However, if you are not in the present moment with an open Heart, while you are giving your attention to the meditation, then you are not meditating. You are fooling yourself. You're dressing duality up as the higher practice of meditation. Without alignment with the right quality of consciousness, it is the performance of a stupid human trick. It is all hand waving and vanity.

Do not let the voice of limitation convince you that you

need to *do* something in order to grow spiritually. As God consciousness, you do not have growth, you are growth. Instead, simply remind yourself to *be* a force of love right here, right now. The inner critic will never admit that you do not have love, you are love. It will only try to trick you into earning love by *doing* things good enough, as opposed to *doing* things the lame and incompetent way.

So what would life on Earth look like if we all let go of our attachments to *doing?* The first thing the ego would have you believe is that everything in the temporal world would suddenly be on a highway to hell. That is utter B.S. Look at the life of Jesus. The miracles, healings, turning water into wine and pulling fish and loaves of bread from inner space manifested when Jesus aligned his attention with *being One.* He was not focused on *doing* things in order to become abundant, he was simply engaged with *being* infinitely abundant in the present moment with an open Heart. The ego, when zeroed in on *doing,* robs us of the power to *be* here now; to manifest as pure God consciousness in a body.

Lax is not the same as Relax – Argisle

Instead of being God, being present, being perfect, being happy, the ego tricks us into thinking we need to *do* something in order to achieve these states of mind. Don't you just love it. **The voice of pure limitation is going to tell us what we have to do in order to have something we already are!** If the charge in your wave is that you have to *do* things to be God, to be perfect, happy, or fully supported, then you will be caught in an endless cycle of *doing.* You are robbing yourself of knowing you already are these qualities and states of mind, right now in this and every present moment.

You do not have love, you are love. Therefore you do not need to *do* any activities in order to deserve love. You do not need to *do* anything in order to become these eternal states of mind. You are these eternal states of mind. Always have been. If you are not presently experiencing the truth of this, then you are presently experiencing the stuff you are here to get over.

Everything in the physical world is here to help us perceive honestly what we are doing with our love. If we are not agreeing to give attention to what Heaven loves, then we are openly and freely choosing alignment with what is not life sustaining. We are *doing* this whether we consciously realize it or not.

The Complete Action of *Being* vs. The Incomplete Action of *Doing*

By focusing on *doing* we are sabotaging *being* One with acceptance, happiness, creativity, and surrender. And, of course, we are ultimately destroying our relationship with Heaven. There is no *doing* in Heaven, only *being*. In Heaven all action is complete, a result of *being* not *doing*. All actions are complete when they occur naturally from a state of being One with the truth in the present moment. If we wish for our Earthly actions to have Heavenly effects, we must complete all actions by being present with an open Heart. Not *doing* the gyrations and contortions of the tiny temporal tyranny master.

Doing is an incomplete action. It has to be repeated. You do not eat one meal that lasts your entire life. (You probably can't even eat just one potato chip, not to mention all that "doing" would make anyone hungry.) You must repeat that incomplete action until you leave the rock.

You do not get dressed only once in a lifetime. That action is determined by the ego. It is incomplete and therefore destined to be repeated. In hell, there is a constant unending *doing*. That is re-creation. *Doing* is incomplete and ultimately ineffectual, because it is all done with no attention, no love given to being present.

So how would things get done in the material world if we all focus on *being* with *what is* in the present moment with an open Heart? First, all violence would end. All conflict would end. This would allow us to finally be able to interact with each other without behaving destructively. No one would be giving their attention to thoughts and beliefs. Everyone would be loving and trusting.

Things in the world can get *done and accomplished* only when we are in our Hearts where we can feel. We have to feel what actions require completing from the place where the human and divine meet: in our Hearts, not our heads. Only in the Heart can we make the necessary connection to manifest a complete action. As we have seen over and over again, our thoughts and beliefs will not help us in that arena. Thoughts and beliefs will only result in an incomplete action.

Look at the life of Jesus. Does Jesus have a reputation for not completing his life's work? Examine the historical Buddha's life. Is there a commentary on a life that is incomplete in any way? If we all lived like enlightened beings how could everything just fall apart? If we all felt from our Hearts what correct action was needed in our lives, how then could the world ever fall into complete and utter chaos?' That kind of crazy making perception does not happen in the life of enlightened beings. Instead of chasing duality in the head, they are living a life of complete action as directed by the wisdom of the Heart.

Complete action from *being,* not *doing* occurs when we are involved in an activity or process. When we find ourselves one with the moment, there is no concept of time, self, or of the stories we are loyal to running. There is simply direct contact with *what is.* All of us have had an experience of this complete action void of *doing.* Reflect on a time when your awareness was completely engaged in an action. You were not aware of time while one with the project. You were not aware of that back pain. You were not focused on what bills you have not paid or how much you hate the ex-husband/wife. When you looked up to see what time it was, you were shocked to see how much time had passed. All you were aware of was the project you were focused on. You were just being in the moment. Innocent. Without a zillion thoughts and beliefs cluttering your mind. It is all simply one action separate from any concept of an individual self, of a *me* that is *doing* the action. There is no *doer* of the action. There is only *being.* There is only a sense of being One with *what is* in the present moment with an open Heart.

Have you ever wondered why you constantly go around and around with some people? Why do some problems in life have no resolution without conflict or difficulty? Each time we *do* something that will fix a problem we are now no longer available for *being* present for what the real problem might be. Giving attention to *doing* something and giving attention to *being* present are opposing movements of mind. When we love being present, we also love giving attention to the truth, which in turn makes us happy, because they are all One. Instead of *doing* to become, we surrender to loving to *be* present. Being present for our mind is what we came here for. That is a complete action. Every complete action contains all the fruitional energy we need to manifest resolution instead of repetition.

The ego can only move the wave into *doing,* an incomplete action. Incomplete action only realizes and empowers the disease of duality deeper and deeper into the wave. It does not give the realization and empowerment of the One. Being present is beyond *doing.* Being in the present moment with an open Heart is love completing the action. What have we learned so far? That only love has the power to complete an action. Not the ego. Not anything temporal. Not your loyalty to duality. When love completes an action, it is whole, complete, perfect, lacking in nothing.

In the same manner that the ego uses ultimate lies to distract our attention from the truth, the ego also uses *doing* to distract our attention from *being.* How can you tell if you are coming from the limitation of *doing* or from *being* in alignment with love? Simple. You know a tree by its fruit. Is your movement through life creating ever-increasing self-witnessing, self-realizing actions that reduce the suffering, difficulty, effort and angst? Do you perceive the movement of mind, of the One, in everyone and everything? Or, is your movement through life fraught with subject/object perception, frustration, anger, resentment, depression, worry, or unhappiness?

You do not have the truth, you are the truth. You *can* tell which tree is producing which fruit. The only thing holding incomplete *doing* in our lives is the perception that we need it. We think that the only way we are going to solve our problems is by building a monument to *doing* with our attention. This is a lie in perception. Only by being conscious of what we are giving our attention to can we realize that this is not the truth. *Doing* is the illusion, the disease, the limited habit we have all come here to discard and replace with real happiness.

Responsibility, Perception and The Ego

Mr. teenie, tiny temporal consciousness, our own personal "mini-me," would have us believe that we need to poison perception with duality, with subject/object, as well as *doing,* in order to maintain and fulfill all of the many responsibilities we have here in life. It is a lie. Just another load of *crap* from the bad boy of the frontal lobe. What a surprise! It is essential in dismantling this lie to ask, "What did I come here to honestly be responsible for?" No one came here to be responsible for saving the world. The world is already perfect. Always has been. Always will be.

The rock is perfectly reflecting everything we need to realize in order to get over all limitation. The world is perfect as are all the very capable life forms on it. Equability is the first law for any successful outcome. We must perceive everyone as equally capable as ourselves. When we believe the world requires our skills alone in order to save it, then we have made ourselves superior to everyone else. The world is perfect. If you are not experiencing that, then "mini-me" has got you by the balls.

The ego will pollute perception with the lie that we are here to give more attention and love to empowering illusion. The ego convinces us that we are not doing it right. That we are substandard in the responsibility department; *not good enough.* We should be making more money, working more hours, and playing less. To the detriment of the physical body, we convince ourselves we need to make bigger and larger investments in the stuff we are here to get over.

"Be still and know you are God!" That adage is the ego's worst nightmare. The ego convinces us that we are irresponsible if we do not work ourselves to death with *doing*. Of course, with all the *doing* the inner critic tells us we are responsible for, there will be no space for love, happiness, relationships, or for being in the present moment with an open Heart. We will have pissed away our God juice by performing a never-ending cycle of stupid human tricks for Asmodeus, without even knowing it!

Right now you are probably asking yourself, "So what am I responsible for?" We are responsible for whatever we are giving our love to and the process that puts our wave through. Period. End of truth. We are responsible for showing up for the evolution of our soul with an open Heart. We are responsible for befriending our mind. We are responsible for ending our loyalty with anything that lives in hell. We are responsible for creating Heaven on Earth with our Ruling Love. We are responsible for practicing living like a good resident of Heaven.

In practical everyday life, it boils down to this: if Heaven has given you a beautiful home, health, family, a nice car, or job, be happy, be grateful. When Heaven is generous, accept the gifts with grace and gratitude, don't complain. If all you do as a response to these gifts is project worry, or fear that "I cannot maintain this, that I am not deserving, *not good enough*," then you are willfully, albeit unconsciously, mastering the practice of turning Heaven into hell, and you will find nothing useful there.

How Perception Gets Distorted Or "You Say You Want a Revolution"... Better Free Your Mind Instead!

The average unrealized wave is addicted to polluting and to bringing disease into perception. Think not? Just look inward. Examine your perception about your temporal body or your life. Most people have incredible judgments and criticisms about both. If you are having a female experience this time around, you know there is a very strong karmic pattern in America to give attention to relentless brutal physical comparison. In the name of beauty, the body is also held to unrealistic and unhealthy standards.

Anorexia is becoming more and more common. It is a disease that starts with the perception that the person is too fat. The perception dictates the need to lose weight in order to be attractive and valuable. As anorexia progresses the person slowly starves to achieve a stark and skeletal standard of beauty and self-control. Anorexia is a perfect illustration of how perception becomes diseased, twisted by focusing on a non-life sustaining story. A starving anorexic person can look at their physical form in a mirror and not even see the bag of bones, close to death, they have become. Instead they see obesity!?!

"I cannot stand to look at myself in a mirror without clothes. My body is ugly. I am fat. Unlovable. I am not good enough. Other people are so perfect. Why can't I be like them? No one could ever love this body, so no one will ever love me." Is any of this sounding the least bit familiar?

It sounds limiting, kind of like hell, doesn't it? Guess who

Many of us give our attention to an inner dialog
that sounds like, "My body would be OK, if only I
didn't have:

1. A flat chest

2. A beak for a nose

3. These ten extra pounds

4. This hair

5. Big feet

is giving you that information? Guess who is contaminating a most important and intimate relationship that awareness has with the physical body? Guess who needs unhappiness to stay alive? Not the IRS. No, not the federal government. No, it is not your mother-in-law. Not your insurance carrier. Well, on second thought, those are good answers. They are just not 100% correct, but you get the picture. Could the source of all this limitation be the ego?

Right Perception Is A Choice

The Eastern self-healing sciences have a completely different perception about the body. The body is actually another being, a temporal being. You are an eternal being. The temporal being you are presently living with knows only unconditional love for you. The Eastern perception is to remember that the physical body is the best friend you will ever know. It does not leave you. You leave the body. When you are giving attention to anything limited such as fear, worry or bad faith, then you are not consciously residing in the body. You are not grounded or present. You get in the habit of energetically abandoning the body every time the ego rattles your chain.

The truth is that you are not your body. This means that when the body gets ill or injured it is the body that goes through the illness or injury not you. That is why in this book we refer to it as *the* body, not *your* body. Your awareness is engaged in an intimate relationship with the experience of having a body. You are closely aware on a feeling level, via the nervous system, of what the body is going through. It is the body, however, that is going through it. You are the witness of what the body is going through. You are neither the body nor the body's limitations or history.

The Eastern perspective requires us to remember that the body loves us so much it would go through whatever we need to experience in order to reach enlightenment. The body goes through pain, hunger, torture, disease, mutilation, fad diets, even bad hair days, and ultimately death. What is eternal cannot die. The body is designed to willingly, unconditionally go through whatever we need to experience, because it loves us that much.

Examining your life's relationships: spouse, children, parents, and friends. How many of them will stay with you in this life until the very end? How many would unconditionally take on any suffering, any pain imaginable or unimaginable if it were ultimately in your highest and best interest? Probably none. Yet look at how we perceive our great compassionate loving life-long body-friend. We perceive our body-friend with disdain, impatience, and criticism, a truly shallow and unrealized relationship. No wonder so many people betray their body with food and substance abuse. They have no love for their body as a great friend and companion.

Most unrealized waves unwittingly value *doing* and *productivity* over the relationship with the body-friend. This is conveyed through unending thoughts and beliefs, "Come on you stupid, ugly, body. Let's get going. There is no time or support for you to feel bad or get ill. We've got places to go, people to see, work to do! We've got to keep up with the ego's demanding schedule." We constantly give attention to our stories of why we cannot accept what is happening with our body. We rarely, if ever, maintain any dialog of gratitude for this completely altruistic friend.

When we get ill, how many of us say to the body, *"Look, body-friend, whatever you need I will provide for you. If you need to rest, I will call work and take a sick day. Feel free to take as much time as you need. You need exercise and clean, pure food and water daily. I will do whatever is needed to provide you with the best, because body-friend you are so good to me. I wish to bring equability to this relationship. Thank you body-friend for working tirelessly for my highest and best interest. Thank you for life-long assistance in liberating the wave."* As Buddhism tells us, the first quality of mind required for any successful outcome is equability and gratitude.

Most unrealized waves threaten the body everyday, "Come on body, there is no time to rest or eat well or exercise, so keep going, and if you do require attention beyond getting the hair, nails, and cosmetic surgery done, forget it . . . there will be no time or money for you. I just drag you around, to do what I want. There will be no consideration for your needs" . . . a very pathetic, ego driven relationship with the greatest, most devoted, loyal friend we will ever experience in this life.

All we have to do to get right with the body is to change our perception of the body *as less than, inferior, not good enough,* and embrace the unconditional love that has been there for us all along. After all, perception is a choice. Sounds simple, doesn't it? Just practice it for yourself. Make separation from this demeaning habit of belittling the body. You will begin to realize the hold that this perception actually has over your wave. It is like a rubber band. It requires a lot of conscious practice to break the memory. If not, it just snaps habitually back to critical business as usual.

Exorcising The Demons of Hell From Perception

On an everyday practical level, this means that we do not ever again use the words, *didn't do it right,* and *not good enough* with respect to ourselves or any other living be-ing. We shift perception to a world where we no longer empower these terms with our love, ever again. We know that both of these lines of discourse are a lie. They imply that this moment is not perfect and that somehow we could create learning experiences that we do not need. These lies imply that divine love and wisdom are no lon-ger the senior intelligence determining everything. These are the roots of all our suffering. These perceptual lies are the very foundation and building blocks of hell itself. And we've all probably used these terms, these "build-ing blocks," enough times to build a four bedroom, three bath home complete with a swimming pool and hot tub - our exclusive personal estate in hell's private subdivi-sion. And you won't see that on *Lifestyles of the Rich and Famous,* but you may catch it on *Inner Lifestyles of the Unenlightened and Unhappy.*

Did not do it right and *not good enough* are never heard, spoken, felt, or experienced in Heaven. In Heaven, *equability* is embodied and experienced as One with Ultimate Truth. As Swedenborg so elegantly phrased it over two hundred years ago, "In order in live in Heaven, you must first be of Heaven." Any time we give attention or love to *didn't do it right,* and *not good enough,* we are wielding hell's most powerful sword. These are the magic perceptual words needed to immediately invoke hell upon the planet. Anyone who utters these words, anyone who wields this sword, shall also die by this sword. For *as it is above, so it is below, as it is within, so it is without.* That is the law of karma, the cause and effect governing a world that is really the story of our unrealized mind being reflected back to itself. So whatever you have done to another, you have done to yourself - what goes around, comes around. Or, as that famous philosopher Pee Wee Herman likes to say, "I know you are, but what am I?

The trauma we experience when we are told that we *did not do it right* or that we are *not good enough* is nature's way of saying, "You are using the inappropriate form of consciousness now." Do we listen, or do we simply give more attention to what we think and believe it all means? Do we add yet one more brick to the wall in the construction of a living hell? That would be the misguided practice of a life that is not worth living.

We all have to create a new response to life minus this crutch. Watch what happens the moment you remove these lies as an option for your attention. You will discover an untapped region of self-honesty awaiting you. When you remove these lies, you will have to get real about what is really bothering you. You will have to take accountability for honestly sharing your feelings, without hiding behind the disease of duality. As Dr. Phil is so fond of saying, *"You will have to stop complaining and start speaking what your needs are."* It may not seem like it now, but removing this diseased facade is a great gift to any wave.

So how might this play out in our every day life? Ladies, suppose you are feeling suffering as a result of a relationship that is not fair. Most of you ladies will not have to really stretch your imagination to see this one, but try. If you are in a relationship where you are doing most of the cleaning, cooking, and household management duties, you want to talk with your partner about the lack of equability, but you do not know how without blasting the other person off the planet with *didn't do it right, not good enough.*

Instead of starting with the reason your partner *didn't do it right,* and is *not good enough,* try starting the conversation with some truth. "Honey, I have a problem that I am hoping you can help me resolve. I am not feeling good about this relationship; I am concerned about my feelings that this is not a healthy relationship for me to be in; I am hurt and disturbed by the unequal division of labor in the relationship; I feel that my time, value and happiness are not considered as important as yours; I'm hoping that you can help; I feel like I am handed the role of "disposable" in this relationship, while you sit back and watch me work twice as hard as you. Would it be all right with you if the roles were reversed, and you had to deal with an unequal division of labor? If it is not all right for you to have the majority of the work, why is it okay when I end up with the bulk of the labor? I am hoping that my feeling good about this relationship is as critical to you as your practice of leaving all of the work for me to do."

Notice that almost every sentence started with *I*, not with finger pointing or making the other inferior. Each of us must cease our contribution to the "blame game" and step forward and honestly begin to speak the truth of what is going on in our Hearts. We must reconcile our differences by sharing what is really going on inside of us, instead of what is wrong with someone else. If you feel the situation is not balanced, say so without destroying the truth that no one here can create a learning experience that they do not need. Once you take *didn't do it right, not good enough* out of your life, you will be free to speak your truth. Imagine how much more effective communication will be when you can break away from symptoms and get down to the real issues.

Our Ruling Love Determines Our Perception Even In Death

The process of thinking and believing one's way through life makes perception very rigid and inflexible. The Eastern sciences of mind suggest that it is this unresolved, unreleased hardness and heaviness in our wave's perception that keeps us trapped in the birth-death reincarnation cycle. Whatever we do not put down while here on the Earth in a body, whatever duality we take with us into the death bardo, is what we will not let go of. (Bardo is a Buddhist term meaning there is an incredibly heightened opportunity happening for self-realization.) After the body dies if there is any unresolved duality, this rigidity in mind will require yet another incarnation, another body for yet another opportunity to practice self-realization. Once in the death process, the bardo, the temporal is stripped from us so that we may fully realize ourselves as only eternal. Buddhism describes death as the entire purpose behind the birth and the life. Why? Because death is where we review our lives from a greater place of clarity. Death is where we realize we are nothing that we have been dreaming, while asleep within the disease of duality. We are the universal white light, free from all limitation. Always have been. Always will be. If there is one thing no one has the power to change, it is the reality that God conscious is perfect, right here, right now.

While in the death bardo, whatever we have come here to get over but have not released, becomes very heavy in the spiritual realm. This burden becomes like an anchor and drags our awareness back down into the heavy vibration of the physical plane. Once again we find ourselves riding on the birth-death carousel. Back on this cycle, we take as many bodies and dream as many lives as we need. Since our true nature is space, anything that has not been transformed back into space becomes heavy and pulls spirit right back down into the Earth plane. It has to work this way. The rock is the place where spiritual creatures that have something to get over show up and practice giving their attention to creating a new response to life. It is just like Bill Murray in the film *Groundhog Day*; only it is extended out over many lifetimes.

Our typical perception is seen in the joke about a man who was about to die. He petitioned the angel of death very intensely to ask God if there could be an exception made to the rule "you can't take it with you." The dying man pleaded with the angel of death to ask God if he could, please, bring just one suitcase with him to Heaven. The angel informed the dying man that this was an unusual request, but he would check-in with God to see if there was any permission for this man to bring one suitcase with him into Heaven.

It seemed the angel was gone only a moment, when he returned in a flash of light. "Good news," the angel said, while handing the dying man a piece of paper. "God has agreed to let you bring in one suitcase. Let's go. Now it is time." The dying man, anticipating a positive response, had a suitcase all packed with gold bars ready to go.

Once at the pearly gates, Saint Peter tells the man that no one can bring anything into Heaven. The man shows Saint Peter his permission form from God that the angel of death had given him at the time of his death. Saint Peter reads the form and tells the man, *"Well, you're right. You do have permission to bring in one suitcase. Go right ahead on in. But before you enter the gates, I am curious to know what you packed? What was so important that you felt you needed to bring it with you? Do you mind if I look inside the suitcase?"* The man replies *"Of course you can see what I brought,"* and he gladly opens the suitcase. Saint Peter looks in at the contents and says, *"I don't get it? You brought pavement?"*

The man with the suitcase perceived gold to be of the highest value. But as everyone knows the streets of Heaven are simply paved with the stuff. So, from the perceptual viewpoint of Heaven, gold is merely the stuff pavement is made of. The man who wants to "take it with him" is the last to see that what he is really attached to is hard, heavy and burdensome. Real value, real worth and power from Heaven's perception would be to show up in the present moment with an open Heart. No luggage, baggage. No burdens.

It may seem ironic but the rock, this whole dog and pony show, *was* constructed to facilitate with ease, the realization of what we are doing with our love. Even more ironic is that we have agreed to stay here until we get it. No wave becomes One with the ocean on the energy of an incomplete action. When the wave is One with the ocean, the action is complete, because we are finally giving our attention and love to what we came here to give it to.

Unresolved loyalty to thinking and believing one's way through life re-creates hardness, inflexibility and rigidity within the wave. The Eastern traditions say that loving and trusting one's way through life creates alignment with spaciousness, with what Heaven loves: honesty, openness of mind without mental charges, acceptance, patience, compassion, tolerance and surrender. It is our perceptual relationship with all of these eternal qualities that heals the inner hardness. It is our perceptual Oneness with Source that transforms the density of our mind into a greater spaciousness, into a divine flow of flexibility, lightness, clarity, expansion, infinite possibilities, and unlimited intelligence. Our job is to constantly keep lightening up the wave with our perception until it matches that of the ocean. It is then they are truly One.

Motion of devotion One with the ocean – Argisle

You Can and Do Take It With You . . . Perception That Is

Swedenborg speaks about a judgment day after the temporal body falls away and the wave enters into the death bardo. He advises us that this is not the judgment day of our thoughts and beliefs. Swedenborg says that *our Ruling Love* determines whether we move into a *higher level of Heaven or a lower level of hell.* There is no gray haired God sitting behind a big desk with a calculator that judges you. You judge *you* according to your Ruling Love. *You decide* where you are most comfortable living: Heaven or hell. You decide.

However, please consider that if you have spent all of your love and attention here on Earth turning Heaven into hell, why would you do anything different when you leave? You are what you practice loving. Why wouldn't we just continue that practice in the next realm? We do, of course, because as *it is above, so it below, as it is within, so it is without.* Whatever we do not put down here while we can, whatever lie we do not let die here, we take with us into the spiritual realm. And Swedenborg has already warned us that it is much, much more difficult to get rid of illusion there.

Hence the purpose of the rock. If we could transform the wave while in a purely spiritual realm, we would not be here. There would be no need for a physical experience of mind. But there is a need. Specifically a need to feel the truth. That is why we are here - to feel the consequences *of our perceptual choices.* This is where we get real about what we are doing with our love, or we do the duality dance until we do.

The outer world exists solely as a mirror to the inner. No one came here to labor themselves to an outer reflection. No one came here to be a slave to a mirage. All of us came here to *be* with the movement of mind in order to realize what we are doing with our love. All of us are responsible for *being* with *what is* in the present moment with an open Heart beyond thoughts and beliefs. That is it. That is all we are responsible for - just showing up from the loving, feeling place, not the *doing*-thinking place. All actions that occur when aligned with this *being* are complete, whole, and fully life sustaining. When you wish your actions to be the most life enhancing that they can be, then that action must come from the Heart, from the only place that is real.

Being with *what is* in the present moment with an open Heart is the definition of embodying one's highest potential. It is the manifestation of divine consciousness actualized in the physical. We make each present moment so difficult, hard, contracted and limiting when we allow the ego to interpret *what is.* The voice of limitation does not know *what is;* it never has and never will. How could it? By nature the ego is pure limitation. The present moment is eternal and unlimited. Only love knows; only love can reveal; only love is real.

Born Again . . . It Is a Perceptual Thing . . . Not A Dogma Thing

If we wish to have a life worth living then we must each be responsible for not giving our attention to the ego's ultimate lies. We must each be responsible for a perceptual rebirth. This is what Jesus meant when he said, *"Marvel not when I tell you that you must be born again to enter into the Kingdom of Heaven."* When you give your attention to the temporal, that is what is meant by being "born of the flesh," born of the temporal world. Here is where the law of what you give your attention to reveals itself. Jesus goes on to say, *"That which is born of spirit, is spirit!"* That which is born from the process of giving attention to the eternal is eternal. Mind is liberated. Mind is born again as pure consciousness beyond the grasp of the limited.

Love! Why Perceive Anything Else?

Since thoughts and beliefs are the most limited and shallow forms of intelligence, there is no way that any wave can heal itself of the disease of duality by using the most fragmenting form of awareness available to it. It is in the complete action of surrendering our attention to a wholeness–creating intelligence that we heal the fragmentation. The only wholeness–making intelligence in the universe is loving what Heaven loves. *That is why Heaven's love is the most powerful force in the universe.*

Whatever Heaven's love touches becomes transformed into Heavenly love. Gayle's letter of forgiveness to the man who murdered her daughter shows that *(See the end of Chapter Five)*. When real love touches grief, the grief is transformed into real love. When authentic love touches worry, *less than* or *not good enough,* the limitation is transformed into authentic love. Whatever unlimited love touches becomes unlimited love. No other force in the universe has this power. Whatever judgment and criticism touches becomes smaller, more divided, more separate, more deeply charged with duality.

The truly appropriate use of awareness, which is eternal, is to give it back to eternal Source. As Jesus said it over two thousand years ago, *"Render unto Caesar, what is Caesar's."* If it is a temporal problem, then give it the appropriate temporal consciousness that it is due. However, if we are *"Rendering unto God, what is God's"* that is an eternal problem. That will require that we render unto God, what is God's eternal due. That will require showing up from an open and innocent Heart, ready to grow beyond what has hurt us, ready to just *be* with *what is.* If it is an eternal problem, then give it eternal consciousness. The relationship we all have with perception is eternal. You can therefore see how useful and spiritually healthy it would be to simply forget the *doing*. Cut to the chase. Right here. Right now. Just surrender to seeing yourself and others as *being* the perfect love you already are.

Swedenborg pointed out that being here now is a remembering and a forgetting thing. *"Remember to give your attention to the truth and forget everything else."* This advice is the absolute perfect wisdom for understanding, in a practical day-to-day way, how we are to *"render unto God, what is God's."* Remember to give your eternal problems eternal consciousness and forget everything else.

Each of us, in order to live right relationship with perception, must practice Ghandi's great cry of freedom, *"non-violent, non-cooperation"* with the disease of duality. Each wave must develop a Ruling Love that organizes all intelligence to serve eternal consciousness solely on a moment-to-moment basis. Each wave must align perception with the One and the movement of the One in all things. Each wave must practice the fine art of separating the shit from the shinola, and return home to loving and trusting the whole of life and all its relationships.

Each wave has absolute free will in its use of perception. A commitment to non-violent, non-cooperation with the ego, with duality, is to choose to no longer invest in the head's neurotic rantings. It is to choose only the truth. This choice is something that only the Ruling Love of each wave can make. Each wave chooses according to what they have trained their mind to love. Each wave chooses according to what they have practiced giving their attention to. If the truth is that we do not exist independently from what we love, then it also holds true that we do not choose independent from what we love.

Similar to divine emotional visitors, perception provides an honest form of feedback about what we are doing with our love. No one needs to go through a death bardo to know that Heaven and hell exist right here, right now on this hunk o' rock. If Heaven and hell are different places or opposing movements of mind, then how can we be seeing, experiencing and feeling both of them right here? Because everything here is inherently neutral. Imagine that . . . (please). What we are really experiencing here is *the charge* we are projecting out onto the world. A charge manufactured by our unresolved relationship with the ego.

The world itself is inherently neutral. It is designed to be that way so that it can reflect back every perception projected by every person simultaneously. Like a giant blank movie screen, the world renders the illusion of a co-existing Heaven and hell. The co-existance is an illusion that Swedenborg explains can only happen here, because here there is a physical appearance that hides the truth. Pretty sneaky. God can be so deceptively clever.

It is the Ruling Love of each wave that determines the individual experience or perception of either Heaven or hell. Here in the physical realm, we can see this dichotomy in action all the time. We can have two people standing right next to each other, same space, same moment. There is no noticeable or measurable difference, but for one person it is Heaven and for the other it is hell. Just observe what happens the next time an Academy Award winner is announced. Even though the nominees appear to be sharing a similar reality, this facade could not be further from the truth. The winner is in Heaven while the losers, no matter how they try to hide it, are clearly in hell. Each person has no access to the other, because the reality is they are living in completely different realms. Each individual's experience is created according to one's individual perception. Swedenborg points out that Heaven and hell can be seen and experienced here, but that neither are the real ones, which are, of course, non-physical states of existence.

Thus we choose according to the charge in our perception whether life is an express elevator to Heaven or hell. We choose according to the charge in our perception, our wave, whether everything that touches us is the perfect food of Heaven rendering liberation, or whether everything we experience is yet another lesson in futility that we could have lived without. Our perception is only as healthy as what we are giving our love to, specifically, our Ruling Love. Do we love the right use of perception? This is a question all waves must ask of themselves. We have established that perception is eternal. That means the right use of perception is to give it back to eternal consciousness. On a practical everyday level, this means loving and trusting our way through life and relationships, without a thought or belief about what it all means.

The following story illustrates the magic of perception, and the need to consciously choose our perception wisely. The story is taken from *Stories of the Spirit, Stories of the Heart* edited by Christina Feldman and Jack Kornfield (Harper San Francisco 1991; p.292-293).

There once was a man who wandered throughout the world seeking his deepest desire. He wandered from one city to another, from one realm to another looking for fulfillment and happiness, but in all his wandering never came to it. Finally one day, tired from his search, he sat down underneath a great tree at the foot of a mountain.

What he did not know was this was The Great Wish Fulfilling Tree. Whatever one wishes for when seated underneath it immediately becomes true.

As he rested in his weariness he thought to himself, "What a beautiful spot this is. I wish I had a home here," and instantly before his eyes a lovely home appeared. Surprised and delighted he thought further, "Ah, if only I had a partner to be here with me, then my happiness would be complete," and in a moment a beautiful woman appeared calling him "husband" and beckoning to him. "Well, first, I am hungry," he thought. "I wish there was food to eat." Immediately a banquet table appeared covered with every wonderful kind of food and drink, main courses, pastries, sweets of every variety. The man sat down and began to feast himself hungrily, but partway through the meal, still feeling tired he thought, "I wish I had a servant to serve me the rest of this food," and sure enough a man servant appeared.

Finishing the meal the man sat back down to lean against this wonderful tree and began to reflect, "How amazing it is that everything I wish for has come true. There is some mysterious force about this tree. I wonder if there is a demon who lives in it," and sure enough no sooner than he thought this than a great demon appeared. "Oh, my," he thought, "this demon will probably eat me up," and this is just what it did.

To See As God Sees

It is your destiny to see as God sees,
to know as God knows, to feel as God feels.

How is this possible? How?
Because Divine Love cannot defy its very
Self.

Divine Love will be Eternally True to Its
own Being, and its being is giving all it can,
at the perfect moment.

And the greatest gift God can give is His
own experience.

Every object, every creature, every man,
woman and child has a soul and it is the
destiny of all,

to see as God sees, to know as God knows,
to feel as God feels, to Be as God Is.

—By Meister Eckhart

Chapter Ten

Agreements

Everything happens by energy agreement. We understand this in the physical world as polarity: positive and negative, North and South poles, electrons and protons, ph balance: acid & alkaline. Energy agreement also happens on a spiritual level within the wave. When we give our attention to temporal consciousness via a thought, word, or belief, these all have a charge. Anytime we give our attention to ultimate lies, our wave re-creates a negative charge. We then experience a polarity match with this energy. Our wave matches the energy of the ego. So if we give our attention to a memory, perception, or thought that we or someone else *did not do it right,* is *not good enough,* or that there is *not enough,* then we, as eternal consciousness, are using our love to re-create negativity within our lives and on the planet.

Negativity does not exist in Heaven. However, it is the very ether and atmosphere of hell. The more attention we give to solving our eternal problems using temporal consciousness, the more charges we are manufacturing, and then re-creating within the wave, as well as on the planet. The unresolved negativity accumulates, and eventually translates into our everyday life as unhappiness. This gradual accumulation of unresolved negativity, places our wave in the slave position of working for the unhappiness – hungry ego. A wave that is loyal to negativity is a wave whose ruling master is diseased, mis-placed wisdom, and self-sabotaging agony.

The consistent re-creation of negative charges projected out by a wave manifests itself as a predictable gateway to hell. Any wave consistently re-creating negative charges will also consistently and predictably live in hell. To whatever degree that we give our attention to: *did not do it right, not good enough,* or *not enough time, love, money, or opportunity,* is the degree to which we live in hell. We put ourselves there by the power of what we are freely giving our attention to. This message was brought to you courtesy of the truth that *you are what you love, and you love whatever you are giving your attention to.*

When we give our attention to positive thoughts and beliefs, we are creating positive charges within the wave. Creating positive charges is a much more life sustaining choice than re-creating negative charges. But if you are creating any charges, you are still bound to an ego/head-limited world. The object is to transcend all charges, to live in the Heart, to give awareness to what is beyond limitation, beyond duality, beyond the smallness of posi-tive and negative charges. The bigger picture is that we, as eternal beings, are beyond any positive or negative charge. What we want to ultimately do with our love, is freely surrender it back to the One, without charges at-tached.

You Know The Energy Agreement Tree By Its Fruits

Because we know a tree by its fruits, if you give attention to negative thoughts, you will attract negative feelings: depressed, hopeless, victimized, unhappy or worried.

Give attention to positive thoughts and you will increase feeling positive: hopeful, looking forward with good intentions and strengthened by imagining a positive outcome.

Give attention to the truth and you will feel beyond the grasp of positive and negative. Loving the truth, *feels* like Heaven. It *feels* like surrender, neutrality to the world's drama, openness, receptive, accepting, flexible, fully supported, carefree and completely equitable. You will not be disturbed by anything on an inner or outer level. You will be beyond all thoughts or beliefs, beyond the tyranny of the ego and the force of limitation. Love is what you came here to realize. No one, not even yourself, could offer you more.

We have to live according to our love as well. That means every wave is agreeing to where it is presently emotionally and perceptually living. If you agree to give attention to ultimate lies then you are agreeing to live in hell. You are signing on the dotted line for a special delivery package of limitation and unhappiness. Whether you consciously realize it or not, this is the nature of energy agreements.

Agree to give attention to the truth, to eternal consciousness, and you agree to live in Heaven: in happiness and infinite abundance. What you are agreeing to on a moment-to-moment basis is also where you must live. Whether we consciously want to or not. If we find ourselves living in hell, then the first thing we need to ask ourselves is, "How did I agree to this? When did I choose ultimate lies? Why am I not trusting life and love? Where am I trying to control the perfection of *what is* by having thoughts and beliefs about what it all means?"

The Highest Agreement We Can Make

Ghandi once said, "*We must be the change we wish to see and not the darkness we wish to leave behind.*" We must match the energy of that agreement with our love before we possess the power to manifest that reality. Why is that? Because *everything happens by energy agreement.* That reality makes it unavoidably necessary for us to figure out what we are agreeing to *consciously as well as unconsciously.* If you truly wish to understand what agreements you have set into motion with your love, then look no further than your own life. Every wave is projecting all the unresolved charges everywhere. Are you agreeing to manifest Heaven? Or are you agreeing to manifest hell? Does your life feel hopeless? Do you feel like a victim to life and relationships? Guess what you are agreeing to? *Everything happens by energy agreement,* so that we can get clear and concise feedback about what we are agreeing to with our love, *consciously as well as unconsciously.* Whatever we are agreeing to is going to find us here on the Earth, and when it does we will have to *feel* it. That way there can be no mistake about what we are agreeing to with our love. What are you agreeing to? Where has it led? Do you want to make any adjustments? If so, what?

Agree to self-mastery and the wave will master freeing the higher self. The higher self is freed when the limited, smaller self we have personally identified with, the ego re-created story of self, has been surrendered into love, without a thought or belief. Personal growth is to work with the temporal positive and negative charges within the wave. It is the process by which we become aware of how giving attention to negativity re-creates more negativity in our life. Giving attention to positive thoughts, to clean up our belief system, also has an immediate impact upon our nervous system, as well. Start to feel better about life, yours and others; we have nerve, rather than being nervous.

Self-mastery comes after personal growth. After we have practiced and organized the wave to focus on the positive rather than the negative, the next step is to go beyond positive and negative. Self-mastery is to let go of all identification with thoughts and beliefs, anything temporal. The next step is living beyond the charge of *good* or *bad*. It does not matter. These charges have no hold over you when you *see* that everything *is* already perfect. With self-mastery comes the realization of self as beyond duality. With self-mastery the wave has realized life beyond any limited positive or negative sense of perception. The wave has mastered how to release its grasp on the comings and goings of the temporal world, regardless of the positive and negative projections of mind that continue to spin and fly everywhere. The death story of Mellen-Thomas Benedict, in **Chapter 8,** illustrates this transformation of consciousness: awareness freeing itself from the grip of ego re-created charges.

This next step is going to require a practiced surrender of all knowing, of all understanding to Ultimate Truth, the eternal. The self-mastery step is all about making separation from the entire thinking and believing addiction process. Self-mastery is about responding unconditionally to the stimulus of life with love, acceptance, tolerance, compassion, patience and loyalty to the perfection of the present moment, to the exclusion of everything else.

"I unconditionally surrender to trusting and loving the perfection of every present moment. This is all I know." That narrative must become the focus of our inner dialog. Liv-

ing the truth that real security and real abundance comes from being with *what is* in the present moment with an open Heart. This is the highest agreement any wave can make.

Authentic security and abundance will never be realized within the disease of duality, the disease of limitation. Agree to real, authentic security and abundance, and you shall humanifest the same. That is the beauty of the law of energy agreements. It clears up any and all confusion about what you might be agreeing to with your love.

Only here on the rock, can we stop lying to ourselves, about whether we are empowering eternal or temporal with our life force. Only here on the rock we can see, taste, touch, feel and directly experience the truth that we are whatever we are agreeing to with our love. Only here can we practice knowing a tree by its fruits. Are the fruits you are seeing, touching, tasting, feeling and directly ex-periencing, are they life-sustaining fruits, or are they life-diminishing fruits? You know. *You can tell, because you do not have truth, you are truth.*

Everything happens by energy agreement. No wave can manifest a higher eternal agreement by aligning its atten-tion with temporal, limited consciousness. Eternal agree-ments manifest wholeness making results and uncondi-tional fruits. Gayle's story from *Chapter Five* exemplifies this. Gayle *agreed,* within her wave, to grow beyond what had hurt her. The result of this agreement freed her to not only forgive her daughter's murderer, but to actu-ally transform that painful relationship into a mutually shared and honored experience of love and respect.

Ego-based energy agreements such as an attachment to

an outcome, the judging and criticizing of yourself and others, controlling or manipulating others, contracting from *what is* - all of these match the energy of you hu-manifesting unhappiness, living an unfulfilled life, and feelings of failure and hopelessness. To manifest eternal fruits we must first agree to match that eternal energy. Eternal consciousness is the energy to match with our attention when we are choosing to solve the eternal quest of *"Who am I?" "Why am I here?" "What is the meaning and purpose of my life and relationships?" "What is my value, power, and worth?"* To align your wave with an eternal energy agreement you must first get out of your head, as the eternal energy agreement is not anything you are thinking. It is what you are feeling.

Why is it so important that we feel it? Simple. It is harder to lie to yourself about what you are doing with your attention when you have to feel the consequences of it. Feeling is the higher agreement, the equalizer, of all life here on the rock. The good news is that this feeling feedback law, is why masturbation works so well for so many of us, because the higher truth is that nobody knows how to do it to you, like you. And if you want happiness, you will have to learn how to take happiness out of your head and into your own Heartfelt hands.

We Choose to Agree Energetically with Either Truth or Illusion

In order to agree to manifest eternal fruits, we must first agree to stop thinking and believing, judging and criticizing our way through life and its many relationships. We must end our present agreement with how much attention we are willing to give the voice of limitation. We must agree with the choice to be awake and watchful for the possible return of Asmodeus. We must be willing to *live* the truth that we do not *have* love, we *are* love.

Anytime we willingly give our attention to charges like, *"It is going to work out for everyone else in the world but me. Everyone else will have success and happiness except me."* We are choosing to live in hell. What we have come here to learn is this: there is nothing useful or life-sustaining for us in hell. Therefore do not continue to go there. The only reason we are re-creating hell is so that we can become aware of our doing it and finally break the cycle; practice surrendering attention to loving, trusting and breathing instead. Choose to freely dismantle and leave forever our re-created hell in this lifetime.

Whenever we make a choice in our lives based on fear, such as, *"I'm going to take this job even though I hate it. Why? Because I'm afraid if I do not, I will end up homeless and unsupported, wandering the streets begging for money."* Or, *"I'm going to marry this person. Not because this is the love of my life, but because I'm afraid I cannot make it in the world by myself. I will end up alone and unloved if I do not take my only pathetic chance at happiness."* Whenever we make a choice in our lives based on fear, we are giving our attention, our love, to manifesting more fear. That translates on a feeling level to more hell on the planet. We know a tree by its fruits. If we plant fear-based seeds, we will grow and reap fear-based fruits. Only you can decide for yourself what you are choosing to learn about. Is it Heaven? Or is it hell? What you are choosing is also a commentary on what you are doing with your love, and the determining factor in where you will live spiritually, psychologically as well as emotionally.

If there is anything in your life that is not working for

you, then you can end that limitation and create a new response to life by simply agreeing to give your attention to matching the polarity of what Heaven loves. Align your affinity with the affections of Heaven, and that is where you will live. If we are having conflict in our relationships, the preferred method of ending the conflict would be to invite all beings involved to live in Heaven. There is no conflict there, only peace, equability and happiness. What greater service to the people in your life than to negotiate unconditionally from a Heavenly position.

When has it ever served us or others to leave the perfection of Heaven and sink into the hell of *not good enough, did not do it right* or *not enough* love, money, time, opportunity? Does it ever serve us or others to embody the pattern of ignorance that is keeping us all in hell? Haven't we all learned everything we need to from unhappiness and limitation? Or do we still need reminding that there is nothing useful for us there? Maybe we are just slow learners, maybe we are just asleep at the wheel, or maybe we just like screwing ourselves. Ah, yes, the beauty of self-discovery, it is why we are here.

It is very useful to ask ourselves on a moment-to-moment basis, *"What am I agreeing to with my love? Is it serving to myself and the many relationships I share in this life?"* Ask yourself these questions from the feeling place, not the thought and belief place. How does what you are agreeing to feel? Your feeling intelligence is an infinitely higher form of intelligence than any thought or belief narrative going on inside the brain. Your rational mind can reason away almost anything. However, it is your emotional truth, your inner feelings that are not easily rationalized away. Just try to tell yourself you are not really feeling something, I dare you . . . I triple dare you!

The unresolved emotions will come back to haunt you, every time.

Anytime you agree to give your attention to worry, that energy agreement attracts feelings of abandonment, lack of support, and unworthiness in love and happiness. You cannot just invite worry over with your attention and not expect to see the rest of the *limiting* crowd of party crashers. There is an energy agreement, a match between worry, abandonment, unsupported, unlovable and unhappiness. They work to energetically attract and hold each other together inside the wave. It is no different from placing two magnets close together. They will either repel or attract each other depending on the energetic charge. Worry is a feeling magnet, charged to attract these other limited states of being, directly into the emotional body.

Ever wonder why enlightened beings do not behave like neurotic unenlightened beings? It is because enlightened beings do not give their attention to anything limited. They are fully conscious, they do not have an unconscious thought or belief attracting other limited charges. Therefore there is no doorway, no energetic match, or connection for anything restrictive to enter into their wave. Unenlightened beings spend most of the their energy attracting that which they profess they most want to get away from. They spend their lives building a monument to worry and unhappiness with their love. If you want to be immune to all negativity, just as enlightened beings are, then do not form an energetic agreement with anything negative. Do not give it your attention. Instead choose to practice being in the present moment with an open Heart. That is the gift that keeps on giving.

We Agree to Remain Asleep, or
We Agree to Wake Up

Enlightenment is the process of detoxifying the limited, the sabotaging addiction of surrendering all of our attention to the thinking and believing process. Each wave must organize its love to agree to break the pattern of *remaining asleep* in the disease of duality. If there is no love for *being awake,* then there will be no *awakening.* If there is no agreement to de-brainwash our dependency on the inner critic for solving our eternal problems, then there will be no movement in the wave to that end.

All of us have been brainwashed since birth to live in our heads, to be loyal to our projections of mind, to our limitations and stories of unhappiness. All of us since birth have been indoctrinated to think and believe that we are the stuff we are actually here to get over. We have all been brainwashed to identify our value, power and worth with our socio-economic status. We live within the boundaries of whatever temporal thing the body has been diagnosed with. We have all been brainwashed to think and believe we are our experiences: marriage, divorce, parenthood, bankruptcy, surgeries, audits, trials, speeding tickets or high school and college degrees. We confuse our true nature with everything, from what kind of car we drive to what beer we drink. We are none of these things. These are precisely what we have come here to leave behind forever. We have come here to liberate ourselves from those forces by agreeing to realize the hold the illusory has on the wave. The truth is we are agreeing to whatever we are loving, and we are agreeing to love whatever we are giving our attention to right now.

Agreeing to *wake up* is to agree to watch what you are doing with your attention. *Awake* is agreeing to let reality reveal something about its self-evident nature, instead of the wave endlessly projecting what it thinks and believes reality to be. *Remaining asleep* is agreeing to give attention to *not good enough, did not do it right* or *not enough time, love, money or opportunity*. (Now you are not just asleep, you are starting to snore loudly!) *Awake* is agreeing to shift attention from the voice of limitation to the expansive voice of eternal consciousness for solving eternal problems. It is understanding that you have two forms of consciousness and knowing which one you are giving your attention to on a moment-to-moment basis. *Waking up* is agreeing to do a *core dump* of all of the information the wave has previously given attention to, in order to understand the value, power and worth of ourselves and others.

Awake is to agree to make Ultimate Truth the senior information that guides the soul through *what is*. It is agreeing to unconditionally love and trust your way through life, no matter what the temporal world throws at you. It is agreeing to surrender attention to what Heaven loves: equability, honesty, mercy, patience and good faith in life and love, as a instinctual response to the whole of life. *Asleep* is giving our attention to what hell loves and indulging anything negative with our awareness. (Now you are snoring so loud you're waking up the neighbors, and hopefully yourself!)

Agreeing to heal the wave means practicing being with *what is* in the present moment with an open Heart. Agreeing to let go of worry is to agree to being joyous right now, because you can. *Awake* is to agree to witness the contents of the wave, to be in the world, but not of it. Agreeing to align the wave with Christ consciousness is to agree to love your enemies. *Awake* is to agree to go *cold turkey* on duality. Agreeing to align the wave with the One, is to give gratitude to Heaven for all of its infinite gifts without ceasing. *Awake* is to agree to creativity as the senior manifesting force in the wave. *Awake* is to agree to end all re-creation and manifest a life worth living. Agreeing to surrender the movement of the wave to love and trust, is to agree to enlightenment. *Awake* is to agree to respond to *what is* with neutrality. Agreeing to empty the wave of all loyalty to limitation and unhappiness, is to freely agree to the truth, that only love *rules*.

Inequality, worry and contraction, all these limited energies agree to bring in other limited energies. Why? *Everything happens by energy agreement.* If we agree to give love to inequality or respond to *what is* with contraction, we are providing the necessary energetic agreement for all other related limiting issues to enter right into the wave. This happens whether or not we are consciously aware of what we are inviting in. That does not matter. The energy agreement is what matters. Anytime we give attention to anything limited we are simultaneously energetically agreeing to infuse struggle, difficulty, effort and hardship directly into our lives and nervous system. All of our "spiritual commuting" occurs directly through the doorway of perception. *You are what you love and you love whatever you are giving your attention to. You do not exist independently from what you love.* And you agree to live in the place that matches the polarity of what you love.

The opposite holds true as well. If you give your attention to equability, to trusting and loving your way through life, if you consciously practice responding to whatever life gives you by expanding into the truth, then you are also agreeing to invite the entire community of Heaven into your wave. When you agree to align your attention with the affinities of Heaven, then your Ruling Love by energy agreement, will be beyond duality. When you, of your own free will, choose divine truth over illusion, you will live in Heaven, because then you will finally be *of* Heaven.

Agreeing to envision *what is* as perfect is to agree to organize the wave into being One with Heaven. If you freely focus on empowering a story of good faith in life and love no matter what the temporal world delivers to your doorstep, you will agree to receive the sweetness of life that has been here for us all along. If you agree to embody the present moment with an open Heart, you agree to manifest Heaven on Earth. Right here. Right now.

We make our own heaven and hell here on Earth
– Sheila Spritzer

The law that everything happens according to energy agreement means that each and every wave is freely choosing their reality according to what they love. Each of us is freely agreeing to be One with Heaven or to be one with our own personal private hell. So if you find that something is coming between you and Heaven, between you and your highest dreams, between you and happiness, between you and the present moment, then whatever that something is, you *agreed* to it.

The New Millennium Agreement

When the calendar changed from 1999 to 2000, everyone on the planet went through a collective energetic agreement shift, because we entered into a new millennium, a new energy agreement. The old agreement was the Piscean Age agreement, which was: the power, privilege and money will go into the hands of the few. If your last name is Gates, that few was you. You do not need to be a brain surgeon or a rocket scientist to see exactly how that old agreement played out.

Noam Chomsky, the prolific writer and linguist from M.I.T., refers to the ultra wealthy as the *opulent* of our global society. In his lectures and writings, he has been warning that this group of elite people has become dangerously concentrated over time. As we have progressed through the Piscean Age and headed towards the new millennium, the Aquarian Age, the *opulent* community has become smaller and smaller. The power and privilege has progressed into fewer and fewer hands. That was the energy agreement.

From the time the planet entered into the Piscean Age, about the time of the birth of Christ, the number of people who have the most money, resources, assets, power and privilege has dramatically shrunk, not increased. That concentration is apparent in the fact that less than ten companies own all the global media: all the newspapers, magazines and radio and television stations. The agreement of the old millennium allowed for this to happen on the Earth plane because of the law that *everything happens by energy agreement.* For those of us on the planet during the old millennium, we agreed to learn more about what happens when we give our attention to hell, to inequality, so that we would realize there is nothing there for us, and abandon it.

The new millennium is about the progression that happens when you realize that unfairness and inequality hold nothing for you. That is the Aquarian Age. The new agreement in this new millennium is that the power, privilege, and money will go into the hands of the many! The tide is turning. This new millennium will not support the outrageous greed, insensitivity, gross inequality, and overt hatred towards the body of the Earth the last millennium allowed for. This new millennium is about each wave putting down the *not enough*, bad faith in life and bleeding love stories that have accumulated in the previous Age. The last millennium was to show us the hell that we love with our attention. This new millennium is about getting over the self-inflicted trauma of the last millennium.

For those of us on the cusp, who physically lived through the millennium change, we agreed before we came here to go through this consciousness shift. We agreed to let go of all the reasons why the power, privilege and money cannot come to us easily, freely and simply right now in this and every present moment. Those born after December 31, 1999, have the benefit of incarnating in an Age where the energy agreement supports fairness and abundance.

For those in a body on the planet during the beginning part of this new millennium shift, this time will be the most intense. Why? Because of the limiting issues we have dragged with us into this new millennium. The burden of dragging hell around with us everywhere is the familiar weight pulling us down. It is the unresolved loyalty to the re-creation of our most familiar scarcity stories that manifests most intensely at first. In order for us to enter into the promised land of the new millennium, first be prepared to put down all of the memories, impressions, and beliefs that we have entertained about our value, power and worth. Master separation from all the reasons why we cannot be One with power, privilege, and abundance easily and simply, right now. Agree to align ourselves with an energy agreement that allows us to live and embody our true birthright, which is infinite abundance!

If you have dragged the energetic agreement that there is *not enough* with you into this new millennium, then reality of the new energy agreement will go out of its way to manifest this lie for you. In your face. In your life. In your wallet and on your credit report, until *you choose to* exchange it for the more updated and stylish infinite abundance agreement. As merry prankster, Ken Kesey, used to say, *"You're either on the bus or off the bus."* You are either swinging with the new energy agreement, or you are dangling from the rope of the old energy agreement.

The wisdom of Swedenborg says we are nothing physical, nothing limited, nothing in duality. What we really are does not even show up here. Only what we are here to get over shows up. In this new millennium, the oldest, densest, most stubborn *shit* we are standing in is going to appear first. Why would it appear first and most virulently? Because we must first free our mind of the old lies, the old energy agreement, in order to be in right relationship with the present millennium energy agreement and what we are doing with our love.

What is so powerful about this new millennium is this: if you love Heaven's infinite abundance, then you have the best energetic agreement to support you in manifesting that love. Right here. Right now. This is the millennium that holds greater potential for each wave to master a life worth living. This is the millennium that says *yes* to creating a new response to the old stuff we are here to get over. This is the millennium that has the energy agreement to support the embodiment of Heaven, not hell. This is the millennium that offers the most accessibility to Heaven on Earth that the planet has seen in thousands of years. There is no better time to know, understand and to ultimately live the truth that *you are what you love and you love whatever you are giving your attention to* than right now.

Infinite abundance has always been available to us whenever we have aligned our love with Heaven's love. This new millennium energy agreement however, best supports us in the practice of *receiving* Heaven's infinite abundance. This is the millennium with the energy agreement that hands every wave, on a silver platter, the invitation to embody the truth that you do not *have* love or power, you *are* love and power. The Power *is* Love, the time is now and all we have to do is agree to it.

When I Was The Forest

When I was the stream, when I was the
forest, when I was still the field, when I
was every hoof, foot, fin and wing, when I
was the sky itself,

No one ever asked me did I have a purpose, no one ever wondered was there anything I might need, for there was nothing I
could not Love.

It was when I left all we once were that the
agony began, the fear and questions came;
and I wept; I wept. And tears I had never
known before.

So I returned to the river, I returned to the
mountains. I asked for their hand in marriage again, I begged – I begged to wed every object and creature.

And when they accepted,
God was ever present in my arms.
And He did not say, "Where have you
been?"

For then I knew my soul—every soul—
has always held Him.

—By Meister Eckhart

Chapter Eleven

Moving Forward

There is a saying in the San Francisco Bay Area, *always forward, never straight.* This saying is the perfect metaphor for life, which requires that we constantly keep moving forward in our lives. Energy that moves is life, energy that doesn't . . . isn't. Moving forward is a life worth living. Moving forward is like Oscar Wilde's definition of the truth, *"The truth is rarely pure and never simple."* Moving forward, rarely, if ever, means moving in a straight line, because life is a dynamic force that must be experienced and mastered on its terms, not on those of the ego.

Moving forward is a choice made in the present. You cannot move forward in the past, nor can you move forward in the future. You can only move forward by being *here now.* Moving forward translates into letting go of a timetable by which life needs to be lived. Letting go of the inner dialog that dictates, "I should be somewhere else in my life by now. I should have the family, the job, the money, the car of my dreams by now!" Life has no timetable, other than the ever-eternal present moment. The ego, however, does have a highly charged schedule and time agenda. Life is simply present *now*, without any attachment to what time it is, or where you think you should be. Life is happening in the present moment; our job is to be in it with an open Heart. That is moving forward with grace at its finest and its easiest.

Moving forward is an active choice; just as remaining stagnant or living in pain or the past is a choice. It is a choice that is determined by what you give your attention to. Why? *Because you are what you love and you love whatever you give your attention to.* Moving forward can sometimes start with a small choice that evolves slowly building upon itself. When something extremely challenging happens in your life, like losing a loved one, receiving a terminal diagnosis, being cheated on and lied to, being injured by an indifferent party, or losing an important legal matter, these can all be very traumatizing events. Moving forward is a choice. Moving forward is choosing to say *yes to life and love.* This can be challenging and difficult, because trauma by its very nature is a paralyzing force, and it is the degree to which we identify with the temporal - the body, financial assets, experiences - that we suffer. This incomplete action of inappropriate identification creates a doorway for trauma to enter into the soul.

One can experience physical trauma without experiencing soul trauma. The body is temporal and limited. It can experience states such as trauma, paralysis, even death. True self, like the soul, however, is eternal and ultimately beyond any limited states of being. How come we do not experience life this way? Because *we* experience life through the most limited filter of what *we* think and believe it is, what *we* think and believe *we* are, what *we* think and believe life is telling us about our value, power and worth, what *we* think and believe others can do or take away from us.

Life will deal all of us a very challenging hand from time to time; that is the way it is, because we all get the whole of life here on the planet Earth. We all have attachments to controlling the outcomes in our lives. But the truth is, there is no short cut in the Tao. We all get the exact lesson we need, when we need it.

There is a story in Buddhism about a woman who seeks counsel from the Buddha. The woman asks the Buddha why her loved ones died and life is so hard. Why did she have to be singled out to receive more than her fair share of suffering? The Buddha asks the woman to go out and get a mustard seed from a family, any household that has not experienced troublesome difficulties and losses, and then return to him with the mustard seed. The woman leaves and goes in search of others. When she returns to the Buddha, he asks her for the mustard seed she has received from a family that has not been touched by suffering and loss. The woman retells her experiences to the Buddha about how each household she encountered had stories of great loss, suffering and pain. The woman leaves the Buddha realizing that there is nothing personal in her suffering here on the rock. No human being is immune from experiencing the whole of life.

Life cannot be manipulated into a flawless, perfect world where we can never be hurt. Why? Because this is the place where the stuff we are here to get over shows up. This is the place where we can be lied to and violated, because this is the place where we practice saying *yes to life and love* no matter what the temporal world throws at us. This is the place where we practice showing up from the Heart without a thought or belief. This is the place where we practice responding with compassion, patience and understanding, because we realize we are relating to our own mind. This is the place where we practice know-ing that everything that touches us is the perfect food of Heaven, and that we have everything we need to digest that food and release the waste. This is the place where we practice aligning our focus of attention with the One, until that is all we feel in an arena that we cannot fake.

Moving forward is a practice like everything else here. If moving forward seems impossible to you now, it may be because you do not practice it enough to make a differ-ence in your life. You may be more familiar with a lack of growth and resiliency. Perhaps the idea of moving for-ward without a loved one, or in spite of a great personal loss seems offensive or meaningless to you. In order for moving forward to have any real power in our lives it must be practiced unconditionally. It must be practiced consciously. You must ask yourself each day when you wake up, "What can I do today to move forward?" Maybe what you do to move forward is just take a shower and look through the mail. That is okay. Moving forward, after trauma, does not always have to be a major move-ment to be highly effective in your life. What it must be is *conscious!* You must actively choose to identify with the truth: I do not *have* love, I *am* love. My power, value and worth is that I freely show up as a force of love right here, right now.

In the practice of moving forward, dwelling on "why me?" is not useful. You agreed to your life's lessons before you physically came here. You cannot create a learning experience that you do not need, and you cannot create it before or after you needed it. "Why me?" is a question from the ego, implying there is nothing in this life lesson that moves you further down the path of enlightenment. That violates the truth that this moment is perfect and sent from Heaven for your benefit. The life lessons you've been given and agreed to are the best evolutionary way for you to wake up to the truth of who and what you are. This is the most efficient way for you to practice separation from the obstacles that limit your love and free yourself to live the truth, to live in the feeling place of the Heart.

It may seem like the jury returned the wrong verdict. It may feel like the drunk driver prematurely took the life of another. It may look like the boss took away the job for no reason. It may appear as if the IRS is determined to ruin your life. The truth of the matter is that divine love and wisdom have decided everything. Higher order wisdom is asking us to practice aligning our attention with the truth: I do not *have* love, I *am* love. Unconditionally. My job is to remember the truth that my power is to consciously show up as a force of love, right here, right now. The jury decided nothing. Drunk drivers do not have sovereignty in determining the length of any spirit's life mission. The boss possesses no power over your abundance or security. The IRS may think they're god, or may try to act like it, but they have no dominion over your alignment with happiness.

Heaven determines everything! Always has. Always will. Heaven sent everything as life's perfect food. Remembering that Heaven is playing the music that you are dancing to is critical in moving forward. Listen . . . Feel . . . If you think and believe others have power over your life and happiness, moving forward will be impossible. Lies always limit and paralyze the wave. The truth always sets the wave free. A wave that is moving forward is always free. That's how the wave gets honest and real about what it is doing with its love. Is your wave moving forward or is it stagnating? Is your wave in bondage? Or is it free?

If you still need to ask "why," ask yourself why you agreed to learn this lesson this way? What limiting stories and charges within your wave are dictating the outcome you are presently experiencing? What did you bring to the table to co-create this life's lesson? Is a *didn't do it right,* or *not good enough* story determining that you end up feeling disposable, unloved and rejected, yet again? Is a *not enough* opportunity story behind your inability to land a job that feeds your soul? Everything you are looking at and experiencing is your inner self coming out so that you can *see* what you are doing with your love. These are the unresolved charges within your wave that you are trying to *realize* and separate from. You know, learning the difference between the *shit and shinola*, and leaving one behind. The comforting news is that you get to choose which force you integrate and which you leave behind. That's free will in action.

Instead of asking "why," try praying to Source to show you where and how this life's lesson is perfect. When you seek the truth, it will set you free. If you are not seeking the truth of what you are going through, you will be re-creating more suffering. Ask Heaven for the strength to see the reality that everything that happens here *is* working for you, or it would not be allowed to happen. Focus on aligning your attention with acceptance, surrendering with neutrality, and expressing gratitude for everything that Heaven sends you. It is all perfect, beyond any thought, belief or criticism. That is all you need to know. Ask for the wisdom to *see* where and how what you are going through is all perfect. Ask for the wisdom to remove the illusion that there is absolutely nothing redeemable in what you are experiencing.

If you are not ultimately aligning your attention with the truth, you will not *feel* the truth. You will not *feel* the perfection of the life's lesson. When you align your attention with what you think and believe it all means, you will be feeling limited. It is nature's way of reminding you that *you are what you love, and you love whatever you are giving your attention to.*

Waiting to move forward is not useful either. Justifying why it is best to remain injured and unhealed is never a life-sustaining choice. Time heals nothing. ***Consciously choosing to move forward heals everything.*** On a thought and belief level there may be some very compelling reasons why focusing on anger, retribution and vengeance appears to be useful. However, the truth of the matter is there is no reason that justifies a stagnant limited existence. ***Nobody pays the price for the ways you limit your life but you.*** You do not need for someone to be arrested and convicted in order to move forward. You do not need for an outcome to play itself out in a specific way, the way you think things ought to turn out, in order to choose life. You do not need the partner, the money, the car, the job, or the 38 double D boobs in order to be happy. What you do need is to keep moving forward - to keep organizing your response to life to support expansion by loving and trusting your way through life.

Practice showing up from the Heart without a thought or belief, and saying *yes to life and love* in an arena your nervous system cannot fake. Practice focusing on the truth to the exclusion of everything else until that is all you feel. Why do you need to practice these things? Because that is why Heaven gave you a physical form and placed your charming butt on the third rock from the sun – to practice giving your *attention* to what lives in Heaven unconditionally, until you find yourself *living* in Heaven unconditionally.

Moving forward is empowered by imagining that you are the space between the atoms and subatomic particles. The benefit of practicing identifying with space, is that when challenging events happen, and they will, knowing that you are the eternal portion of the program will allow you to witness the temporal world move by. If you do not identify with the temporal, you do not take anything personally. When you identify with being the space, the eternal, not only will your experience of suffering be greatly diminished, but you will not feel the need to control, manipulation, contract or respond to life with fear. Instead you will feel gratitude, unending Heartfelt gratitude.

To practice identifying with space, means living a fearless existence, beyond the limitation of the temporal world. It means relating to *what is* as the One, for there is no duality in space, only space. To practice identifying with space means relating to *what is* as perfect, as there is no imperfection in space, only space. When great physical or emotional pain is present in life, to imagine being the space, frees spirit to *see* and completely understand that we are not the physical body. We are not the experiences that come and go like a dream. We are the *observer*, the force of awareness that is conscious of the movement of life going by, consciously choosing to show up, identifying with love, right here, right now.

When we realize we are the space reality, not the atomic structure reality, then we can relax, trust, let go of our attachments to an outcome. We can free fall into being One with the present moment without a thought or a belief. When we align our attention with the truth that we are really immortal and unchanging space, then we can fully communicate real love and understanding to all of our relationships.

When in great physical pain, if we identify with being the space and not the matter, we can communicate to the body from a place of peace, beyond agitation, that everything is indeed fine, as well as working for our benefit. Everything is indeed perfect and is just as it should be. The *observer consciousness,* from the *Heart,* communicates this to the body. The *observer* communicates a deep abiding love and trust for *what is.* The *observer* communicates complete confidence in the body's natural healing intelligence. The *observer* communicates to the body that the body is perfectly capable of healing from whatever it needs to. The *observer* communicates to the body that whatever is presently happening is all part of Heaven's plan and therefore we can show up for it with an open Heart. The *observer* also communicates to the body the truth of infinite abundance: "Please, body, take all the time and healing love energy you need, because there is always infinite abundance. As I do not *have* love, I *am* love!"

Moving forward requires right perception. Moving forward is rarely, if ever, linear. It therefore requires right relationship with perception to order to even *see* it. The best way to imagine right relationship with moving forward is to visualize driving a car in traffic. The red and green lights we encounter while driving determine our forward movement. So it is in life. If we are showing up in each moment with an open Heart, without a thought or belief, it begs the question, "How do we know when we should move, and in what direction?

Since Heaven, otherwise known as love and wisdom, determines the movement of *everything*, what we are really asking is, "Where do I have a green light from Heaven?" What you will find is that Heaven's green lights are a lot like our traffic lights; they are changing all the time. You may find you have a green light for a job interview or for a date, but that green light may not last long. It may be for only one interview or for one date. Then the light may turn red.

Our job is not to criticize the lights. Our job is not to find fault with a red light when the ego says, "But, I want it green. Now!" Our job is not to have a thought or a belief about how long any given light is going to remain red or green. Our job is to show up from the Heart and say to Heaven, "Show me the lights. I will move forward as long as the light is green, and I will stop and let go of all attachments when the light turns red." Notice there is no provision in our job description for throwing a temper tantrum when the lights change.

Since we do not know what reality is, how do we know where we should be and when? We know by the red and green lights. Our job is not to relate to these lights as being governed by any power other than love and wisdom. We would be well served to let go of the habit of thinking and believing that what other people do and say has any real power in our lives. We have aligned our wave with the truth that Heaven determines the movement of *everything*. If you were hired for any given vocation, it was because Heaven determined it, not because the people who interviewed you felt you had the right qualifications. Heaven wanted you there. Heaven runs every human resources department everywhere. If the person you went out with last week never called you back, Heaven is sending you a clear red light. There is no need to have a thought or belief about your power or lovablity or what a jerk the other person is. There is only a need to show up from the Heart and pay attention to where and when Heaven is directing you.

Let go of the notion that you choose anything other than how you respond to what is. You choose the attitude. You choose what you will give your attention to. That is it! Everything else is determined by love and wisdom. There is simply no greater force or power on the Earth, or anywhere else in the universe for that matter. Since Heaven determines *everything,* we would be best served to let go of our stories. Simply show up innocent in this moment and ask for the strength and wisdom to see Heaven's perfect instructions.

When we come from what we think and believe, we cannot understand why Heaven would have us go from one place and one relationship to another. We cannot see the wisdom in the sequence of red and green lights given. Life on Earth is for the practice of realizing mind. It does not exist for the sole purpose of solving temporal problems or for accumulating material things. Life on Earth is for practicing neutrality, surrender and unconditional acceptance through the mastery of loving and trusting one's way through life. This means that each wave is to practice moving forward according to the red and green lights given by Heaven, not by what we think and believe and not by what the ego demands. Each wave must ultimately surrender to **the truth that only love is real and the movement of love determines** *everything.*

Unrealized waves are simply practiced at ignoring Heaven's traffic signals. The only reason we do not obey the higher order of life is because we have not practiced it. We have not practiced listening to the wisdom of love from the Heart. We have not practiced surrendering to the perfection of Heaven's red and green lights. Instead we have practiced listening to the ego. We have practiced giving attention to limitation, bad faith, manipulation and control, which is the same as running red lights, speeding and making illegal lane changes. We'll call it **D.U.I.E.** – *driving while under the influence of the ego.* It is time to master the practice of aligning our wave with Heaven's lights, without a thought or belief, without a judgment or a criticism, without contraction or re-creation.

Heaven's red lights and green lights will not change simply because a wave has not learned to recognize them. If a wave chooses to ignore the lights, it does not mean it is immune to Heaven's direction. A wave focused only on the ego's agenda will feel frustrated, depressed, angry, impatient and resentful when presented with Heaven's higher order. Again the ego brings only limited results, because it is a limited form of intelligence. No surprises there!

Surrendering to the red and green lights as they are presented without any other agenda is its own reward. Since life is inherently neutral, nothing that happens to us here is good or bad. It simply *is.* It is nothing more than a red light or a green light. We choose with our free will to embrace it as Heaven's perfect food of enlightenment, or to experience it as something less than what it is - absolutely perfect.

If you did not marry your high school sweetheart, if you never became the person you thought you'd be, the athlete or the artist, if you find yourself living somewhere unpredictable, doing something unimaginable, then that is what you have received from Heaven. Those are the red and green lights for your life. Instead of finding fault with our lives, with the red and green lights, with moving forward, what if we aligned ourselves with gratitude for what we *do* have, for what *is* given? Remember Heaven chooses the red and green lights, but you choose your response to that gift.

If we do not practice moving forward as a natural response to life, when the challenging events in our lives do unfold, and they will, we will only put into motion what we have practiced. And that will not be very useful. Practicing moving forward in our everyday lives assures us the talent and skill will be there when we most need it. Practicing moving forward will keep the wave in alignment with acceptance intelligence and surrendering to the whole of life, because the wave cannot be resisting *what is* and be moving forward at the same time.

When we practice giving attention to whatever nurtures moving forward, we practice loving moving forward for no other reason then we love moving forward. This is a relationship with moving forward that cannot be distracted, contaminated or diminished by any other influences. *When you love moving forward because that is what you love, with no other reward, then and only then will you be inseparable from that action.* Why? Because *you are what you love, and you love whatever you are giving your attention to.*

Your job is not to judge, criticize or have a thought or belief about the life lessons you agreed to go through while here on the rock. Your thoughts and beliefs are limited and temporal. Your life lessons are eternal and unlimited. Your job is to keep moving forward through those lessons. To keep consciously accepting Heaven's perfect food, which is everything that touches your mind, life and nervous system. Your job is to align the wave with the truth, to focus on what is equal, fair, and of good faith. It becomes clear and self-evident that without a well developed love and practice for moving forward, you are "asleep at the wheel." What you want, as the performer Meatloaf puts it, is "to see paradise by the dashboard light."

What Is It About "No" You Fail To Understand?

Socrates had many years of practice at moving forward as a response to *what is* in his lifetime. When he was in his fifties, about twenty years before his famous trial, a nearby military group took over Athens where Socrates and his family lived. The invading military had rounded up all the people in Athens that they felt had significant influence among the general population. The hostile military leaders then informed the small group of Athens' finest citizens that they were to go out and arrest a group of innocent people the invading military had identified and listed. The threatening military power explained to the Athenians, of whom Socrates was among, that if they did not arrest the people on their hit list, the invaders would kill them and their families.

Socrates knew some of the people in this military group. As a matter of fact, the ones he knew were former students of his. He understood, as did the other Athenians, that arrest meant a death sentence for these innocent people. The message behind this "arrest action" for the rest of Athens, was they better comply with the new rulers whims or else. Socrates would not be coerced into doing anything he knew in his Heart was wrong. Period. End of sentence. Not up for negotiation. If the voice in your head sounds limiting, tastes limiting, and looks limiting, guess who is talking to you? Socrates refused to placate the ego's voice.

Startled, shocked and probably very frightened, the group was released to do the dirty work of the invading military. This small group of people stood together in the street talking quietly amongst themselves about what to do. Socrates, however, had already started walking down the streets towards his home. Surprised by Socrates' lack of concern for what appeared to be a seriously life-threatening predicament, the group called out to him, asking him what he is going to do about the situation. Socrates, the picture of composure, responded, "Why, I'm going home and having dinner of course. I will not be talked into doing something I know is not right."

Socrates' answer to moving forward, when someone has a gun to your head, is to recognize that only Heaven has the power to decide when your life is over and when it is time for you to return home. No one else decides. Only Heaven. Always has. Always will. Socrates is fearless, unwavering and deeply practiced at only giving his attention to the truth and nothing else. As Heaven and history would have it, the threatening military force was overthrown shortly thereafter, so there was, in actuality, no punishment for not arresting the people cited to die.

In addition to being a model for how to live a conscious life, Socrates left us with the wisdom that *the unexamined life is not worth living.* Imagine a world where the inhabitants were authentically interested in *creating a life worth living.* It would be a world where no one could commit any action they knew was wrong or in any way life-diminishing, no matter what the temporal world threatened. It would be a world in which a Hitler could not exist. A world in which lying could not happen. A world where children could speak freely to anyone, where all the shelters for abused people had been transformed into dance halls and recreational centers. A world where jails aren't used and where people are treated and respected as a force of love. Hearts are full of trust, heads are empty of criticism and everyone is equal to everyone else.

This is what is so powerful about Socrates' story. He didn't care what the violent military power threatened. Socrates could not be talked into doing *anything* that he knew was wrong. Case closed! Do not pass GO and do not collect $200.00.

Most of us in all likelihood will not be faced with Socrates' exact dilemma. However we all have a great deal to learn about how to continue moving forward unconditionally, without flinching, from Socrates' practice of right perception in an arena he could not fake.

NO is ON backwards – Argisle

When we do move forward we practice leaving everything behind us, and that is exactly where the ego's advice on everything eternal belongs. The only thing that is useful for us to bring into each new moment is an open and innocent Heart. Babies are resilient and heal faster than adults, because they do not have a thought or belief system about themselves, others or *what is.* Babies simply show up in the moment from an open Heart. They fully experience *what is.* They digest it, let go of the waste, then they move on and show up innocently for the next given moment. I'm sure all baby changers can verify just how fast and how often babies do *let go of the waste.* Imagine what the world would look like if we could all let go of our waste like babies do. It does beg the question, would we need to wear diapers too? Probably, *Depends.* (wink, wink, nudge, nudge.)

Babies are so well practiced at being with *what is,* without a thought or belief, that they are naturally aligned with innocent, playful and light-hearted. That is a state of mind we sadly lose when we leave this place of ease and flexibility, for the presumed safety of the strategically manipulating head, otherwise called adulthood. Aligned with innocent, playful and light-hearted, our true natural state by the way, is what provides babies with their resilience advantage. Every wave would be better served to expand the qualities of innocent, playful and light-hearted in their Ruling Love - to be child-like in nature, without being childish. As Jesus has already reminded us, *"Truly I say to you, unless you are converted and become like children, you shall not enter the kingdom of Heaven."*

Before we can be converted and become like children, we must first value and honor innocent, playful and light-hearted - a quality deeply frowned upon throughout most of American culture. If you are the average American, unless you are a standup comic or on some very powerful pharmaceuticals, you value and honor responsibility and being serious far more than being innocent, playful and light-hearted. Case in point, Senator Robert Dole is a man with an astonishingly great sense of humor. Any politician wise and insightful enough to publicly advocate the brilliance of *South Park,* will always get my vote.

However, when Senator Dole was running for the office of President of the United States, no one in the public arena knew the man was so incredibly light-hearted, playful and free. After he lost the election, he came out of his "humor closet" as he no longer needed to maintain any campaign etiquette posturing. After the election many people were greatly impressed by his authentically lovable nature, and when interviewed, he would be asked why America *never saw this Bob Dole,* the funny down to Earth guy that clearly does not have a dis-honest bone in his body. His reply was that he was warned many times by the professionals that guide and groom public image, that funny people were not taken seriously and that his easy going nature would not be considered by our cultural standards, a positive trait. What a truly sad commentary on what we value and consider worthy of trust.

Swedenborg advises us to ask ourselves if what we are giving our attention to lives in Heaven, a place beyond limitation, or not? If not, simply stop giving it your attention, and shift your awareness back to the tree that produces unlimited fruits and results. Consider that valuing responding to the temporal realm over and above the eternal, is not a state or condition that exists in Heaven. "Serious as a heart attack," is a common enough American slang expression. Hard to imagine serious in Heaven, a place defined by its light-hearted, free and unconditional state of being.

Indian and Tibetan Ayurveda, as well as Chinese Medicine, warn us that anything that contributes to a hard, rigid or inflexible mind is deeply unhealthy and will have seriously negative health consequences. Serious perceptions and inappropriate responsibility attachments to the exterior world re-creates tremendous density, hardness and inflexibility within the wave. Remember you are really space: nothing but absolute free openness. No one can be aligned with innocent, playful and light-hearted and be re-creating destructive actions within the wave at the same time.

In America we confuse serious with *focused*. We can be focused on giving our attention to something, without being serious. We can be compassionate and take care of business, without getting in bed with serious. Speaking of getting in bed, next time you are considering a serious response, please reflect back upon Sean Connery as *James Bond*. After a particularly stressful, often times life-threatening moment, James will recover his neutral composure and consciously move forward by sharing some playful and light-hearted witty quip. The playful attitude is what gives James Bond his acute and heightened sense of savvy, just as much as his numerous mechanical fashion accessories embellish his *I be the man* aura. If playful and light-hearted are good enough "tools of the trade" for James Bond to get in bed with, it would seem monumentally obvious that there is an equally liberating gift in there for the rest of us.

Batter Up!

Life is like baseball "batting practice" and the rock is like a giant baseball "batting cage." While we are here, our job is to keep the bat of truth knocking the balls of illusion out of the ballpark of our life. No mature player gets in the "batting cage," and then protects themselves from the practice of knocking out the balls. Lord knows as long as you are in the "batting cage," the balls are going to keep coming. While in the "batting cage" it is not useful to take the balls personally, and it is not useful to relate to the balls as being more powerful than you are.

What is useful is to align ourselves with the truth that we are pure love! No one here can create a learning experience that they do not need. Do not be disturbed by anything that touches you here on the rock. Instead understand that this place is the cosmic, universal water closet, because this is where the unserviceable, the functionless, the useless, and the futile *shit* that we give our attention to shows up!

Elimination equals Illumination – Argisle

Remember to posture your awareness in the present moment (which is home plate). Pick up the bat of truth with your unwavering attention on what Heaven loves, and knock every ball of distraction the ego pitches at you right out of the ball park of your mind and nervous system. As long as you find yourself here, you need the batting practice. So let us take a page from Solomon's book. Instead of getting pelted by Asmodeus in the "batting cage," let us knock out every obstacle thrown at us until we find ourselves liberated from the toilet and restored to our true throne!

By the way, life is not a test, if it were we would all have been given the answers at the beginning. Life is a practice. Life is what you practice giving your attention to. Life is the practice of realizing *we do not have love, we are love*. Life is the practice of aligning our will, our love, our service and our life purpose with the love and affections of Heaven. Life is for practicing the realization that whatever you have done to another, you have done to yourself. Life is comprised of Heaven's perfect food. It is a daily dining on the Heavenly blue plate special. Our movement through life is completely dependent on our practice of seeing it, receiving it, and digesting it as the prefect food that it is. May we all live the realized life of the One. May we all consciously celebrate life's perfection. And may we all shine on as the Universal White Light that we are! So it is and so it goes.

The sayings of the Buddha

The thought manifests as the word;

The word manifests as the deed;

The deed develops into habit;

And the habit hardens into character.

So watch the thought and its ways with care . . .

As we think, so we become.

–From the Dhammapada

Suggested Readings

Anything by: Leo Bascalia

Lenny Bruce

Fritjof Capra

Pema Chodron

Meister Eckhart

Matthew Fox

Thich Nhat Hanh

Bill Hicks

Dali Lama

J. Krishnamurti

Jerry Mander

Dr. Phil McGraw

Jacob Neddleman

Emanuel Swendborg

Sir Oscar Wilde

Brian Breiling, *Light Years Ahead*

Antoine De Saint-Exupery, *The Little Prince*

John G. Fuller, *The Ghost of Flight 401*

Dr. Elson Hass, MD, *Staying Healthy with the Seasons, 21st Century Edition*

Neil Douglas-Klotz, *Prayers of the Cosmos*

Dr. Stephen LaBerge, *Lucid Dreaming*

Dr. Stephen LaBerge and Howard Reingold,
   Exploring the World of Lucid Dreaming

James F. Lawrence, *Testimony to the Invisible: Essays on Swedenborg*

Robert A. Monroe, *Ultimate Journey*

Brian Narelle, *Living In Vertical Time*

Sogyal Rinpoche, *The Tibetan Book of Living*

D. T. Suzuki, *Swendenborg Buddha of the North*

Seth Series, *New Awareness Network, Inc.*

Michael Talbot, *The Holographic Universe*

Wilson Van Dussen, *The Presence of Other Worlds*

Dr. Brian Weiss, *Many Masters, Many Lives. Only Love is Real.*

Glossary

Aba Gayle – Is a living, walking, talking, sharing testimony to the power of divine love and wisdom. Her miraculous story of forgiveness and growth, after her daughter was brutally murdered, appears at the end of chapter five. Her story can be found in its entirety at http://www.forgivenessday.org /default.htm. Look under "Heroes" for Aba Gayle.

Acceptance – Being with "what is" in the Present Moment with an open Heart. The action of making mind available to receive Heaven's perfect gifts, in each moment without a thought or belief.

Asmodeus – Considered to be the king of demons, he was a real nasty one. He boasted of "hatching plots against newlyweds, I mar the beauty of virgins and cause their Hearts to grow cold." (Testament of Solomon 5:7). He was beaten by the Archangel Raphael! Yeah go God go! His most famous encounter was with King Solomon, who had captured him to provide him with information he needed in order to build the Holy Temple in Jerusalem.

Bardo – A Buddhist term referring to events that occur which are not what they appear to be, in respect that what is actually happening is not really drama. What is really happening is an opportunity for self-realization that is incredibly heightened. Buddhism says that the truth is, that every Present Moment is a bardo. However, some bardos are more charged than others. Buddhism also says that the two most important bardos we will ever experience are the birth and death of bardos, the coming and the going.

Beatles – Considered by some to be the greatest rock-n-roll band of all time. The Beatles certainly had their place in influencing the sound and growth of recorded music in their lifetime. The Beatles are as follows: John Lennon, guitar. George Harrison, guitar. Paul McCartney, bass guitar, and Ringo Star, drums.

Beliefs – The shit we are here to get over. Projections made by an unrealized mind.

Bitch Slap – Relax. This expression had nothing to with women. It is a male prison slang term. It denotes a type of slap involving striking back-and-forth with an open hand. It is used strictly in this book for the sole purpose of invoking a visual image.

Buddha – Which means The Enlightened One. Was named Siddhartha at birth, by his father who was a great King. The Astrologers prediction for Siddhartha, which was a commonplace request at the time of a persons birth in those days, informed the King that his son was destined to become either a great King, like his father, or Siddhartha would grow up to be a great spiritual leader. The King was determined that his son should take his place as a worldly ruler, so he did what he could to ensure that outcome. He kept Siddhartha in the palace at all times surrounding him with wealth and luxury, as well as keeping him insulated from the harsher realities of life on Earth. Siddhartha in search of truth scaled the walls of his father's palace where he soon after encountered for the first time, people of old age, illness and death. He also so encountered a monk. He was suddenly exposed to all the things that he had been shielded from. Siddhartha choose to learn, to seek out spiritual truth and enlightenment. Upon reaching enlightenment he took on a new

Spiritual name Sakhy Muni. Vaishali is the town where the Buddha lived and taught for many years.

Cesar Chavez – 1927-1993, born in Arizona, Cesar began his life as migrant worker at the age of ten. He grew to be the most influential labor leader bring forth the greatest changes and improvements to the lives of migrant farm workers in America.

Cheech and Chong – A counter-culture comic duo. Famous for a series of comic recordings and comedy films based on nontraditional counter-culture characters and situations.

Cold Turkey – A slang term for cutting oneself off suddenly and immediately from a substance and/or habit or behavior.

Contractions – The exact opposite of expansion. A response that happens within the mind, within the nervous system, when attention is given to illusion or lies. **One of the three great negative kamic response along with re-creation and stagnation.**

Creativity – Healthy God Consciousness. Consciousness that has the power to manifest something from nothing. Creativity is a natural by-product that happens when Spirit aligns itself with Source.

Dalai Lama – Is a Tibetan Buddhist monk, that in addition to being the reincarnation of divine love and compassion intelligence humanly embodied, is also the spiritual and diplomatic leader of the Tibetan people and culture. The Dalai Lama and many of the people of Tibet, were forced to flee their native land in 1959, due to the invasion of the Chinese military. The Dalai Lama now travels the globe teaching, enlightening and healing the planet and its occupants.

Duality – The disease that infects perception with subject/object orientation. The original dis-ease that all other diseases stem from. The disease enlightened beings no longer suffer from.

Earth – The rock, specifically the third rock, from the Sun. Look down under your feet.

Edward R. Murrow – 1908-1965, is an American broadcaster of iconic, legendary stature. He covered World War II on radio, during the bombings of London, as well as American involvement in the Korean War. He would sign off his broadcast with this signature closure; "Good night and good luck." Murrow on his *See It Now* television show during the late fifties, exposed Senator Joe McCarthy, for the fascists he was, marking the beginning of the end of McCarthyism. Murrow will always be remembered for his unparalleled, incorruptible, fearlessness as a newsman who pioneered and set the standard for television journalism when it was still in its infancy.

Ego – The limited form of secondary consciousness we inherit when coming to the Earth plane. All information learned on the rock. Information for solving only temporal problems in a temporal world. Also known throughout this book as "the voice of limitation," "the inner critic," etc.

Ghandi – A native of India, famous for his passive, non-violent, non-cooperation philosophy that was highly successful in the liberation of India from the rule of the

English. Ghandi, in many ways, is the Eastern Indian version of America's great peacekeeper, Martin Luther King Jr.

Grandma Moses – 1860-1961, she was a self taught American painter, she started her now famous career at the age of seventy, when her health became to frail for much physical activity.

Groucho Marx – To say he was one of the funniest people who ever lived would be to damn the man with faint praise. He was born one of four brothers, and they all went into show business collectively. They were successful on Broadway, but gained International acclaim in films such as: *Duck Soup, A Night At The Opera, A Day At The Races* and many more. Groucho was easily recognizable with his classic black painted on mustache, baggy pants and quick delivery accompanied by animated eyebrows. His most famous line is; *"I shot an elephant, in my pajamas, this morning. How he got in my pajamas, I'll never know!"* Groucho died in 1977 at the age of 86.

Heaven – A quality or state of existence beyond any limitation, beyond everything physical, beyond all suffering, beyond duality. A state or condition where mind is aligned unconditionally with Ultimate Truth.

Hell – A quality or state of existence inseparable from limitation, one with unhappiness and suffering. An inflexible place of fear, "less than," unequal, and unfair. A state or condition of atrophied growth and paralyzed self-perception, due to the unresolved disease of duality of mind.

Homer Simpson – A cartoon character created by Mat

Groening. Homer is known for his out of shape physique due to his weakness for donuts or any food or non food item he can consume. He has a large bald head with only a few stray hairs on the top, and an amazing talent for the stupid, the lame brain, the self sabotaging. Homer is the ultimate comical boob. He is the father of three cartoon children; Bart, Lisa and Maggie. He is married to the blue haired Marge. Fewer things are funnier than Homer and the entire Simpsons' clan.

James Bond – A fictional, secret agent character based on the novels by Ian Flemming. Many films have been based on these novels, the first of which starred actor Sean Connery, va va voom!

James Dean – 1931-1955, born in Marion, Indiana he was raised mostly by his grandparents after the death of his mother. Although his career was extremely brief, he made an indelible mark on the World. He raised the bar for actors everywhere with his natural ability to perform with a remarkable quality of emotional availability. He made only three films which are: *East of Eden, Rebel Without A Cause, and Giant.*

Jimi Hendrix – 1942-1970. Rock-n-rolls' greatest guitar player ever! No need to say anything more! Listen and feel!

Jimmy Durante – A beloved comic actor from film history. Best known for his large nose and running gag about his jokes which was, "I got a million of 'em!"

Karl Marx – 1818-1883, German born philosopher. He is widely acclaimed to be the primary theorist of socialism and communism. His reputation spread in his life time as a socialist representing the working class of economically suppressed countries in Europe.

Krishnamurti – A spiritual teacher from India, author of many spiritual-based books. Krishnamurti is famous in his lifetime for being the first "just say no" guru. He would not assume a leadership role offered him by the then very popular and large Theosophy Society, in the early part of the 1900's. Instead, he advocated for each person alone has sovereignty over their own attention. For more information, contact the J. Kirshnamurti Foundation based in Ojai, California. (805) 646-4773. www.krishnamurti.org.

Madonna – The Madonna referred to in this book is not the mother of Jesus Christ, but rather the popular recording artist and dancer. The Queen of MTV. A woman known for her wild and original creativity, now called Esther of the Kaballah!

Mark Twain – An American iconic humorist. He came to be born with the once every seventy five year appearance of Haley's comet, and he left seventy five years later with its reappearance. He was born on November 30, 1835 and died on April 21, 1910. He outlived his wife and three of his four daughters. Mark twain was only his pen name, he came up with as a Mississippi riverboat pilot, his real name was Samuel Clemens. His most famous books, which should be required reading for anyone with a body, are: *Tom Sawyer, Huckleberry Fin and Connecticut Yankee.* Clemens was as prolific a pipe smoker as he was a writer.

Martin Luther King, Jr. – Born, January 15, 1929 he was assassinated on the morning of April 4, 1968. He was a

Baptist minister, and the most profound leader of social change during the civil rights movement in the 1960's in America. He led many marches throughout the South supporting the end of segregation. He was imprisoned many times for his nonviolent advocating of equality and fairness. His now famous *"I Have A Dream,"* speech given originally in Washington DC, is still one of the most timeless inspirational tributes to the power of unconditional love.

Meatloaf – A popular rock-n-roll singer from the 1980's.

Meister – A title such as "mister" or "sir."

Meister Eckhart – A monk and native of Germany, born in 1260, died in circa 1328. His teachings of God and the truth where considered radical in his time. His eloquent Spiritual brilliance is still a modern time marvel. A few of his poems appear at the end of every chapter.

Mellen-Thomas Benedict – A personal reformer of world views, Benedict was clinically dead for over an hour. His amazing account of the death experience, and life after death story appears at the end of *chapter eight.*

Mini-Me – A character from the Mike Myers' *Austin Powers* movie series.

Mother Teresa – 1910-1997, A Nobel Peace Prize winner, Mother Teresa was a Catholic nun, world renowned for her Saint like work with the sick and the poor, primarily in Calcutta. Often referred to as the *"Angel of Mercy"*, or *"The Saint of the gutters".*

Neutral – A mind aligned with the truth that *everything* *is as it should be.* A mind beyond the grasp, pull, and distortion of charged thoughts and beliefs. A mind not disturbed by anything inner or outer.

New Dimensions Radio Program – To order any archived program, call (800) 935-8273, or write PO Box 569, Ukiah, CA 95482. www.newdimensions.org

Noam Chomsky – Born in 1928, Noam is one of the most prolific writers of the twenty first century. He has worked as an educator and linguist at Massachusetts Institute of technology since 1955. Noam is so densely concentrated in his verbal communication he is good only for "sound boulders," not "sound bites."

O.J. – Is short for Orenthal James Simpson, no relation to Homer or Marge Simpson. The reference in this book to O.J. is whether or not he "did it." This is referring to the murder of his ex-wife Nicole Brown Simpson and Ronald Goldman in 1994. He was acquitted in 1995 in criminal court, however he was found liable for the two deaths in 1997 in civil court. If you lived through this one, you will remember it as a time when everyone and his brother had an opinion about whether or not O.J. "did it."

Oprah – Oh come on! Do you really need Oprah defined? She is the conscience of America. She is every woman's best friend whether we have met her personally or not. Oprah is the only person to transform daytime television from a barren wasteland of mindless banter to *The Angel Network*! Need we say more?

Oscar Wilde – Born in Ireland in Oct. 16, 1854 as Oscar Fingal O'Flahertie Wills Wilde, to a wealthy, well educated family. Oscar's father was a famous eye surgeon, his mother a writer. Oscar has been called the greatest literary genius of the last century. Wilde lived his life with Saint like generosity and kindness to others. He could speed read both sides of a page simultaneously. He graduated from Oxford University with honors. He was accused of "gross indecency" by the British Government for his relationship with another man. Oscar was sentenced to prison. The government sized ownership of all his creative writings, forcing his family into financial exile. Oscar died on November 1, 1900 of complications due to spinal meningitis. His last words, while dying in an shabby hotel room were; *"Either the wallpaper goes or I do!"* Long live the brilliant gifts of Sir Oscar Wilde!

Princess Diana – 1961-1997, One of the world's greatest philanthropist, Princess Diana married and then later divorced Charles Prince of Wales. Diana worked tirelessly to support charities, often auctioning off her gowns worn to public and private events for donation money. She was also a champion for helping those suffering from Aids/ HIV virus. She died in a car crash that is still somewhat surrounded by mystery and uncertainty. She is survived by two sons.

Re-creation – Unhealthy God consciousness. Awareness that does not create a new response to any problem. An incomplete action destined to be repeated until ended by creativity. A neurotic form of response(s) over and over again. Unhappiness. **One of the three great negative karmic responses along with stagnation and contraction.**

Rod Serling – The creative genius behind the ground breaking television show *The Twilight Zone*. Serling was a gifted highly prolific writer of fictional stories designed to open the mind, educate the soul and enhance human development.

Rosa Parks – 1913-2005, A young black woman, in the spirit of just say "no," changed the course of history when she said "no" to a white man in the winter of 1955, marking the beginning of the civil rights movement in America. Parks, a seamstress, was traveling on a public bus in Alabama, when asked to relinquish her seat, so that a white male could sit down. Rosa refused, was promptly arrested and that action inspired the Rev. Martin Luther King Jr. to begin his; "Stride Toward Freedom." Rosa has been called, "the mother of the civil rights movement."

Samskaras – The impressions made in a wave by the disease of duality. Memories, stories, and charges we are here to get over and heal the Mind from.

Shania Twain – A female country-western singer who rocks the rock!

Socrates – Ancient Greek philosopher and teacher, a citizen of ancient Athens. Famous for coining the phrase; *"The unexamined life is not worth living."* Sentenced to death for treason, for the crime of corrupting the youth, Socrates was forced to drink hemlock.

Sogyal Rinpoche – A Tibetan Buddhist monk, born in Tibet. Educated in Delhi and Cambridge University. World renowned teacher, speaker and author. Famous for his work on death and dying.

Solomon – Son of King David and Bathesheba. Legendary for his divinely guided wisdom as a worldly ruler and as a spiritual mystic. He was the builder of the famous Holy Temple in Jerusalem, which took seven years to build and was covered with inlaid gold. Solomon became King somewhere around 967 BC. It is believed he contributed to the writings of the Bible, in the books of Kings I, Chronicles II, Song of Songs, Proverbs and Ecclesiastics. His empire reached from North of the Euphrates to the South of Egypt. Solomon ruled as King of Jerusalem for forty years and was laid to rest in the City of David.

Stagnation – Energy that does not move and is therefore not life. Any part of a person's mind or life that is already dead, even while the body appears to still be alive. **One of the three great negative karmic actions along with re-creation and contraction.**

Stephen LaBerge – Dream guru extraordinary. A graduate of Stanford University, Dr. LaBerge is the founder of the Stanford based Lucidity Institute. Dr. LaBerge is the author of many books, and a much sought after speaker on the subject of dreams and dreaming. For more information contact the Lucidity Institute or visit their web site.

Steve and Terry Irwin – Otherwise known as the Crocodile Hunter and Family. Steve and Terry Irwin own and operate a Zoo in Australia, host a cable television program, and advocate for animals everywhere. The Irwin family is the "love the planet and every life form on it" family. Long live the Irwins!

Surrender – The conscious action to letting go of what you think and believe, while simultaneously returning attention to the Truth: We do not have love, we are love. No one can create a learning experience they did not need. Everything is coming to us from Heaven, and it is therefore Perfect beyond any judgment or criticism.

Suze Orman – Is a Internationally renowned finance expert. She is an author, she has her own question and answer television show, as well as providing many other resources to the general public to help organize a healthy and conscious financial life.

Swedenborg – (1688-1772) A Swedish mystic, also renown as a great scientist. He wrote many volumes of scientific and spiritual information. Swendenborg was famous for his shy, and exceedingly gentle and compassionate nature. Ship captains used to love to sail with him, as they said the weather was always better when Swedenborg traveled with them. Also, he could always inform captains of the exact day and time of arrival and docking. www.swedenborg.org.uk.

Tao – Sometimes spelled "dao." The literal translation from Chinese is "the way."

Thoughts – Temporal consciousness for solving temporal problems. The voice of the ego. Charged consciousness we are designed to give attention to only 5% of our day for resolving mundane problems.

Ultimate Lies – The ego's version of the Truth. The first half of ultimate lies is that you are separate from love because you "did not do it right" and "you are not good enough." The second half of the lie is that there is not enough: time, love, money, and opportunity. These lies are the source of every single person's suffering. These lies are what we have come here to practice being immune to with our mind because our perception recognizes them for the useless lies they are.

Ultimate Truth – Heaven's version of the Truth. The first part of the Truth is that we do not have love – WE ARE LOVE! There is only the One, and the One is love! Because there is only One, and it is love, that makes us One with love as well! The second half of the Truth is that there is always Infinite Abundance! Of course, if there is only the One, and the One is love, then how could we not be Infinitely Abundant as well?

Wave – Swedenborg's expression or illustration or individual consciousness, including the conscious and unconscious mind. The metaphor for an unrealized person.

About the Author

Vaishali describes herself as the only spiritual teacher you will ever meet who dresses like a stripper and talks like Lenny Bruce. She graduated Magna Cum Laude from both the Religion and Philosophy Department as well as Radio and Television Department from San Francisco State University. Her entire life has been devoted to the learning and sharing of Esoteric wisdom. She has been teaching and providing Spiritual individual consultations since the early nineties. She refers to herself as a "dead head", but only from the neck up. She has worn only the color purple – exclusively, for over a decade as her Spiritual uniform of choice. If you ever meet her, have a good joke to share, and an extra ticket to the next Grateful Dead show.

Also Available from the Author

The companion book to You Are What You Love:
The You Are What You Love Playbook

Excerpts from:
You Are What You Love Book
on CD

Available at:
www.purplehazepress.com
www.youarewhatyoulove.com

You can also contact Vaishali by going to either website
and clicking on contact us.